RENEWALS 458-4574

DATE DUE

GAYLORD			PRINTED IN U.S.A

WHO CAN COMPETE
AGAINST THE WORLD?

*Power-Protection and Buddhism
in Shan Worldview*

*For Honora S. Guerin, Barbara Baird Tannenbaum,
Deborah Tannenbaum Thapa, and Honor Devi Thapa*

May the line continue.

WHO CAN COMPETE AGAINST THE WORLD?

Power-Protection and Buddhism in Shan Worldview

Nicola Tannenbaum

Published by the Association for Asian Studies, Inc.
Monograph and Occasional Paper Series, Number 51

© 1995 by the Association for Asian Studies

Published by the Association for Asian Studies, Inc.
1 Lane Hall
The University of Michigan
204 South State Street
Ann Arbor, Michigan 48104

Library of Congress Cataloging-in-Publication Data

Tannenbaum, Nicola Beth, 1951–
    Who Can Compete Against the World?: Power-Protection and Buddhism in Shan Worldview/Nicola Tannenbaum.

    p. cm—(Monograph and Occasional Papers Series/Association for Asian Studies; 51)
    Includes bibliographical references and index.
    ISBN 0-924304-29-4

    1. Mae Hong Son (Thailand: Province)—Religious life and customs. 2. Shan (Asian people)—Thailand—Mae Hong Son (Province)—Religion. 3. Buddhism—Thailand—Mae Hong Son (Province)—Customs and practices. 4. Animism—Thailand—Mae Hong Son (Province). I. Title. II. Series: Monograph and Occasional Papers (Association for Asian Studies); Number 51.

BL2077.M34T36 1995   95-43510
294.3'089'9591—dc20   CIP

The publication of this volume has been financed from a revolving fund, supported in part by the Luce Foundation. A full listing of the AAS Monograph Series appears at the end of this volume.

Printed in the United States of America on acid-free paper.

Contents

Plates

Figures

Tables

Acknowledgments

I have received considerable support from a wide range of people and institutions. My research has received financial support from the Midwestern University Consortium on International Activities—the International Fertilizer Development Center, the Social Science Research Council of New York, and a Franz Fellowship and a Class of '68 Fellowship from Lehigh University. I am also indebted to the United States Department of Agriculture, whose food stamp program provided support for a brief period of time. While in Thailand, I received support from the Thai National Research Council and was affiliated with the Social Science Research Institute at Chiang Mai University and with Sukhothaithamatiraat University.

I owe an intellectual debt to E. Paul Durrenberger, who introduced me to Southeast Asia and Shan studies and developed my sense of anthropology. To paraphrase a Shan saying, one can never repay the debt one owes one's professor. I received intellectual and emotional support from Cornelia Kammerer, both in and out of the field, which I gratefully acknowledge. And I thank Hjorleifur Rafn Jonsson, who continues to read and think critically about Southeast Asia and my writing while managing to squeeze some fun out.

I also owe an unrepayable debt to the people of Thongmakhsan and Mawk Tsam Pe for their help and willingness to teach me. Without them, none of this would have been possible.

CHAPTER ONE

Introduction

My interest in Shan worldview is an outgrowth of my study of the structure and use of knowledge as it related to farming. To understand and contextualize the goals that structured the agricultural decision process, I had to understand Shan religion and worldview in Shan terms. Initially I accepted the characterization of Shan religion as Buddhist. Shan, like other "Buddhists," supported temples and monks and also propitiated a host of spirits. They separated these two aspects of their practice, saying that spirits had nothing to do with Buddhism. Yet Shan used metaphors of shade and spheres of protection to explain the power of humans, spirits, and the Buddhas, and the effectiveness of using Buddhist elements in treating spirit-caused misfortune. The more I explored these ideas, the more I realized that, while Shan and others often characterize animist and Buddhist practices separately, the two derived from a single underlying worldview. With this insight, I began to explore Shan religion as an integrated whole, which incorporated and synthesized both "animist" and "Buddhist" practices. This monograph is the result of those explorations.

THE SETTING

Southeast Asian peoples are usually categorized based on where they live—on the hills, or in the valleys, or on the coasts. Shan fit none of the categories: they are people of the hills and valleys, living in the mountain valleys of southern China, northern Burma, and northwestern Thailand. Like other valley dwellers they grow irrigated rice; like hill peoples they also make slash and burn—swidden—fields.

Politically and ideologically they resemble lowland peoples. Shan are members of states, albeit today smaller states than those of the Thai, Burman, and Lao. They identify themselves as Buddhist, and recognize other lowlanders as their coreligionists with whom they share same scriptural traditions. However, each group practices a variant form of the religion with different festivals, religious scripts, and ordination lines.

Their identification as "Buddhist" distinguishes lowlanders from uplanders. Lowlanders see uplanders with their various animist practices as having no religion (*sasana*). Buddhism is important as a sign of difference and as a mark of civilization. However, this Buddhism is not necessarily the Buddhism of the Pali canon. The label "Buddhist" does not illuminate the nature of Shan religion, or that of other lowlanders. One of my concerns in the rest of this text is to explore Shan religion and examine the place of Buddhism within it. (I return to this issue in the next section.)

Shan in Thailand live primarily in Maehongson, Chiang Mai, and Chiang Rai provinces. Those in Chiang Mai and Chiang Rai are relatively recent residents, refugees from the fighting and confused political situation in Burma. My discussion is limited to those in Maehongson who are long-term residents of Thailand and, unlike the recent refugees, Thai citizens. Their political incorporation into Thailand occurred around the turn of the century. Prior to that time they owed allegiance either to small Shan states in what is now Burma or to a prince in Maehongson Town. The Maehongson ruling family had married into the ruling family in Chiang Mai although the prince probably paid tribute to both Chiang Mai and Mawk Mai, a large Shan state nearby in Burma (Wilson 1985; Durrenberger and Tannenbaum 1990).

The Thai administrative structure of Maehongson is the same as that of any other Thai province. It is subdivided into three districts: *amphur mนuong*, the capital district, Mae Sarieng, and Paay. A fourth district is being established and will include the northern part of the capital district. Each district is subdivided into village clusters, *tambol*, which contain from five to fourteen villages. The provincial governor, district officers, and their assorted assistants are all appointed from Bangkok and are periodically rotated to serve in other areas. The village cluster headmen are elected from among the headmen of their constituent villages.

Maehongson Town, Mae Sarieng, and Paay are the only urban areas. Maehongson Town, the provincial capital, is the smallest of the three with approximately 10,000 people. People in towns are primarily Shan, northern, or central Thai. Villages in the outlying areas are primarily Shan although they may have a few northern Thai, Chinese, or Burmans living in them. Rural Shan refer to Maehongson Town simply as "Town." There are also scattered villages of Karen, Hmong, Chinese, Lahu, Lisu, and Pa-O.

Most Shan are farmers. The basic crop is rice, ideally grown in irrigated fields, which are two to three times more productive than hill fields (Durrenberger and Tannenbaum 1990). The area that can be turned into irrigated fields is limited. Before 1900, when Maehongson Province became directly administered by Thailand, people had usufruct rights to irrigated fields in return for performing corvée labor. Now people can secure legal title to irrigated fields but are responsible for land taxes. In villages near mountains, those without sufficient irrigated land can grow rice in hill fields. Although mountain lands belong to the government, people are allowed to use it make hill fields. These fields are made new every year and the ideal fallow period is ten to fifteen years. Access to hill fields is becoming more limited as the forestry department is actively planting teak trees, which removes the land from agricultural use. In villages without nearby mountains, those without sufficient irrigated fields work as hired labor or produce other products to sell. People grow rice for household consumption and sesame, garlic, and soybeans as cash crops to meet their money income needs. In villages near towns people may grow vegetables to sell in the market.

My analysis draws on research in two Shan villages: Thongmakhsan in *tambol* Huay Pha and Mawk Tsam Pe in *tambol* Mawk Tsam Pe. I began doing research in Thongmakhsan during the summer of 1977 when E. Paul and Dorothy Durrenberger were doing research on Shan farming. I returned in June 1979 and remained until January 1981, doing research on agricultural decision making (Tannenbaum 1982). In 1983 I briefly visited Thongmakhsan. In August 1984, I returned to the area, to live in Mawk Tsam Pe through December 1985. At that time I focused my ethnographic work directly on Shan worldview and religion. Finally I returned to Thongmakhsan in July 1988, staying through December 1988 to begin a pilot study of intercommunity relationships. Altogether, I have spent slightly more than three years in the area. In the rest of the text I refer primarily to Thongmakhsan, with references to Mawk Tsam Pe where they differed.

Thongmakhsan

One reaches Thongmakhsan by travelling north from Maehongson Town on a paved road for approximately 27 km and then taking an unpaved road that branches off the highway for another 3 km. The village lies at the edge of a narrow valley of the Mae Ngi River bounded by mountain ridges to its east and west. Houses are located near the base of the eastern ridge while the Mae Ngi River defines the western limit of the irrigated fields. The valley behind the village contains the largest cluster of irrigated fields, although there are fields in two more smaller valleys to the north. Approaching the village, travelling north, one first sees the irrigated fields, then a cluster of houses, the school, the temple, more houses, and finally more fields.

Thongmakhsan is a small, relatively poor village. In 1977, it had 38 households with a population of 161; by 1988, the households had increased to 56 with a population of 213. Most of the growth resulted from people getting married, having children, and establishing their own households. Some of the growth is a result of spouses from the surrounding area marrying into Thongmakhsan. Only four households had migrated into Thongmakhsan between 1977 and 1988.

Although it is small, the village is further subdivided into neighborhoods. Households near the school form one group, those in the middle near the stream another, and the newer houses in the northern "suburbs" another. Neighborhoods are led by assistant headmen. When there is village work such as cleaning the village or working on the temple, it is allocated to the neighborhood groups. Usually each household is responsible for sending one worker. If the work will take all day, often the men do the work while women prepare food for lunch. The neighborhood as a group is also responsible for contributing kerosene or wood to the temple.

In addition to the neighborhood groups, the village is divided into a number of other more or less formal groups based primarily on age. There is a youth group that draws its members from those young adults who are involved in productive work but still living with their parents. This is an informal grouping; people of this age and status are expected to help prepare festival food, serve it, and clean up. These young people participate as a formal group when they organize into sports teams and work together to raise money to buy equipment. A formal youth group was organized recently, in 1986 or 1987.

In 1987, the married women started a formal "housewives' group," *klum mae baan* (Shan, *kum me waan*), under the auspices of the Norwegian Save the Children Foundation, *Redd Barna*, and the district agricultural office. While membership is open to any married woman, only older women without small children joined; younger married women said they would join once their children were older and they had more time. With *Redd Barna* money the group operates a loan program advancing money to women to buy piglets and pig food. The interest from this and money raised through other activities goes into two loan funds, a general purpose one and an emergency one with lower interest rates. Informally older married women supervise the preparation and serving of festival foods and this continues separate from the formal *klum mae baan*.

There are also a number of committees that operate on a village level. There is an informal advisory committee to the headman, which includes the assistant headmen and respected wealthy or knowledgeable men. The headman consults these before scheduling villagewide festivals or planning village projects. Once these ideas are worked out with the informal committee they are presented to the rest of the village at a village meeting. Each household sends a representative to the meeting. Often the men on this committee also serve on the temple and school committees. These committees organize events involving the temple or school in consultation with the monks or teachers and manage the locally raised funds for both.

An indication of Thongmakhsan's smallness and relative poverty is that it lacks both noodle shops and village-based minibus transportation. While people have more cash now than in the recent past, no one can afford a minibus, and their disposable income is not sufficient to support a noodle shop.

People in Thongmakhsan rely on minibuses based in Naapaatsaat, 7 km north, and Huay Pha, 4 km south. If their need is urgent, they can either walk the 3 km to the main highway and flag down a minibus or hire one of the motorcycles in the village. There are two small shops that provide sundries such as shampoo, soap, batteries, and kerosene. Neither shop provides a full-time occupation for its owner.

The village temple has been under construction since 1978. In 1980, the temple was finished enough to use and it was formally opened in 1987. In 1988, all that remained to do was finish window shutters and put in the glass panels above the windows. The wood, roofing, nails, and labor were all donated by the villagers. In larger wealthier communities it is likely there would be a number of major sponsors, making it possible to buy wood, hire workers, and finish relatively quickly. Here work is done during the agricultural off-seasons and has proceeded slowly.

The school, which originally provided a fourth grade education, opened approximately thirty years ago. At that time Thai law mandated six years of elementary education (Steinberg et al. 1971:402), but few Thongmakhsan children bothered to walk to Huay Pha to continue school. In 1979, the school added fifth and sixth grades. Now, with the mandatory six years of education possible, the school faces an enrollment crisis since there are usually too few children to justify teaching all six grades. In 1988 the school taught second and fifth grades and parents of kindergarten-age children paid an older village girl to teach kindergarten.

A few children have attended or are attending secondary school in the provincial capital. However, it is expensive since it requires transportation to and from Town or a place to stay, tuition, pocket money, and proper school uniforms. When the students finish school there is no work for them in Town and since they have been in school they do not have the farm skills their age mates have. Most ninth grade graduates eventually settle back into farm life.

People make their livings farming. In 1988, 8 households did not grow rice; 6 households made only hill fields, *hai*; 31 made only irrigated fields, *naa*; while 10 households made both (this does not total 56; two different pairs of households worked irrigated fields together). Soybeans, garlic, and sesame are the cash crops and all except two households grew at least one of them. One household relied on wage labor and the other had not yet separated from a parental house.

There are few costs associated with farming. People typically do not use fertilizers and rarely use herbicides or insecticides on either rice or cash crops. People purchased the first "walking tractors" in 1984; in 1988 there were ten tractors. Before, they used water buffaloes to plow and harrow the irrigated fields. The walking tractors have not completely replaced the water buffaloes, but more people are buying tractors or hiring them to prepare their fields. In the past, households without access to irrigated fields could hire out as contract laborers to plow and harrow the fields of others. Since people with irrigated fields own the tractors, others now hire them to prepare fields. This source of income is now unavailable to poor households.

The tractors and the diesel fuel they need are the first major and recurring expenses associated with irrigated rice production. Lately people have bought grass cutters to more easily prepare the irrigated fields for planting garlic. People are more likely to use fertilizer and other cash inputs on their cash crops than on the rice crops since the cash crops return money (Tannenbaum 1982).

The school headmaster brought the first rice mill in 1975. It has since broken but there are two other rice mills in the village. People say that the mill and the school that supervised small children freed women to work in the fields, since they no longer had to stay home to watch the children and pound the rice in foot-operated rice pounders. Rice mill owners make money from milling the rice and selling the removed bran as pig food.

There were no costs associated with preparing cash crops for market until 1986 when it became possible to have one's soybeans mechanically threshed. It then cost 8 *baht* (1 *baht* = U.S. $0.04) per 20 liters.

Mawk Tsam Pe

If one goes over the ridge west of Thongmakhsan, one reaches the fields surrounding Mawk Tsam Pe. Crossing the ridge is the most direct route but it is steep and the usual route is to go south along the road until it joins the highway and south on the highway through Huay Pha to another small road and to follow that road west. Mawk Tsam Pe is about 7 km south and west of Thongmakhsan in a broad valley watered by both the Mae Ngi and Mae Nga rivers.

If one approaches Mawk Tsam Pe from Maehongson Town, one turns off the highway earlier and follows a road that goes through the valley. This road goes by two other Shan villages with a turnoff to other Shan villages. There is also a path, which connects the road to a nearby Karen village. Mawk Tsam Pe is approximately 25 km from Town.

Mawk Tsam Pe is much more cosmopolitan than Thongmakhsan. Mawk Tsam Pe got electricity in 1984; Thongmakhsan was scheduled to get electricity in 1990. There are a number of noodle shops, a small dry goods store associated with one of the stores in Maehongson Town, three or four smaller stores, and at least six minibuses. Thongmakhsan and Mawk Tsam Pe began their new temple construction on the same auspicious day in 1978. The Mawk Tsam Pe temple is long completed and the village has started another construction project, building a chedi on a mountain overlooking the temple. The Thongmakhsan temple rarely has more than one monk, while Mawk Tsam Pe supports a large temple with five or six permanent monks and currently has a young and energetic abbot.

Mawk Tsam Pe consists of approximately two hundred households in three contiguous villages: Mawk Tsam Pe proper, with the temple; Waan Kang to the west; and Waan Yawt to the north. These three communities form a single administrative village within *tambol* Mawk Tsam Pe. Because it is the *tambol* village its headman is the *tambol* headman, *kamnan*; he is responsible for recording births, deaths, and other administrative details, helped by an assistant headman and a clerk. The three communities are subdivided into ten groups, each with its leader. Villagewide meetings are rare; usually the neighborhood leaders are called to consult with the *kamnan* and decisions and plans are announced over the public address system.

The youth group and the housewives' group are more formal and have more structured activities. The head of the youth group receives a small salary and is responsible for organizing work groups on national holidays; he reports to the *kamnan*. As in Thongmakhsan, the youth group is informally responsible for preparing festival food, serving it, and cleaning up under the supervision of the housewives' group.

Wealth differences are greater in Mawk Tsam Pe: some households own many irrigated fields and minibuses; others must rely on selling their labor; some are government officials, either police or health workers, whose salaries support them at a relatively high standard of living. Because of the greater wealth and access to transportation, more children study in Maehongson Town; some go to the private kindergarten in Town, others to elementary school, and still others to the high school. Wealthy Mawk Tsam Pe individuals have connections with Maehongson Town so that the Town people contribute to and participate in village ceremonies, especially large or unusual ones.

The population is also somewhat ethnically diverse, including northern and central Thai, a few Burmans, and Chinese. The northern and central Thai are policemen and schoolteachers, the Burmans and Chinese mostly traders.

These differences make Mawk Tsam Pe more cosmopolitan and perhaps less "Shan." People have travelled to and worked in Bangkok. Most young adults are fluent in Central Thai. Sermons at large temple events are likely to be given in Central Thai. Some people do not follow the restriction about not doing loud or heavy work on Buddhist holy days. During the annual ceremony to rid the village of bad influences, the village should be closed to traffic, but I observed the traffic proceeding as usual. Nonetheless the village is primarily Shan and the ceremonies and traditional activities are still "Shan."

BUDDHISM AND ANIMISM

Initial scholarship on religion in mainland Southeast Asia focused on Buddhism and the perceived conflict between Buddhist and animist practices. In one interpretation, doctrinal Theravada Buddhism appears as an esoteric, austere, otherworldly religion focused on the achievement of nirvana through meditation and nonattachment to the mundane world. Many observers note that it is difficult for ordinary people to grasp these notions and follow proper Buddhist practices. Some invoke this observation to account for the existence of animist practices. As Gombrich (1971:48–56) points out, this analysis has more to do with the Western interpreters' own sense of doctrinal Theravada Buddhism than with the doctrine itself (see also Spiro 1982:xi–xiv, and Almond 1988).

More recent scholarship, recognizing the problem, focuses on practical religion in Leach's (1968) sense of religion as it is practiced rather than as it is articulated in the doctrine. Analyses in this framework emphasize Buddhist interpretations of village practices and the subordination of animist beliefs and practices to Buddhism (M. Nash 1965a, 1965b; J. Nash 1965; Tambiah 1970; Keyes 1971, 1977a, 1977b, 1984; Kirsch 1975, 1982; Pfanner 1965; Piker 1968; Smith 1966; Van Esterik 1982a, 1982b). However, Buddhism is assumed to be the key element in the religion.

This assumption is a natural extension of the everyday rhetoric. Theravada Buddhism is the state religion in Burma and Thailand and was the state religion in Laos and Cambodia. The countryside is dotted with Buddhist temples and chedis; monks in their saffron robes are a common sight. Most lowlanders, asked about their religion, say they are Buddhists. In fact, it seems to fly in the face of commonsense observations to question the basic Buddhist nature of lowland religion.

"Buddhist" carries multiple meanings. At the state level it is a rhetoric of justification for the unequal distribution of power and resources (Jackson 1989). It also carries connotations of civilization and order. When lowlanders state they are Buddhist they are making an appeal to this civilizational aspect along with any religious claims. It identifies them as civilized along with members of other world religions and separates them from uplanders, "hill tribes," who have no religion. This sense of Buddhism makes no reference to doctrine or practices and is best understood as a marker of civilized identity or a rhetoric of justification.

The label "Buddhism" obscures the analysis of religious ideology and practices. Even those working within the "practical religions" framework assume the basic Buddhist nature of everyday religion, and their analyses are phrased in Buddhist terms. The meaning of "Buddhist" remains unexamined in this context. This makes it impossible to understand village religion in its own terms or to examine the relationship between practices that can easily be labelled Buddhist or animist.

My work suggested that rather than presuming the central role of Buddhism, I should begin by analyzing religious practices and ideology in their own terms. Thus, my perspective differs from that of scholars operating within a Buddhist framework. I am not claiming that Shan are less "Buddhist" than any of their coreligionists, only that it is necessary to understand Shan religion in Shan terms.

Shan religious practices include the obviously "Buddhist," such as supporting Buddhist monks and temples and celebrating Buddhist holy days, and the obviously "animist," such as making offerings to assorted spirits associated with fields, households, and villages. While people can and do distinguish between these two kinds of observances, they explain the actions of Buddhist and animist beings in similar terms and interact with them in similar ways. Rather than taking this separation at face value, I examine the logic that underlies and explains both practices.

For Shan this logic is structured in terms of power and protection, which mutually imply each other. If one has power one can behave as one chooses without fear of the consequences of one's actions, and if one is protected one can also behave without fear of the consequences. (I explore this in much more detail in following chapters.) Focusing on power-protection made sense of both "Buddhist" and "animist" practices from the Shan perspective rather than the Western perspective based on doctrine, and provided a principled way to examine the place of Buddhism in Shan worldview. This monograph is an analysis of power-protection and its implications for Shan life.

ANTHROPOLOGICAL KNOWLEDGE

How can I assert that Shan religion is based on power-protection rather than Buddhism as everyday Shan assert? Analyzing power-protection and its implications for Shan life raises questions about how one identifies cultural principles and the kinds of evidence necessary to ascertain that one has discovered them. For power-protection to be a more plausible analysis of Shan religion than Buddhism, it needs to account for local explanations, "Buddhist" practices, and practices that are anomalous in "Buddhist" terms. I devote the rest of the monograph to the argument that power-protection is the underlying principle for understanding Shan religion.

Here I want to raise and answer questions about how and why I find it both necessary and plausible to make this claim. To do so I first raise the question of knowledge and how it is to be understood and explained, and then examine the role of ethnography in answering those questions.

Whose Knowledge?

A traditional doctor in Thongmakhsan described an offering basin as representing the Buddha: the coconut in it was the Buddha's head; the rice, his body; the two hands of bananas, his hands; the red cloth, his tongue. Neat, I thought, until I noticed these offering basins were given to carpenters and to men who supervise cremations. Neither of these occupations could be associated with the Buddha. It turns out that traditional doctors, men who read Buddhist texts out loud, and anyone else who learned a skill from a teacher all receive these offering basins. In general these offerings are said to be for teachers.

What can we make of the man's analysis? Is it wrong? Is he lying? For those whose skills rely on the Buddha's power, as do traditional doctors', the interpretation of the offering's contents as parts of the body of the Buddha makes sense. However, this traditional doctor's analysis is idiosyncratic: other traditional doctors do not describe the offering basin in this way. His analysis is not implausible; he constructed an explanation for the contents in response to my question and used local concepts to do so. This traditional doctor's account is neither correct nor incorrect; it is merely part of what needs explanation. Local accounts are part of what needs to be understood and explained and one should not accept informants' analyses at their face value.

Informants' explanations are culturally produced behaviors and, like other behaviors, need to be interpreted. The traditional doctor had no vested interest in proposing one explanation instead of another; little was riding on his account except, perhaps, his need to demonstrate his knowledge to the anthropologist.

This may not be the case with other explanations. Leach suggests that people present different interpretations of events, saying for Kachin "each lineage head tells a version which puts himself and his group in the most favourable possible light" (1954:98). While anthropologists and others have been skeptical of informants' economic or political analyses (see Scott 1985, Colburn 1989), this same skepticism has not generally been part of informants' symbolic analyses (Turner 1960, Geertz 1973, but see Roseberry 1982). To be skeptical about statements of belief or symbolic interpretations seems ethnocentric. After all, what is the appropriate interpretive framework, if not that of our informants?

How do we judge and interpret what our informants do and tell us? What sorts of evidence are their self-reports? Minimally they are culturally plausible explanations. The traditional doctor's symbolic interpretation of the offering basin drew on locally relevant constructs derived from his understanding of the world. His analysis provides some insights into the nature of these constructs. It points to the importance of the Buddha for traditional curing (see Chapters 6 and 10, where I discuss this in more detail). Informants' statements and explanations are part of the puzzle and also clues for its solution. They provide pointers to the assumptions and underlying conceptual organizations that informants use to construct their statements. Informants' explanations are not those assumptions or conceptual organizations but they provide paths for identifying them.

This type of analysis parallels the methods of linguistics. Informants' statements are an important source of information but not necessarily of analysis. The underlying principles that structure their statements may not be obvious to the speakers. Chomsky's remarks on the nature of transformational grammars are pertinent here. He states:

> Any interesting generative grammar will be dealing, for the most part, with mental processes that are beyond the level of actual or potential consciousness; furthermore, it is quite

apparent that a speaker's reports of viewpoints about his behavior and his competence may be in error. Thus a generative grammar attempts to specify what the speaker actually knows, not what he may report about his knowledge. (1965:8)

Or as Foster put it when he developed his analysis of limited good,

The members of every society share a common cognitive orientation which is, in effect, an unverbalized, implicit expression of their understanding of the "rules of the game" imposed upon them by their social, natural, and supernatural universes. A cognitive orientation provides the members of the society it characterizes with basic premises and sets of assumptions neither recognized nor questioned which structure and guide behavior in much the same way grammatical rules unrecognized by most people structure and guide their linguistic forms. (1965:293)

The objective is to specify the principles that make statements and explanations plausible for the speakers, not merely to report what they say.

Not all statements point to cultural principles in the same way. Lehman (1972) identifies cultural clichés, standard cultural accounts for interpretation of phenomena or actions. If I ask almost any adult Shan what his or her religion is, he or she will tell me it is Buddhism. This statement has the sense of cultural cliché. In order to interpret it, one needs to know the context of the statement and the audience. "Buddhism" defines Shan in contradistinction to both uplanders, whom they perceive as having no system of religion, and those Shan who have become Christian. It further serves to associate them with the more powerful lowland states. Westerners may evoke the "Buddhist" response as Shan imagine Westerners place low value on "animist" practices. Beyond this, if anthropologists assume Buddhism is the religious framework then their questions may also evoke "Buddhist" responses. In all these cases the construction of the interaction and the nature of the relationships among the people involved constrain possible statements and their meaning becomes an interpretive problem.

Spiro's (1982:23) "blue ribbon sample" of experts on Buddhism may have felt constrained to present Spiro with

Buddhist accounts, since they were consulted because they were judged to be the most knowledgeable about Buddhism. Anthropologists who work in Thailand make similar assumptions about the centrality of Buddhism for understanding all aspects of Thai culture. Keyes provides a good statement of this with reference to gender:

> In Thailand, like other Theravada Buddhist countries [Sri Lanka, Burma, Laos, Cambodia] fundamental understandings of the world have been constructed on the basis of Buddhist dogmas communicated through ritual, instruction in the *dhamma* [Sk. *dharma*]—the teachings of the Buddha—and practice of the *dhamma*, most notably by members of the order of monks, the *Sangha*. It is to be expected, then, that the culture of gender in Thailand has been shaped by Buddhist assumptions regarding the nature of reality. (1984:223)

(For a similar perspective, see also Kirsch 1985:305.) The assumption that Buddhism is the key factor for understanding constrains the questions the anthropologists ask and establishes an ethnographic context where they are likely to evoke the Buddhist answers they are seeking.

One needs to know more than the context that evokes the response and the cultural principles that inform that response to understand and interpret what is going on. One needs to know how and why people appeal to particular principles and cultural clichés. Some informants' reports may have more to do with ongoing arguments about claims to positions of value, judgments about others, and self-justifications, as Leach (1954) suggests. Nevertheless these arguments and judgments invoke or imply principles that structure arguments (Leach 1954, Scott 1985).

These underlying principles are what I take to be culture. My understanding of culture parallels Kuhn's (1962) paradigm or Wallace's (1961) mazeway for individuals. Cultures or paradigms provide a sufficiently shared framework for actions, interpreting events, defining appropriate goals, and arguments (see Keesing and Keesing 1971:123). The problem becomes how one discovers these cultural principles and how one knows one has discovered them.

Ethnography

Ethnography becomes key. Without it, we do not have the information necessary to discover the principles, ideas, and assumptions that inform peoples' behavior. Nor do we have sufficient information to sort out contexts to understand why people make the claims they do and whether those claims are reasonable in local cultural terms.

Current anthropology is deeply concerned with questions of the relationships among anthropologists, their assumptions, the interactional context with their informants, and the consequences these have for ethnographic accounts. It is fashionable to question whether any author can describe reality, much less describe different cultures' realities. Any author has values, fears, and biases, and must accept the limited nature of what can be seen, understood, and recorded. Any authorial voice is suspect, especially those of the classic anthropologists whose understandings and presentations are suspect because they were unexamined (see Clifford and Marcus 1985, Marcus and Fisher 1986, and the citations in both).

Yes, anthropology is an interpretive enterprise, because reality is not something we can know directly and we are always constrained by our own backgrounds, goals, and theoretical and political stances. Yes, it is good to be concerned with the anthropological fieldwork experience and the fieldworkers' relations with the people being studied. But these are not sufficient reasons for abandoning the anthropological enterprise of describing, analyzing, and comparing cultures. Careful attention to just those issues acts as a corrective on naive anthropological interpretations and analyses, and strengthens the resulting ethnographies.

Careful ethnographies do capture something about the reality "out there." Recent work by Weiner (1988) on the Trobriand Islanders and Errington and Gewertz (1987) on the Chambri (Mead's [1963] Tchambouli), demonstrate the enduring validity of Malinowski's and Mead's observations. Weiner notes that Malinowski's work has omissions, most seriously about women's activities, and she disagrees with his analyses, but not with his ethnographic reporting. Authoritative and unexamined voice or not, Malinowski captures something of the Trobriand culture. His extensive writings and detailed accounts are of enduring value, providing sufficient information to allow others to construct alternative interpretations. Malinowski's questions and mode of writing are of his milieu but there is more to Malinowski's work than insights into his time and culture. Errington's and Gewertz's analysis of Chambri makes a parallel case for Mead's ethnographic skills while disagreeing with her analytic accounts.

Examination of Mead, Malinowski, Benedict, and others from literary or biographical perspectives provides interesting insights into the nature of anthropology, its political concerns, and styles of analysis. Nevertheless, their works are also enduring contributions to ethnography—the description and analysis of cultures. The concurrence with Weiner and Malinowski and with Errington and Gewertz and Mead suggests that there is some ethnographic reality "out there" that we can approximate. Their works reinforce one's confidence in the general ethnographic enterprise.

How one frames an ethnography presumes answers to epistemological and anthropological questions about the nature of the enterprise. No ethnography can account for everything; one makes choices on what to use to construct an argument leaving aside other information, questions, and analyses. I see anthropology as a "science," as an exercise in description and explanation, in trying to explain some reality, however imperfectly perceived. The question I ask is how to describe the Shan understanding of their religious system. I assume that the analysis I make of Shan religion can be tested in some way against Shan "reality."

If I have discovered the logic that underlies one set of activities, say tattoos, the logic should continue to illuminate anything more I learn about tattoos and, hopefully, illuminate other actions that are not related to tattooing. One understanding derived from the power-protection analysis is why Shan translate the Pali Buddhist term *anatta* as "lack of control." *Anatta* is one of the four noble truths of Buddhism and is standardly translated into English as "no self." Shan monks, when they translate this term into Shan, do so as "no control." This is anomalous in terms of Western scholars' understandings of Buddhism. Yet the "no control" translation fits logically in a universe where power is protection and evidence of power is one's control. I discuss this analysis in more detail in Chapters 6 and 10. *Anatta* was not an issue when I began my analysis of tattoos. But the analysis of tattoos, and my understanding of power-protection based on that, illuminated the Shan understanding of *anatta*. Clarifying another issue, not directly related to the analysis at hand, strengthened my sense that power-protection captures something that is real about Shan religion and worldview.

I walk between the empiricists who assert that we can only know through numbers and behavior (see Tannenbaum 1984a, and n.d.) and those who appeal to human universals as explanations (Lévi-Strauss 1963, Douglas 1973), and so have no need to test their analyses. I assume that there are patterns to people's behaviors and that these patterns are a consequence of cultures, particular ways of organizing, interpreting, and interacting with the world. The approach I take is a rationalist one that assumes one can, through analysis, discover the patterns that underlie people's behaviors. In discovering these patterns one relies on speech, behavior, observations of structures, layouts of communities, informants' explanations, and anything else that helps one understand.

In this monograph, I show how power-protection works and the place it plays in Shan worldview. Ethnography is central in this enterprise. It provides both the information that my analysis needs to account for and the test of the goodness of fit of my analysis. There are no particular discovery procedures. The goodness of fit of my analysis comes from the structure of the evidence and its ability to account for anomalies that others leave unexplained. In the rest of the monograph I present considerable ethnographic detail to show what needs to be explained and to demonstrate the utility of the power-protection analysis. This is necessary to demonstrate the overall explanatory power of the analysis. There may be alternative explanations for each particular case, but the strength of the power-protection analysis is that it provides a coherent account for all the cases. This parsimony is another line of evidence for the analysis. Here I can only assert these as my claims for the explanatory power of my analysis; I return to these issues in the conclusion.

OVERVIEW OF THE STUDY

Festival preparations and celebrations highlight the practice of Shan religion. At a festival one notices that Shan sort people into different categories based on what they do, how they are dressed, where they sit, and how they are treated. Festivals raise questions about how people and other beings are categorized and the consequences this has for interaction.

I begin with the description of the end of the rains retreat festival held in Thongmakhsan in 1988. Following the festival I turn to a discussion in Chapter 3 of the organization and use of space, focusing on the village and its constituent parts: the temple, households, the cadastral spirit (*Tsao Mūong*) compound, and the heart of the village. The organization of space and definition of access to it provide one way to sort beings into categories and help define the nature of those categories.

Having associated beings with places, I begin in Chapter 4 the analysis of beings by examining events during which they are offered food. An understanding of food offerings and the beings to receive such offerings then provides another line of evidence for the categorization based on the organization of space and yields initial behavioral information on how Shan interact with the various beings.

In Chapter 5, I examine the nature of power-protection, locating the beings identified above on the continuum of power-protection. Beings have different capacities for and ability to acquire power-protection. Differences in power-protection structure interactions, and making offerings or providing feasts is one aspect of this interaction.

In Chapter 6, I begin to explore the place of Buddhism within this analysis. A first step is to determine what people know about Buddhism. The major source of information about Buddhism is sermons delivered by monks. In sermons, monks present their understanding of Buddhism and how it is related to village life. People attending events have the opportunity to hear sermons, although the audience does not necessarily listen closely. The sermons determine the maximum extent of information about Buddhism Shan villagers are likely to have, although depending on one's attentiveness one may learn less.

In Chapter 7, I discuss power-protection throughout the life cycle to show how capacity for power-protection structures one's activities and status as one matures. I continue this discussion in Chapter 8 to show how distinctions based on power-protection persist after death, focusing on differences in ceremonies and kinds of spirits created at death.

In Chapter 9, I return to a discussion of space and places and show how powerful beings act on them to create bounded protected areas; I go on to discuss how units of time form similar bounded units containing power. Since human beings may also be powerful, I examine their ability to create bounded protected areas and relate it back to the life cycle and one's changing capacities for power-protection.

In Chapter 10, I return to the discussion of the nature of Buddhism raised in the introduction and examine the relationship between power-protection and Buddhism. I show how power-protection structures Shan understanding of Buddhism, focusing on the Buddha, his teachings, and the monkhood; *karma*; and *anatta*, which Shan understand as "lack of control" rather than as the doctrine of "no self," an issue first raised in Chapter 6.

In most of the monograph, I refer primarily to Shan materials. In Chapter 11, I briefly examine other lowland "Theravada Buddhist" societies and present evidence that suggests power-protection is more than a Shan heresy. I go on to consider anthropological approaches to Buddhism to explain why these indications have been ignored. Finally, I return to the issue of anthropological enterprise raised in this chapter.

CHAPTER 2

Awk Waa Festival

Festivals highlight Shan community life and provide insights into Shan culture and worldview. People use the lunar calendar to schedule festivals and ceremonies. The year is divided into twelve months; even-numbered months have thirty days, odd-numbered months twenty-nine. An intercalary eighth lunar month is added every third year to keep the calendar synchronized with the solar year. Each month has two periods, a waxing moon of fifteen days and a waning moon of fifteen or fourteen days. There are four *Wan* (day) *Sin* (precept) in each month on the full, dark, and half-moon days (Tannenbaum 1984b).

Minimally each Shan village hosts a festival at the end of the rains retreat (*Waa*, Shan; *Phansa*, Thai), usually sometime from November to January. *Waa* is a period of intensified religious practices for both the monks and laypeople. It lasts three months, from the full moon day of the eighth lunar month to the full moon day of the eleventh lunar month. Ideally all men spend at least one rains retreat as a novice or a monk. The temple population is highest during these three months. During this time monks and novices should remain in the temple studying Buddhist scriptures. Their movements are restricted and there are few festivals. Old people also enter *Waa*, keeping the eight precepts (see below) and spending the day and night of each *Wan Sin* at the temple. More laypeople attend temple services during this period and the service usually includes a sermon, something that is less common outside of *Waa*.

The festival after the end of the rains retreat celebrates the monks' and community's completion of this period of increased religious activity. The festival may be called *poy awk waa*, the festival (*poy*) for leaving (*awk*) *Waa*. At the beginning of *Waa* people offer large candles to the temple to provide light for the monks while they study. So the *Awk Waa* festival may be called

21

poy pawt phay tin, the festival of extinguishing (*pawt phay*) the rains retreat candle (*tin*). It is also *poy koiy tsawt*, the festival at the end (*koiy*) of the teachings (*tsawt*), commemorating the return of the Buddha from the Tavatimsa heaven where he taught his mother and other celestial beings.

Other festivals may be celebrated in conjunction with this festival. There may be a robes offering to the monks, *kathing*, and so it can be called *poy kathing*. They may also celebrate a *poy mahatuk* (great suffering) where the villagers invite a large number of monks and individual households invite monks into their homes to receive breakfast. This festival commemorates a poor man's invitation to the Buddha to receive the morning meal at his home and the celestial help he had in preparing the meal. A *poy mangkapa* (maze) can also be held at this time, although it is rare and only held regularly at one temple in Maehongson Town.

The festival can be held any time from the end of *Waa*, after the full moon day of the eleventh lunar month, until the beginning of the second lunar month, *lūūn* (month) *kam* (observe, keep), when no festivals are held (Tannenbaum 1984b). Poorer villages may delay their festivals until after the rice harvest in December, when they know how much rice is available, and hold them in the twelfth or first lunar month. Thongmakhsan held its *Awk Waa* festival for 1979 in the first lunar month (January 1980). In 1988, the villagers started their festival on October 31, soon after the end of *Waa* (October 25).

Planning begins long before the festival is scheduled. In August and September 1988, people were talking about starting another three-year cycle of offering *poy mahatukh*, although in the end it did not occur. The village headman and his informal advisory committee made the initial plans. This committee includes men on the temple committee and the leaders of the three neighborhoods in Thongmakhsan. Together the headman and committee decide on the number of temples to be invited. This determines the size and cost of the festival since each temple will receive a money offering. Each village temple invited means that villagers from that temple will also come, increasing the size of the audience and the number of people the hosts have to feed at midday. In 1988 each temple received an offering of 100 *baht*, approximately U.S. $4.00; in 1980 the offering was 60 *baht*, at that time U.S. $3.00.

The committee can plan the size of the festival because it knows the probable range of contributions. There are two kinds of contributions: one of rice and money to buy foodstuffs and one of money to offer the monks. The village is divided into four contribution groups based on the prosperity of each household. There are five households in the first or wealthiest group and each household contributes at least 100 *baht*, enough to offer to a temple. There are twenty-five or twenty-six houses in the second group and each house would contribute 50 *baht*. The ten houses in the third group would contribute 20 to 30 *baht* while the five or six houses in the fourth group would contribute 10 to 15 *baht*. In 1988 the contributions to the cost of the festival were set at 60, 30, and 20 *baht* for the first three groups and firewood from the fourth. Households in the first group would contribute around 20 liters of rice. These figures are not absolute and some households do not contribute at the expected level; still it is enough to calculate the size of the festival.

The 1988 committee decided to invite thirteen village temples. These thirteen include all of the villages in their same subdistrict, *tambol*, plus villages from the two subdistricts in the immediate neighborhood. The invited villages include those that invite Thongmakhsan to their festivals and villages where people in Thongmakhsan have relatives.

Once the probable size is determined, the committee consults local experts to determine an auspicious day to start the festival. In 1988 it decided to start the festival on the sixth day of the waning moon of the eleventh month (October 31) because it was the only good day available. At the *Awk Waa* service on October 25, the headman announced that the festival would begin on the sixth waning moon because it was a good day, that they would invite thirteen temples, and that the richer households should contribute 60 *baht* to the festival expenses, the middle group 30 *baht*, and the poor 20 *baht*.

Once the basic outline of the festival was decided, two villagewide meetings were held at the temple. The meetings served two purposes: announcing contributions and organizing for the festival.

The festival has two parts: a temple fair held at night and the offering itself. The temple fair is a way to raise money. There are such games as knocking cans down with a ball, ring toss, and bingo. The most popular event is the *lamwong* dancing, a Thai dance form. Teenage girls form the dance troupe. The villagers build a stage and recruit a band. People who want to dance buy a ticket for a *baht,* which allows them to go up on the stage and dance with one of the troupe. Both men and women dance, although young men predominate. Some of the girls dance with three or four people at one time. The band leader blows a whistle approximately every 30 seconds, the dancer shreds the ticket, and that segment of the dance is over. Most people will buy ten or more tickets and remain on the stage dancing until the tickets are all used up. People also sell refreshments: noodles, sweets, boiled peanuts, soft drinks, and alcohol. Older people I spoke with characterized the fair as the young people's festival and said that when they were young there were no fairs, just food preparation and the offering the next morning.

At the first meeting, the housewives' group, *klum mae baan*, the youth group, and the older men made plans. The housewives' group discussed what they would sell during the nights of the festival, who would go to Town to buy the goods, who would do the preparation, and so on. The young people's group talked about who would be the *lamwong* dancers, the dance they would perform before the *lamwong* started, and what kinds of games to have. The men discussed how much each household should contribute to the festival. When the meeting proper began, each household announced how much it would contribute. The informal committee used this meeting to solicit contributions for robes for the Buddha images in the temple. Nothing was decided about the length of the festival.

There were scheduling problems. A nearby village was holding an ordination festival on the eighth of the waning moon and people in Thongmakhsan needed to go to a districtwide agricultural cooperative meeting in Maehongson Town on the ninth. One other factor was the availability of a band to play for the *lamwong* dancing. Thongmakhsan wanted to invite the local Border Patrol Police band since the members would contribute their time. (The band had no police functions.) Finally, the committee had decided to celebrate the festival for two nights. The festival would start on the sixth but the fair would be on the nights of the eighth and ninth and the offering on the tenth (November 4, 1988).

The second meeting was held on the thirtieth. This meeting was organizational. Most of the adults and young adults were assigned to various committees: young adults were to be in charge of the games; men took charge of "security," to watch for drinking and potential fights; most married women were assigned to the housewives' noodle stand; and the older men and women were to be in the temple to receive representatives from the invited villages when they came.

At this meeting the abbot of the Thongmakhsan temple suggested inviting a temple from Maehongson Town, because it has a pick-up truck and would provide transportation for the other invited temples. The committee calculated that it would have enough money and so it agreed. In the end fourteen temples were invited to the festival.

At this meeting it was announced that the festival would begin on the next day at 4:00 P.M. If people would be in the village at that time, they should come to the temple and bring popped rice with them. In addition, the youth group should come to the temple in the morning; the young adult men would build the *lamwong* stage while the women cleaned up around the temple yard.

By 3:30 P.M. on the thirty-first, the festival preparations were well underway. The *lamwong* stage was finished and four of the five large pine torches were set up throughout the village. These torches are around ten feet tall and are lit the last night when delegations from the invited villages arrive.

As people were coming to the temple to open the festival, a group of men finished putting a pine torch together. They formed a procession led by men playing drums and gongs with six men carrying the torch. The people coming to the opening stopped and threw popped rice at the torch procession. The procession went once around the temple clockwise and brought the torch to the south entrance of the temple compound. The people went into the temple.

By 3:50 there were around a dozen adults and as many children in the temple. The headman asked about the *phu*

mūong, the caretaker of the cadastral spirit, *Tsao Mūong*, saying
it was about time to begin. The *phu mūong* was at the cadastral
spirit altar informing him about the festival plans, inviting him
to the festival, and asking him to keep misfortune and fighting
from it. Around 3:55 the headman lit candles and incense on the
Buddha altar. The headman's wife was sent to bring the robes
for the Buddha images. When she returned, the headman
dressed the images in their new robes.

A woman brought a basin filled with rice and other
offerings, *phūūn poy*, for the Buddha image. While the
Thongmakhsan monk sat formally with his legs folded behind
him and his hands together held at chest height, *way*, an old
man offered the basin to the Buddha image. This old man is one
of the local experts consulted to determine the day and time to
begin the festival.

The opening ceremony began around 4:15. The old man
who offered the basin began by saying, "All the people of
Thongmakhsan invite all the spirits to come to the festival
which is starting today." He asked the spirits to ward off all
dangers and then went on to invite the spirits to the north and
the south, the east and the west, to come to the festival. After
the spirits were invited, he led the audience in the request for
the five precepts. The monk gave the precepts and then
volunteered to recite an auspicious chant. He finished chanting
around 4:45. After the monk finished, the *phu mūong* sprinkled
naam moon, sacralized water, over the Buddha images, the
drums and gongs, the headman, and the old man who led the
opening ceremony. During the ceremony, the audience sat
formally with flowers and popped rice in their hands. There
were a number of children running around shouting; people
tried to quiet them but finally the headman's wife went and sat
on the temple porch and her presence was enough to bring some
order.

While the ceremony was going on in the temple, the young
men brought the electric generator, borrowed from Huay Pha, a
village 3 km south of Thongmakhsan. Men from the youth
group were wiring the *lamwong* stage and the area around the
temple.

That evening about fifty villagers, mostly young people,
came to the temple compound to watch the girls practice

lamwong. The girls used a tape recorder to provide the music. A number of older people lit candles at the temple compound spirit altar, *tao tang ha*, at the rest house Buddha altar, and at the altar in the temple (*see* plates 3.1 [p.42] and 3.3 [p.46]). An old woman explained that they do this because it is the festival. There were no other fair activities.

The first official night of the festival was the eighth of the dark moon of the eleventh month, November 2. By 7:30 P.M. the *lamwong* stage was set up and the housewives' group was prepared to sell two varieties of noodles, candy, soft drinks, and beer and whiskey. The dancing began with two dances from the schoolchildren: one with the fifth graders and the other with the kindergarten class. They both danced to recorded Central Thai songs. Then the *lamwong* dancers, a group of twelve Thongmakhsan girls, took over while the Border Patrol Police band provided Thai rock and roll music. Underneath the temple the youth group had booths for ring toss and knocking down milk cans. Near the temple a number of people sold assorted snacks. The schoolchildren sold candy and fish balls while three people from Huay Pha sold sweets and boiled peanuts. The bingo game was set up near the temple's southern gate. Outside the southern entrance to the temple, a Thongmakhsan woman set up her own noodle and drink stand. As on the opening night, old people lit candles at the temple compound spirit altar, in the temple, and at the rest house. The people coming to the festival were from the surrounding area. The festival lasted until 2:00 A.M.

The next day was busy as people began to prepare food to feed the guests on the following day. In the morning the young adults met at the house of one of the assistant headmen. They prepared coconuts to make the sweet to be offered to the monks. Young adult women prepared food for the band, which had spent the night in Thongmakhsan. Others peeled garlic and onions for tomorrow's main dish of *kaeng hang le*, a pork curry. *Kaeng hang le* is the archetypal festival food. It is a rich concoction of pork and spices simmered in its own juices overnight. While women typically prepare the other foods, a man skilled in making *kaeng hang le* supervises its production.

Older women prepared new flowers to freshen the offering basin originally presented when the festival opened. Near the headman's house another group of women prepared the noodles to sell that night at the housewives' booth. These preparations were finished by 2:00 P.M., although the *kaeng hang le* was left to simmer the rest of the day.

By 6:30 the *lamwong* dancers congregated at a nearby house to prepare for the "revue," which opened the dancing. By 7:15, people had gone to the temple compound to set up the stalls. More people from Huay Pha came to sell snacks. The housewives' group was sponsoring a money tree, which was set up at their noodle stand; people buying noodles would contribute to the money tree.

This was the night to formally receive the invited villages. When the village delegations arrived, some older men and women from the temple met them and escorted them to the temple. Invited village delegations are expected to bring small money trees, which are offered to the host's temple. They offer the trees, receive a blessing, and then go to participate in the fair.

The pine torches were lit throughout the village. Inside the temple, the group of older people waiting to receive the village delegations prepared plates with cigars, pickled tea, and betel, and the lime and pepper plant leaves that go with it. Others prepared trays of glasses, boiled water for tea, and made sure there was drinking water available. These are the standard polite offerings to guests. Some of the invited monks had already arrived, either by regular minibus service or with the people from their village.

The youth group performed the dance revue around 8:00 and the *lamwong* dancing began about forty-five minutes later. There were the same games as the night before. However, the bingo game was moved under the temple to be closer to the crowds.

Delegations came from a number of the invited villages. Two villages brought along traditional Shan dance performers. *To* (animal) dancers and musicians arrived with the people from Kahan, a village 12 km to the north of Thongmakhsan. The *to* has been variously described as a yak, a lion, or a deer. There are two dancers inside: one dancing the front legs, the other dancing the hind legs. This one resembled a deer; it had a white mask with horns, battery operated lights for eyes, and a yellow, green, and red striped neck—the colors of the Tai (Shan) Revolutionary Army. The drum was also decorated with yellow, green, and red stripes. People crowded inside the temple to watch the "deer" dance. They placed coins and bills on the floor in front of the "deer," and the "deer" picked up the money in its mouth as it danced. At one point the "deer" danced to where the monks were sitting and, on its knees, touched its head to the floor three times to pay respect to the abbot of the temple. The dancing lasted approximately fifteen minutes.

The other dancer was a young girl from Pang Mu, a village 7 km north of Maehongson Town. She danced the *nok* (bird) dance. The costume consists of a mask and a pair of wings that the dancer manipulates with the hands. The people from Pang Mu circumambulated the temple, and she danced at two or three points while they were going around the temple and then again in the temple. As before, people flocked to the temple to watch the dancing. Generally the *to* dancers are male, while either men or women do the *nok* dance.

Starting around 10:30 the *lamwong* public address system was used to announce that the minibus from this or that village was leaving. The bingo and other games closed down. The housewives' group offered its money tree around 1:00 A.M. It totalled approximately 500 *baht*, 300 *baht* donated from the housewives' group's treasury and 200 or more from customers throughout the evening. The *lamwong* dancing continued until 2:00 A.M.

Around 1:00 A.M., people began cooking rice at the home of the assistant headman nearest the temple. The *kaeng hang le* and the sweets were finished in the morning. Around ten young adult women, a few younger men, and two or three older women to supervise stayed up to cook pot after pot of rice. Altogether people donated around 6 *thang* (1 *thang* = 20 liters) of milled nonsticky rice. Households that made hill rice fields donated hill rice. Because this is more fragrant and tasty, it was cooked separately and served to the monks. Rice cooking lasted all night.

Early in the morning, women began preparing other curries to be offered to the monks for breakfast and to be offered for lunch to both the monks and laypeople. They made *kyasan*, bean thread soup, a standard festival food because it is easy to prepare and inexpensive. The *kyasan, kaeng hang le*, and *khanom phawng*, fried water buffalo rinds, would be offered to everyone. They prepared *phak kat up*, a stew of greens, *tom cūūt*, a bland soup, and *taeng sa*, a cucumber salad, for the monks.

After breakfast, people gathered near the headman's house to form a procession to carry the small money trees, *ton ngen*, and other offerings to the temple. To make a *ton ngen*, people take a piece of soft wood, decorate it with colored paper, split small pieces of bamboo and insert money (new bills if they have them), decorate one end and stick the other into the soft wood. The "tree" is placed in a glass filled with milled rice. In other villages, rolls of toilet paper or bunches of garlic form the base of the tree. The money, tree, and glass are all donated to the temple. Young adult women dress in their best clothes, and donors often give their *ton ngen* to these young women to carry in the procession.

The man who had donated a toilet for the temple led the procession. He carried a bowl with popped rice and flowers. A schoolboy carrying robes to be offered to the abbot of the Thongmakhsan temple followed. People carrying *ton ngen* followed the boy. Three people donating Shan texts also carried them in the procession. Young men playing drums and gongs brought up the end. The procession included around thirty to forty people, counting children. People not participating in the procession stood along the road or waited to greet it at the temple. When the procession reached the temple entrance, the man leading it broke away from the procession and joined the people throwing popped rice on the offerings. The people circumambulated the temple clockwise, three times, and carried the offerings to a table in front of the altar.

The procession was over by 9:00. Soon after, laypeople and monks from the invited villages began arriving. In the temple, young adults set out trays containing teapots, glasses, pickled tea (*miang*), salt to mix with the *miang* and which Shan put into their tea, betel and the lime and pepper leaves that go with it, and cigars or cigarettes. The same hospitality items were offered to guests the night before.

When people enter the temple they climb stairs, since the temple is elevated, and leave their shoes on the verandah (*see* figure 3.2 [p.47] for the temple layout). On entering the temple proper, they face the main image and bow down three times— once each for the Buddha, his disciples (the *sangha*), and his teachings (the *dharma).* Then, turning toward the monks, they repeat the three bows.

Those attending a festival usually offer a small amount of money, anywhere from one to ten *baht* (U.S. $0.04 to $0.40). By this generosity they share in the merit made at the festival. People carefully place their money contributions in a monk's bowl in the center of the temple.

Around 9:30, one of the two men skilled in reading Shan (*tsale,* literally "clerk," but here men who read texts out loud in the Shan style) began reading Buddhist religious texts to the laypeople. When the people from Mawk Tsam Pe, a village 7 km southwest of Thongmakhsan, arrived, their *tsale* took over the reading. The *tsale* receives an offering basin, *phʉʉn poy,* similar to the one for the Buddha, but which also includes an envelope with 20 or 30 *baht.*

Older men and women, guests and members of the host community, stayed in the temple chatting with friends, drinking tea and eating *miang* or betel, and listening to the *tsale* read. Younger people wandered through the village, visiting friends. In larger villages, the visitors may shop in the local stores, but Thongmakhsan's store does not offer any goods not generally available elsewhere. Often people sell sweets, boiled peanuts, or Shan medicines near the temple on the day a festival is offered. However, Thongmakhsan's festival is relatively small and there were no vendors.

Most of the invited monks and novices arrived together as they received a ride from the monk from Maehongson Town. As they entered the temple they too removed their shoes and paid respect to the Buddha image and to the abbot of the temple. They remained in the temple, seated on the elevated area surrounding the Buddha images, and visited with other monks or with laymen sitting near the elevated area.

Two older women dressed in white and with shaved heads arrived with the visiting monks from Huay Pha. These are *mae khao,* literally "women in white," and are often referred to as Buddhist "nuns." Unlike Catholic nuns, these women are not ordained; however, their subservient role and their self-appointed tasks of cooking and keeping the temple compound clean make a functional identity with nuns elsewhere. The Buddha is said to have reluctantly established an order of female monks, *bhikkhuni*, but it died out and there is no one to ordain new female monks. (I return to a discussion of women and religion in Chapter 10.)

Around 10:00 there was some panic as people worried whether there would be enough *tom cūūt* for the monks, and *naam phit nawk*, a hot and spicy pork dish, was prepared at the last minute. Monks, novices, and *mae khao* cannot eat solid food after 12:00 noon; they usually eat their lunch around 11:00. The food has to be prepared and ready by then.

Around 10:40 the activity level at the temple increased as people brought the rice and curries from where they were prepared. In the kitchen area in the temple, women prepared plates of sweets and started making up trays of curries. Men set up small round tables on the elevated area and others on the floor nearby. The tables on the elevated area were covered with tablecloths and set with the best dishes and cutlery the Thongmakhsan temple owns. The other tables were not covered and were set with everyday dishes and cutlery. Men took the trays of curries and plates of rice and set them on each table. They also placed a basin of cooked rice beneath each table.

Monks were now invited to eat at the tables on the elevated area. At each table, a layman formally offered the food by using both hands to slightly raise the table, the monks touching the table to acknowledge the offering and accept the food. Each table seated five or six monks. The food offered to the monks included the festival foods, any foods prepared especially for the monks, and any curries people may have brought to the temple that morning. Usually monks are offered fruit and sweets for dessert.

Novices ate at the tables placed near the elevated area. The food was not formally offered to them. Novices were served after the monks and generally received the same range of foods. If there is a small amount of a particular dish, it is offered only to the monks. If there are enough fruits and sweets, the novices are also served dessert.

Mae khao sat in the middle of the temple. They were served their lunch on trays set on the floor. Their food is usually the same as will be served to all the laypeople. Nuns are not offered a dessert unless it is going to be served to all the laypeople. Occasionally the hosts almost forget the *mae khao* and there is a last-minute flurry of activity to prepare their trays so they can eat before noon.

While these groups were eating, preparations were underway to serve lunch to the laypeople. The cooks, assisted by young adult men and women, dished up and served the food. Trays were filled with dishes of curries, and plates were filled with rice.

Once the monks, novices, and nuns had finished eating, food was served to the laypeople. Old men were served first, and their trays of curries were likely to include leftovers from the monks' meal. Other men were served next, and then women. There was a little time lapse once the serving started, so that all the laypeople began eating at much the same time. People sat in a circle around the trays of curries. Generally old men ate with other old men, younger men with younger men, and women and children with women and children. As people ate, young people carrying serving pots with more curry refilled empty dishes and saw that everyone had more than enough to eat. They also made sure that water jars were placed throughout the temple. The laypeople were served around 11:30.

The people preparing and serving the food ate last, after everyone else had finished. The eating groups were more informal, with people clustering around the preparation area, men and women together. After they ate, they washed the dishes and swept the eating area. Guests might then remain in the temple or visit in the community.

The servers finished eating and cleaning up around 12:30. People were anxious to start the ceremony and they kept checking to see whether the people washing dishes had returned.

Once the cleanup was finished the preparations for the ceremony proper began. Monks straightened their robes and put on their shoulder cloths. Trays with cones of flowers were brought and placed throughout the temple. People took three cones of flowers and some popped rice to offer, placing them on three trays near the middle of the temple. One tray was for the Buddha, one for his teachings, and the third for the monks.

One of the men got up and struck a gong with a mallet to call the last stragglers into the temple. The monks finished straightening their robes and began to assemble on the raised area in front of the Buddha images (*see* plate 3.3 [p.46]). Monks seat themselves based on their seniority, the monk who has been in the order for the most rains retreats sitting on the front right. The other monks in descending rains retreat order sit to his left and, if necessary, form second or third rows. The novices arrange themselves in rains retreat order to the left of the "youngest" monk.

Men took the trays containing the flower and popped rice offerings and placed the one for the Buddha in front of the main Buddha image, the one for the teachings in the northwest corner to invite the spirits to hear the teachings, and the one for the monks near the preaching chair for the monk who would lead the service.

The ceremony began with the *tsale* from Naapaatsaat announcing that today was the day when Thongmakhsan was offering its festival. It is somewhat unusual to have a man from elsewhere lead the ceremony. Any older man who knows the words can lead the audience in formally requesting the monks to begin the service. The request begins with the man leading the people in paying respect to and asking for forgiveness from the Buddha, his teachings, and the monks. The leader begins the request and the audience recites along with him. Young people are not likely to know all the words and they recite the parts they know; otherwise they remain silent. This is followed by the formal request to receive the five precepts. Both of these are in Pali, the sacred language of Theravada Buddhism. People may not know the meaning of the chants but recognize which ones are used for what.

The oldest monk, here the abbot from Naapaatsaat, indicated that the monks had selected the abbot from the Pang Mu temple to perform the service and give the sermon. Some monks, like the abbot of Pang Mu, are known for their skills in delivering entertaining sermons. If one of these monks is at the festival he is likely to be invited to give the sermon.

The abbot from Pang Mu bowed three times to the Buddha image and then to the "oldest" monk, left the elevated platform, and seated himself in the preaching chair. The *tsale* from

Naapaatsaat offered him the tray of flowers and popped rice, which he accepted by touching the tray.

Holding his fan in front of his face, the Pang Mu abbot led the lay audience through the chants that are part of receiving the five precepts. As all temple services, it began with *"Namo tassa bhagavato arahato sammasambuddhassa,"* homage to the Exalted One, the arahant, the Buddha perfected by himself (Khantipalo 1983:2). This was repeated three times, followed by the request for the three refuges and the five precepts. The three refuges, also repeated three times, are "To the Buddha I go for refuge, to the Dhamma I go for refuge, to the Sangha I go for refuge" (Khantipalo 1983:2). This is followed by the five precepts: I undertake to refrain from taking life, stealing, improper sexual behavior, lying, and intoxication.

Precepts (*sin* in Shan; *sila* in Pali) are rules for behavior. Keeping the five precepts is an ideal. Unlike the Christian commandments, people do not have to follow the precepts all the time; good people strive to do so but people recognize that it is generally impossible to do so all the time.

The chants were followed by a formal request for a sermon, again in Pali. The monk put down the fan and began his sermon with *"Namo tassa . . ."* repeated three times and added another passage in Pali. He then went on in Shan mixed with some Thai. As is usual, he began by listing the sponsors of the event, in this case all the people of Thongmakhsan, the people who had donated books, and the man who had donated the bathroom. He explained what the event was, that it was an *Awk Waa* festival held during the eleventh lunar month. He went on about how this was an occasion for relatives and friends to get together, in contrast to ordinary days when it is hard to get people together because they are working. The festival was a chance to invite friends and relatives from far away; and it was important and good to have friends.

He also talked about the merit and benefits of offering and, in particular, the benefits accruing to the household that offered the toilet. "People might think," he said, "that offering a toilet does not have much merit, that it's not very important. However, after a long trip, what is the first thing you want? A toilet." Anything useful brings merit. People offering the books and the villagers offering robes to the monks receive merit. The villagers provide the monk with the four necessities—food, clothing, shelter, and medicine. Laypeople and monks both need these. People offering them receive benefits in this and future lives. The monk ended with a blessing asking that powerful beings protect all the laypeople. The sermon lasted approximately twenty-five minutes. (I discuss sermons in more detail in Chapter 6.)

From the start of the service through the beginning of the sermon, the laypeople sat formally with their hands together at chest height holding popped rice and flowers and with their legs bent back. People do not necessarily pay much attention to the sermon. As the sermon progresses they begin to sit more comfortably. Some people dozed, leaning against a pillar or the raised platform. The sleepers were a source of amusement for the rest of the audience. As the sermon drew to a close, people cued by the increased speed of the blessing sat up and resumed their formal posture. Throughout the service there was a fair amount of noise with children playing and people whispering; this is not considered disrespectful.

After the sermon, the monks were presented with offerings. Each monk representing an invited temple received a *ton ngen*. The Pang Mu monk was presented with a special offering, a plate filled with goods monks need such as detergent, incense, soap, candles, and matches, all wrapped in translucent gold paper with 20 *baht* attached to the top. These offerings cost 15 *baht* on up; stores in Maehongson Town make them to order or people can buy the contents and put them together themselves. Men presented the offerings, placing one before each monk. Novices were presented with envelopes containing their offerings. Envelopes with money were also given to *mae khao*. If monks receive 50 *baht*, novices are likely to get 20 *baht*, and *mae khao* 10 *baht*.

After the offerings were made, the monks and novices chanted a blessing. Usually the *mae khao* either chant quietly along with the monks or repeat a blessing they know. After the monks chant the blessing, the abbot announces that they will chant for pouring water, *yat naam*. During the chant, old people and the major sponsors take a small bottle of water and pour it either through a hole onto the ground or into a container that they later empty on the ground. The chant and water pouring are to share the merit made with all living beings. The laypeople again pay respect to and ask forgiveness from the Buddha, his teachings, and the monks, and the ceremony is over. The Thongmakhsan festival finished around 1:15.

Monks and novices gathered up their offerings to return to their home temples. Guests returned to their own villages. The temple committee members remained briefly at the temple counting money and sorting offerings. A few villagers remained to sweep the temple. Most went home to sleep. Soon the temple yard was deserted.

The work of the temple and festival committees was not finished. They still had to total receipts, calculate costs, and make arrangements to return the unused portions of the goods to stores in Maehongson Town to be reimbursed. The housewives' noodle stand earned 1,394 *baht*, bingo and other games 1,027 *baht*, and the *lamwong* dancing 5,473 *baht*, for a total of 7,894 *baht* for the two nights of the fair. The committee decided to give the Border Patrol band 1,000 *baht*—not as wages, but to help them because they came and helped with the Thongmakhsan festival. After deducting other costs, the total income was 6,001 *baht*.

This money was divided between the housewives' group, which received 3,000 *baht*, and the youth group, which received 3,001 *baht*. Each group donated 500 *baht* to the village beautification and development (*phatana*) committee. The housewives' group planned to use its money for low-cost emergency loans, while the youth group planned to buy sports equipment. The village beautification committee decided to use its money to buy nails, paint, and other materials to make signs.

The temple received a total of 2,259 *baht* from the money trees brought by village delegations, the excess *ton ngen* not required for the invited temples, and the small contributions guests made. No festival costs were deducted from this money. Some of this money would be used to make the small money trees that the Thongmakhsan villagers would take to the host temples when they were invited to festivals. They planned to reciprocate with trees of the same value as they had received. This would be the first year they had enough money to do this. Before, they had to collect money from the villagers, and the trees varied from around 40 to 100 *baht* in value.

While thirteen villages and their temples had been invited to the festival, two of them did not attend the festival at all—no one came on the night to receive guests or on the day the festival was offered. One of these is a very poor Pa-O village, which used to be close to Thongmakhsan but had moved further away. The other is the small Shan village of Huay Khan, which Thongmakhsan does not normally invite. Since neither monks nor villagers came, they did not receive the *ton ngen* set aside for them and the money went into the Thongmakhsan temple fund. A temple committee member explained that if they sent the trees, it would appear that the nonattending temple was greedy. One village came to the festival but did not send a delegation with a small money tree; its monk came when the festival was offered. People were unhappy that the village had not sent a delegation and there was some talk that Thongmakhsan would not send a money tree to its festival. This village's festival was held after I left and I do not know whether Thongmakhsan sent a tree or not.

CHAPTER 3

Organization of Space

Empty, the temple itself hints at important dimensions of organization and differentiation. The temple layout defines areas and structures the arrangement and interactions among people at festivals. The different areas in the temple and the people associated with them point to important distinctions among kinds of beings and their roles. The cadastral spirit compound, the heart of the village, and houses and house compounds are other areas in the community that help to identify important distinctions among kinds of beings. After describing these places, I present the Shan concepts of space, its division, and how these help identify different kinds of beings. In the next chapter I analyze the roles of these beings and their similarities and differences.

PLACES

The Temple Compound

The temple compound is enclosed by a more or less substantial fence. Shan temples are located, ideally, on the edge of the community. They are part of the community but should be physically separate from it. When first built the temple compound may be at the edge of the community; however, as the village expands, houses may surround the temple compound.

Inside the compound are a number of buildings (*see* figure 3.1 [p.40]). Minimally each compound has the temple building, *kyawng*, and a small enclosed area that contains the altar for the spirit lord of the temple, *tao tang ha* (the official [*tao*] to whom five [*ha*] offerings are made [*tang*]). The compound may contain an ordination hall, *simh* (Thai, *bot*); a special kitchen and food preparation area; rest houses, *sarap*, where devout

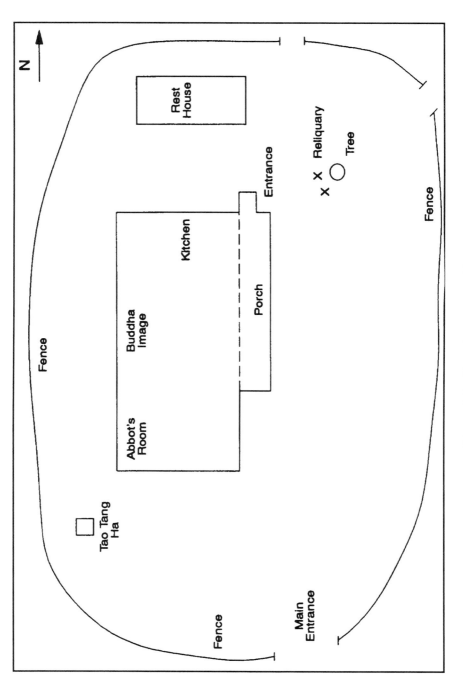

Figure 3.1: Temple compound layout

laypeople stay on *Wan Sin*; and small houses, also called temples or *kyawng,* where monks may live and sleep separate from the monks in the main temple. In addition to these buildings there may be a stupa or chedi, *tsati,* a reliquary containing the remains of a Buddha, paraphernalia associated with a Buddha, or precious objects such as gold or gems. The chedi is enclosed with its own fence. Around the chedi are reliquaries, *umang,* containing ashes and bones left from laypeoples' cremations. These may also be set into the temple compound wall. Temple compounds in well-to-do communities have the full range of buildings while those in poorer communities, like Thongmakhsan, may only have the *kyawng,* the *tao tang ha* compound, and reliquaries (*see* figure 3.1 [p.40]).

The *tao tang ha* is a post approximately four feet tall with four arms placed about two-thirds of the way up (*see* plate 3.1 [p.42]). There is a small platform at the end of each arm and offerings are placed on these and on the top of the post. Offerings to mother earth, *mae thorani,* are placed at the base of the post. Women are not allowed to enter the fenced area surrounding the post. Since the Thongmakhsan temple's *tao tang ha* was not fenced, women could and did place their own offerings. (When I visited in Thongmakhsan in the summer of 1992 the *tao tang ha* area had been fenced and women could no longer place their own offerings.)

Shan temples, *kyawng,* can be splendid buildings with layers of roofs and spires (*see* plate 3.2 [p.43]). The temple is elevated ten to fifteen feet above the ground: ideally it is higher than surrounding houses. This building, technically a *sala kanparien,* is where temple services are held and is the focus for Shan festivals because of the Buddha images and monks that reside there. As in the *Awk Waa* festival, when people parade offerings, they circumambulate the *kyawng.* This differs from the Central Thai arrangement, in which the ordination hall is both the place for services and the focus of the temple (O'Connor 1985). I describe the Thongmakhsan temple; other temples have similar layouts but may be oriented differently.

The entranceway into the *kyawng,* situated on the north side, has its own layered roof leading to the verandah, which leads to the temple proper set a step higher than the porch (see plate 3.2, and figure 3.2 [p.47]). Inside along the south and west

Plate 3.1: The *tao tang ha* compound in Thongmakhsan.

Plate 3.2: The temple in Thongmakhsan.

sides is another raised area approximately fifteen feet wide, which extends along two-thirds of the walls. The west side contains the major Buddha images, placed on a raised altar, and is the sleeping area for most monks. In other temples there may be cabinets for storing extra bedding and the temple's books. This is where monks sit to chant during regular services and ceremonies. The southwest corner contains the abbot's room. Monks eat seated on the southern raised area. Visiting monks might also sleep here.

The abbot and other monks receive lay visitors here; monks sit on the raised area while laypeople sit on the temple floor. Except when placing offerings, laymen do not go onto the elevated area unless invited. Women do not go onto the elevated areas at all. In some temples there are signs in Thai and English warning missionaries, Thai, and the occasional Western tourist that it is forbidden for women to ascend to this platform.

At the northwest corner is another room where the novices sleep; the floor is the same level as the temple floor. Novices sit on the raised area near the altar when there is chanting; otherwise they need an invitation from a monk to ascend to it.

Along the northern side is the cooking and storage area. It is a step lower than the rest of the temple area. This is the area where the festival food is served. Dishes are stored here and there is a small cooking area.

The rest of the temple forms one large open room. In front of the main Buddha image but set on the temple floor is a chair where the monk sits while preaching (*see* plate 3.3 [p.46]). People attending ceremonies sit on the floor in the open area. During a temple service, one can clearly see the orderly arrangement of people. Older men cluster near the elevated areas while younger men sit behind them. There is usually an empty space marking a boundary between men and women. The nuns form the front edge of women. Old women sit behind the nuns while younger women sit along the outside edges. "Old" is a social, not necessarily an age, category and old men and women can be identified by a cloth or towel on their shoulders. Small children, regardless of sex, sit wherever they choose. At any temple service there are usually more women than men and few younger men. Often during a festival service, young men do not enter the temple proper but remain in the entryway or in the temple yard (*see* figure 3.2 [p.47]).

The *kyawng* can be a home for monks, men who have been ordained and keep the 227 monastic rules; novices, men and boys who have been ordained and keep ten precepts; a temple caretaker, *phu kyawng*, who takes care of the temple and serves the monks; and temple boys, *kapi kyawng*, young boys who are sent to live at the temple because their parents cannot afford to feed them, because they have discipline problems, or in order to give them access to better schooling.

The Thongmakhsan temple has only the one monk, who did not want novices staying at the temple. There were no temple boys. When I left in 1988 there was no formal *phu kyawng*; the job was being rotated among all the houses in the village with each house sending one person to serve as *phu kyawng* for twenty-four hours. At other times there had been a regular *phu kyawng*, paid in rice collected from each household. There has to be someone to offer meals formally to the monk. Where there are novices, they can perform the *phu kyawng* functions.

Regular temple services, villagewide festivals, large household festivals, and some village meetings are held in the *kyawng*. The *kyawng* serves as a storehouse for such items as plates, teapots, and large cooking pots. Villagers may borrow these when they sponsor household ceremonies and need more dishes or larger pots.

The temple compound can also be a home for what are called "Buddhist nuns," *mae khao* (literally, women in white; Thai, *mae chi*, female ascetics). These are women who have retired from village life, dress in white robes, shave their heads, and keep the eight precepts for devout laypeople at all times. These women live in their own small houses within the temple compound, where they cook and prepare their own food. They may prepare food for the monks and novices, clean the temple, and take care of the temple grounds. Unlike monks and novices these women are not ordained. In general they do not receive much respect (see Van Esterik 1982a).

If the temple compound has another substantial building, it is the *simh* (Thai, *bot*) or ordination hall. Shan use the *simh* for events limited to monks. These include the regular reciting of the 227 monastic rules (Pali, *pattimokkha*) and confessions of

Plate 3.3: The Buddha altar in the Thongmakhsan temple. The chair in the right

from gram li ruh ye the monk sits to give a sermon

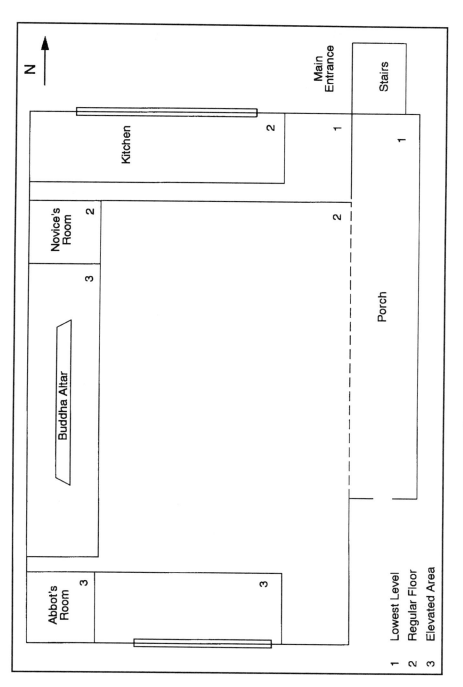

Figure 3.2: Temple layout

breaches of them; the beginning and ending of special retreats, *khao kam* (Thai, *pariwat*); and ordinations. During these times novices and laymen cannot enter the *simh*. During the other times monks and novices use the *simh* as an extension of their living space. Women do not enter the *simh*. When Shan communities celebrate Central Thai festivals (usually those sponsored by the school) with a procession, they circumambulate the *simh*.

Many of the areas are identifiable because people make offerings to beings associated with different parts of the temple compound. Households usually send someone every day to bring food to the temple. The majority of the offerings are placed on the full and dark moon *Wan Sin*. The *tao tang ha* and *mae thorani* receive offerings from monks, novices, and laypeople. If women want to place an offering here they must rely on male intermediaries. People also place offerings at the chedi and their relatives' reliquaries, particularly those of parents and grandparents. They may also place them on the Buddha altars in the *kyawng* and *simh*. The *phu kyawng* or monks place daily offerings to the Buddha images in the *kyawng* and *simh*. When there is a service in the temple, people bring offerings of flowers and popped rice to place on three offering trays, one each for the Buddha, the teachings, and the monks.

Having a temple is an important part of Shan community definition. The size of the temple and its quality are public statements of the community's wealth and well-being. Many ceremonies that mark the village as a unit take place at the temple. Having a temple means that the community exists as a unit separate from other communities, and can participate in the exchange of invitations among communities. If it does not have a temple, it cannot sponsor these ceremonies nor participate as a separate entity in the invitations from other communities.

The Cadastral Spirit: *Tsao Mūong*

The *Tsao Mūong* compound is placed in a tree-shaded spot away from residential areas (*see* figure 3.3 [p.51]). It is a small elevated building, which has an open porch and a closed room. Offerings are placed in the porch area (*see* plate 3.4 [p.50]). When the *Tsao Mūong* comes to the village, he stays in the inner room.

Inside it there is bedding, water, and flowers. Underneath this room or nearby are posts to which other spirits hitch their horses and elephants. There may also be another small building where guests of the *Tsao Mūong* stay. Women cannot enter the *Tsao Mūong*'s compound.

The *Tsao Mūong*'s role is to protect the village from danger, keep out evil forces, prevent trouble during festivals, and generally preserve the well-being of all the human and animal inhabitants. The *Tsao Mūong* or his representative is said to descend to the village on *Wan Sin*. He is invited to receive the precepts and listen to sermons at temple services. He is also said to enforce restrictions against heavy or noisy work on these days. The *Tsao Mūong* is informed of weddings, births, and ordinations and invited to villagewide ceremonies.

There is a reciprocal relationship between a community and its *Tsao Mūong*. In return for his protection, the *Tsao Mūong* receives offerings on full and dark moon *Wan Sin* and is feasted, *liang Tsao Mūong*, once in the seventh lunar month or, if twice a year, less elaborately in the third lunar month. If a household does not participate in this, then it is not included in the *Tsao Mūong*'s protection. The community's relationship with its *Tsao Mūong* is similar to that with the temple. Like monks, the *Tsao Mūong* is presumed benevolent and unlikely to withdraw his protection. By being respectful and making offerings, villagers receive protection. The consequence is a happier and more peaceful community.

Because of their age and devotion to Buddhism, some *Tsao Mūong* receive only white (*phūūk*) offerings of cooked rice, hard-boiled eggs, sweetened condensed milk, sweets, and fruits. Other younger *Tsao Mūong*, like the one in Thongmakhsan, receive red (*leng*) offerings of chickens and liquor in addition to the offerings of cooked rice and sweets. The kind of offering depends on whether the *Tsao Mūong* is a precept keeper; it does not affect the *Tsao Mūong*'s role or power. Food that has been offered to the *Tsao Mūong* is considered particularly wholesome, and villagers of all ages eat it.

In each community there is one man, the *phu mūong*, whose duty it is to keep the compound clean, place the regular offerings made to the *Tsao Mūong*, supervise his annual or semiannual feasts, and act as the intermediary for villagers

Plate 3.4: The *Tsao Mūong* compound in Thongmakhsan.

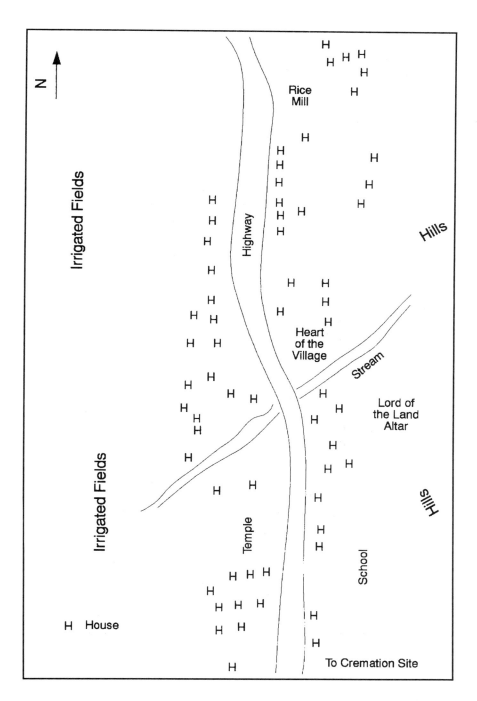

Figure 3.3: Village layout

who wish to make a special request of the *Tsao Mūong*. He will also make the offerings if the *Tsao Mūong* grants the request.

Villagers do not interact directly with the *Tsao Mūong*. When households prepare offerings, they are taken to the *phu mūong*'s house. The *phu mūong* takes all the households' offerings and places them on the porch of the *Tsao Mūong*'s house while reciting the appropriate words. Any man not born on a Monday, and who knows the proper words, can be the *phu mūong*. Monday is tiger day; a Monday-born man as *phu mūong* causes tigers to enter the village, endangering the inhabitants and their animals. In villages where the *Tsao Mūong* receives offerings of chickens, the *phu mūong* is a young man. Because the job involves killing chickens, when the *phu mūong* gets older and actively keeps the five precepts, he will turn the job over to a younger man.

Any collection of Shan households contains a Lord of the Land altar. Each hamlet of Mawk Tsam Pe has its own *Tsao Mūong*. The three *Tsao Mūong* are brothers, of whom the *Tsao Mūong* of Mawk Tsam Pe proper is the eldest.

The Heart of the Village: *Tsaū Waan*

The *Tsaū Waan*, the heart of the village, is a post that resembles the Central Thai country post, *lak mūong* (Terwiel 1978). Unlike the *Tsao Mūong* compound and the temple, the heart of the village tends to be in the center of the village among the houses. Associated with the post is a tower room, the floor of which is higher than the temple floor and neighboring houses. All independent Shan villages have a heart of the village, but some may not have the tower room and may not perform the annual ceremony associated with it. Usually the tower is empty. Women cannot enter this room.

Thongmakhsan does not actually have a post (*see* plate 3.5 [p.56]). They had one in the past but it either decayed and was not replaced or it was buried when the road was built. Nonetheless the villagers treat a spot near the tower room where the post was reported to be as if the post were still there.

The heart of the village comes into prominence once a year in the seventh lunar month, when people ask monks to chant for the village, *suut* (chant) *moon* (blessing) *waan* (village) (see Durrenberger 1980 for the description of one such ceremony).

People also refer to the ceremony as "repairing the village," *mae waan*, or "closing the village," *pik waan*. The ceremony serves to rid the village of all bad things—diseases, bad spirits, bad luck, and misfortune. Ideally the village is closed during the ceremony; people can leave but no one can enter since people entering may bring bad influences in with them.

Underneath the tower people place baskets with sand, pine kindling, spirit shields (*taa liao*), milled rice, white thread, a bucket of water, and other items in everyday use. A Buddha image is placed in the tower room. Monks are invited to chant in the tower. They hold a white thread, connected to the Buddha image, which encircles a monk's bowl with water in it and the area beneath the tower with the baskets. After the monks chant, the senior monk sprinkles the baskets and the people with the water. The water and the baskets the monks chanted over acquire the power to chase out bad influences and ward off their reentering.

People take their baskets and buckets of water home. They sprinkle the milled rice in the house and the sand in the house compound, put the spirit shield up over the door, connect the white thread to the shield, and encircle the house. The rice and the sand chase away bad influences; the spirit shield and thread create a barrier preventing bad things from reentering the house.

Houses and House Compounds

Shan houses are built up off the ground. Substantial houses are made of hardwoods such as teak; others are made of bamboo or a combination of hardwoods and bamboo. In old-style houses, the area beneath the house was used to keep water buffalo, for storage, and as a place to work. In newer Thai-style houses people often lay cement floors, wall in the area, and use it as general living space. The house is divided up into a number of separate identifiable spaces—porch, room to receive guests, kitchen, and bedroom.

As one comes up into an older house, there is an unroofed porch area. The floor is made of boards placed about an inch apart. Here rice is dried on mats, clothes hung to dry, knives sharpened, babies bathed, and so on. People leave their shoes on the porch before they come up the step into the "room to receive guests," *hawng hap khaek*. Most of daily life is lived

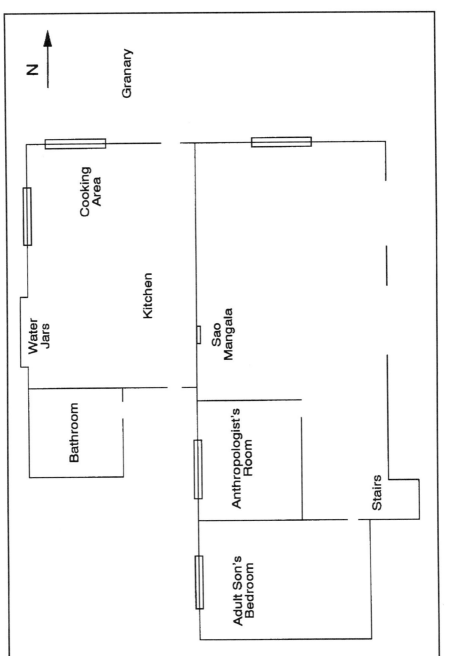

Figure 2.4: House layout: First floor living area

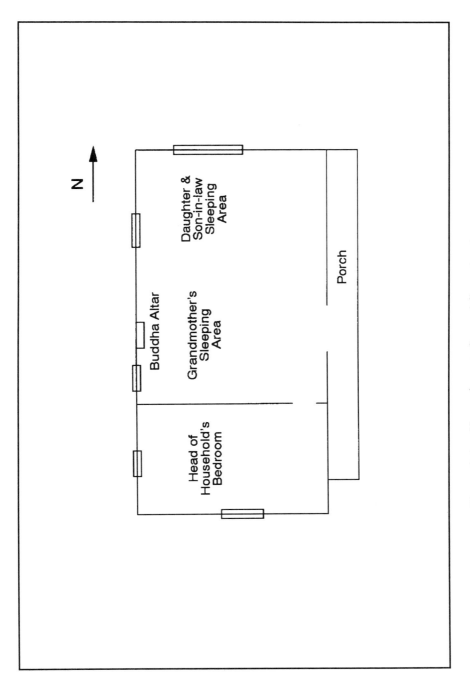

Figure 3.4a: House layout: Second floor sleeping area

Plate 3.5: The heart of the village compound in Thongmakhsan. If there was a "heart post," it would be placed near the elevated room.

here. Here householders eat, children play, people nap, guests sleep, and visitors sit. The room, walled on three sides, opens onto the porch. Behind the guest room is a walled sleeping room, *hawng nawn*, for the couple, girls, and small children. Young adult males of the household may sleep in the outer guest room. Generally only household members enter the sleeping room and they keep their personal possessions there. The floor of the sleeping room is on the same level as the outer room but the door cut in the wall may not go down to the floor level. One must step over the door sill into the sleeping room. The kitchen, *sawng phay*, is on the same level as the porch; however, the flooring is complete and it is roofed over. The kitchen may be placed on the side of the porch or at the back of the house. Inside the kitchen are the firepots, concrete buckets. Most houses have two of these; poorer houses may just have an iron ring. The firepots or rings are set into a box filled with sand or ash.

In newer houses, the cement floored first story serves as the major living area, although the upstairs room is formally the room to receive guests. The enclosed bedroom is also upstairs (*see* figures 3.4 [p.54] and 3.4a [p.55], and plate 3.7 [p.59]).

Attached to one side of the house or on its own elevated platform, approximately at the same level as the house, is the household's rice granary. Traditionally this contains baskets made of bamboo and chinked with a mud and dung mixture to seal the cracks. They are approximately six feet tall and five feet across. One can gauge a household's wealth by the number of baskets in the granary. A few households have built tighter granaries of wood.

The household's Buddha altar, *khing phara*, is usually placed high on the east or north wall in the room to receive guests (*see* plate 3.8 [p.61]). It is attached to the *sao mangala* (literally post, *sao*, blessing, *mangala*). The *sao mangala* is the center post and is the first house post erected; offerings to the *tsao naam tsao lin* (lord of the water, *naam*, and land, *lin*) are placed in the post hole and auspicious plants and a white cloth covered with a red cloth tied to its top. The cloths are said to mark the house as a place of human, as opposed to spirit, occupation. This is important lest the *naga*, associated with the earth, enter and cause misfortune for the human inhabitants.

Plate 3.6: A new style Shan House in Thongmakhsan. This is the house where I stay.

Plate 3.7: The *hawng hap khaek*. The ropes in the foreground support a cradle. The TV is in the corner. The *sao mangala* is the post with the large pictures of the King and Queen of Thailand.

People sit so their feet do not point at the Buddha altar. When they sleep they lie with their heads pointing toward the Buddha altar. Where there are a number of sleeping areas, people are careful to lie so their feet do not point at the heads of other sleepers or at the Buddha altar.

People occasionally place the altar on the west side. One consequence of having the Buddha altar on the west wall is that people sleep with their heads pointing west, an inauspicious direction. The Buddha altar in the house I stay in is on the west wall. Since we had to sleep with our heads pointing to the west, I asked the man of the house why he had done this. He explained that the household Buddha image, like the ones in the temple, would face the sunrise in the east.

The altar may be more or less elaborate (*see* plate 3.8 [p.61]). In poorer households it is simply a wooden platform attached to the main house post or a box set into the wall. Richer households have more elaborate altars decorated with fancy woodwork. Minimally the altar contains three vases of flowers, one for each of the Triple Gems—the Buddha, his teachings, and the monks. Most households have a Buddha image or at least a photograph of a Buddha image on the altar. Other items on or around the altar are pictures of famous monks, photographs of relatives while they were monks or novices, pictures of the King, the Crown Prince, or other members of the royal family, and Shan texts. Additionally people may have images of famous monks, particularly Lung Paw Waen, and of the King, since these have been mass produced and sold door to door. The offering to the Buddha image is placed on a small plate and removed before noon, since the Buddha, like his monks, cannot eat solid food after noon. Wealthier households may have special miniature monk's bowls for this offering; others use a regular plate. There is usually a small glass of water offered to the Buddha; it remains throughout the day.

There are a number of spirits associated with particular places within the house or compound identified by the placement of offerings. The offering for the spirit lord of the house, *tsao ye tsao hūūn* (literally, the lord, *tsao*, of the granary, *ye*, and house, *hūūn*) is placed where the *sao mangala* comes through the second-story floor. The spirit owner of the land (*tsao naam tsao lin*) offering is placed at the base of the post.

Plate 3.8: The household Buddha altar. The image in the center is of the reverend monk, Lung Paw Waen.

The offering for generalized ancestors, *paw tao mawn mae tao mawn* (literally great-grandfathers and great-grandmothers), is placed upstairs either in the southeast or southwest corner. The spirits of the rice granary, the kitchen and the firepots, the gate into the compound, heads of stairs, and wells receive their offerings at their named places.

DIVISIONS OF SPACE

There are a number of features used to divide space. The first is height. Different floor levels in the temple and household mark off different areas of the building. The general principle is higher areas have more prestige. Low areas do not have much prestige. This is clearly seen in the temple. Within the temple, monks are spatially isolated from other kinds of people. Their normal living space is the elevated area surrounding the Buddha altar; when interacting with laypeople, even informally, this height distinction is maintained. The height prestige distinction is less marked for novices, who interact at the same physical level as laypeople and whose living space is at the same height as the rest of the temple.

Generally the higher or more enclosed the area the more private it is. The sleeping room in a house is private, restricted to members of the household. There are two private rooms within the temple: the one for the abbot and the one for the novices. The abbot's room is private. The temple boys, temple caretaker, and novices all have access to the novices' room, although generally laypeople do not.

A second feature is not marked by physical dividers but is seen in the order in which people sit in the temple and also when there are visitors in the house. In the temple, older men sit up front, followed by younger men, an open space, "nuns," then older women, and behind them younger women and children. When people come visiting, the men are called to sit nearer the Buddha altar. In the newer houses where guests are received in the downstairs room, men and important people are called to sit in the inner area, away from the entrance. Generally men sit close to men and women close to women. Children, young adults, and others without much prestige sit near the outer edges, although young children or grandchildren may sit on adults' laps. "Inner" has some of the same connotations as "higher."

A further distinction is based not on the place itself, but on the kinds of beings allowed to enter it. This is a distinction based on kind of death, on gender, and, to a lesser extent, on ordination. Ordination status is ultimately based on gender since women cannot be ordained.

Beings who have died violent deaths are said to be unable to enter the temple. When people make merit for those who died violent deaths, the offerings have to be made outside the temple, otherwise the spirit cannot receive the merit. This contrasts with those who die a normal death and beings like cadastral spirits who are regularly invited to the temple.

Women cannot enter the ordination hall (*simh*), the raised areas within the temple, the *tao tang ha* altar in the temple compound, if it is fenced, the cadastral spirit compound, and the tower room associated with the heart of the village. Men, in contrast to women, can enter all these places. However, young men, before and after their ordinations, are physically marginal to these places. They are unlikely to attend regular temple services and during ceremonies sit at the edges or on the temple porch, or do not come up into the temple at all. This contrasts with their leading role in temple fair activities and the gambling that takes place at funerals and merit making for the dead. This distinction, between where women are not allowed to go and where men are allowed to go but young men do not, points to how Shan construct gender and how gender-appropriate behavior changes through the life cycle. I discuss this in more detail in Chapter 8.

Some spaces within the temple compound are further restricted to ordained monks. When there is a monastic service in the ordination hall, only monks are allowed to enter. Laymen and novices have access to the raised areas within the temple, but this is limited to particular errands, to presenting offerings to monks, and for the novices chanting during a temple service.

There is a further spatial distinction between laypeople and those residing at the temple. Residents of temple compounds, with the exception of the temple boys, are restricted primarily to the compound. People may visit monks at the temple but monks, novices, and nuns rarely visit peoples' homes. In most cases they visit only to perform a service for which they have been invited. Laypeople may visit at the temple, but this is rare and usually limited to people who have close relatives at the temple, people who are discussing a problem with a monk or are inviting monks to a ceremony, or visiting anthropologists.

Spirits associated with various places are similarly restricted. They stay in the places associated with them unless they are formally invited to attend an event, as when the cadastral spirit and a number of other spirits are invited to the temple to hear the preaching of the Dharma. Otherwise, if one wants to interact with them, one goes to the sites associated with the spirits, places offerings, and makes a request or announcement.

These places and the distinctions among them, based on such general features as height, inner or outer areas, gender, and ordination status, indicate a range of beings and suggest some of the dimensions of difference that sort these beings into categories. In the next chapter I present more behavioral evidence for these distinctions and then analyze the categories of beings.

CHAPTER 4

Beings

S han mark differences in status with a range of behaviors. Who gets served when and with what range of dishes provides one line of evidence about distinctions among kinds of beings. Other evidence comes from examining the beings one makes offerings to or formally pays respect to and asks for forgiveness.

Shan meals consist of rice (*khao*) and curries (*phak*). There are two kinds of rice, glutinous or sticky and nonglutinous or nonsticky. People like to eat sticky rice for breakfast and lunch and nonsticky rice for dinner. Like other Southeast Asian cuisines, Shan cuisine is spicy. Shan use of soybean cakes, *tho nao khep*, distinguishes their cuisine from others.

Normally a household eats its meals together. Each person has his or her own plate of rice. The curries are placed on the center of the table. People either make a small ball of sticky rice and dip it into the curry or transfer small amounts of the curry to their plates. Small children may be served curries on top of their rice. On festive occasions this pattern changes.

FEASTS AND OTHER OFFERINGS

Food preparation and feasting are central aspects of all temple events except regular *Wan Sin* services. Feeding people also plays a part in household-focused life cycle ceremonies such as funerals, weddings, and ordinations. When a household organizes a work force that includes more than its own members, its members provide the curries for lunch. In cases of general exchange labor such as house building, the sponsoring household provides the whole meal, often including liquor for the men.

Temple ceremonies provide a chance to observe the full range of people—monks, novices, *mae khao* or "nuns," old people, young men, women and children, and visitors from other communities. The description of who eats with whom and who gets served illustrates Shan concepts of different statuses within the community.

Monks, novices, and nuns are offered food first. They are separated from laypeople because they keep Buddhist precepts. Anyone who keeps eight or more precepts cannot eat solid food after noon. However, even when festivals occur early in the morning or at night these three groups are offered refreshments before others. People who keep different numbers of precepts cannot eat together; monks eat with monks, novices with novices, and nuns with nuns. Laypeople, non–precept-keepers, eat together. People keeping more precepts are offered their meal first and are provided with better food. On nonfestal occasions, monks and novices eat cooked food people bring to the temple. Nuns prepare their own food.

Once the precept-keepers have eaten, food is served to laypeople. Young men and women take plates of rice and trays of curries to all the people. The pattern of service at the *Awk Waa* festival (see Chapter 2) is standard: first the old men then, almost immediately, the rest of the lay audience. Men tend to eat with other men, women with women. This follows from the seating pattern within the temple since people eat with the people sitting next to them. The people serving the food eat last; these include the event's sponsors, the women who prepared the food, and the young adults who do the serving.

These distinctions among kinds of persons can be seen in the seating pattern of events held in a house. A special seating area is prepared for the monks, usually near the house's Buddha altar. The monks' slightly raised seats are made from mattresses. The audience sits on the floor, men in front, then nuns, and other women behind them. This seating pattern is repeated whenever there are events including all these kinds of persons. During all public events men and women sit separately.

The patterns of seating and food service indicate the way Shan sort people into ranked groupings. The broadest division is into two groups: continuous precept-keepers and laypeople. The precept-keeping group is further subdivided on the basis of the number of precepts they keep. Laypeople are divided by male and female, with each group further subdivided based on precept-keeping. *Mae khao* are anomalous; they are precept-keepers but they are also female. Because they are precept-keepers, they are served before laypeople; because they are female, they sit with the women. After the analysis of power and its relationship to Buddhism, I resolve this anomaly in Chapter 10.

People who choose to keep the five precepts at all times and the eight on *Wan Sin* during the rains retreat are generally old people, the men in their sixties and the women in their forties. The eight precepts are to refrain from killing, stealing, sexual behavior, lying, intoxication, solid food after twelve noon, bodily adornment, and sleeping on a wide or high bed. It is only the older people who have the opportunity and interest to keep these precepts. Men find it more difficult to do so because it implies no drinking, hunting, or fishing. In the temple, one can identify old people because they have a cloth or towel draped over a shoulder. Old people do not continually keep eight precepts and do not eat separately from other laypeople. However, because they do keep eight precepts on holy days during *Waa,* and continually keep five precepts, they have some of the abilities of precept-keepers.

Precept-keepers, including old people, are the focus of any ceremony or festival. Because they keep precepts they are able to give merit, *khuso*, and blessings, *mangkala*. The same phrase—to come *"ao khuso"* (take or receive merit)—is used to call people to a service in the temple or to request a blessing from old people. The more precepts a person keeps the more powerful the blessing. People use the number of precepts kept to determine the size of their offerings. Monks receive larger offerings than novices and so on; old people rarely receive offerings other than their meal. The same offering given a monk creates more merit than if it were given to an old person. Precept-keepers are presented with offerings and they return blessings. Precept-keepers form a superior group and this superiority makes them deserving of offerings from laypeople.

Only precept-keepers give regular blessings; other beings give blessings when people come to pay respect and ask for forgiveness (see below). However, these other beings are only the focus when people come to pay respect; most ceremonies focus on precept-keepers.

At any ceremony there are two groups of non–precept-keepers: the people who sponsor the event and the audience. Old people fit into the audience category in that they normally no longer help with serving the food and cleaning up; however, they do return blessings for their meal. The household or group sponsoring the event are the *tsao* (literally, lord) or owners of it. They are responsible for organizing the event and seeing that there is plenty of food for everyone. The audience consists of two groups: old people who keep the eight precepts during the rains retreat and so are superior to the sponsors, and the rest of the laypeople who are, temporily at least, inferior to the sponsors. The sponsors' superior position requires that they be generous to both helpers and audience. For this group, giving, rather than receiving, is a mark of superiority. This relative superior/inferior relationship is part of all such activities including exchange labor. The household whose work is being done is the *tsao* of the event and temporarily superior. Tomorrow another household will be in charge.

The audience's task is to receive the food. With exchange labor, the people working are called to come eat and the sponsoring householders serve them. Regardless of the event there is considerable pressure placed on audience members to come and eat. People serving the food encourage others to eat slowly and to eat until they are full. With temple ceremonies, some people are reluctant to go up into the temple to eat. They may eat elsewhere; if they return to the temple before the meal is over they will be cajoled into eating. People coming into the temple while food is being served are called to come eat. This is in contrast with everyday behavior. If someone passes by while a household is eating, he or she is inevitably called to come eat. However, the passerby is not expected to stop and eat, a fact known to both parties.

With communitywide festivals there is a sense of balanced reciprocity among villages. The same group of villages tends to invite each other to annual festivals. Invited villages send a money contribution to the festival and generally some of its villagers attend its last day when the festival is offered and people fed. People attending festivals have a good idea of the kinds and quantities of food that should be served and they tend to be critical if the food does not come up to expectations. The shared expectations and the general reciprocity of money offerings suggests that these communities strive to maintain relatively equal relationships vis-à-vis one another.

Food is one medium for expressing superior/inferior relationships. Receiving food has two possible interpretations, depending on the giver and the receiver. When precept-keepers accept food it is a mark of superiority; when the audience receives food it is a mark of inferiority. Sponsors make claims to superiority by feasting guests. These claims are temporary in most life-cycle ceremonies and exchange-labor events. One expects to be invited to participate in the ceremonies sponsored by other households. As with villages, the reciprocal sponsoring of events establishes relative equality among households. Richer villages and households sponsor larger and more frequent ceremonies and make larger contributions to events sponsored by others. People are aware of these differences, but are willing to accept others as being members of the same sort, if not the same rank, as long as they are able to participate in sponsoring events at some minimal level. Some households are so poor that they cannot afford to sponsor their own life crisis ceremonies. One household in Mawk Tsam Pe was too poor to pay for the funeral of a member; a richer household sponsored it. Households that never sponsor events maintain a continuing client relationship with other households.

The sponsors of a festival or ceremony admit inferiority to the precept-keepers to whom they offer food. Feasting guests establishes a temporary superiority but makes a long-term claim to equality among peers. Giving and receiving have different meanings depending on the prestige of both parties. Shan need to know more than that food was served in order to interpret its meaning.

So far I have argued that Shan divide humans into precept-keepers and non–precept-keepers and that precept-keepers have higher status. Within the precept-keeping group, rank is determined by the number of precepts kept. The criterion "precept-keeping" makes a difference in the way individuals within and between groups interact. It defines a group where receiving food and other offerings is a mark of superiority. For non–precept-keepers this same behavior is a mark of inferiority.

The Shan universe includes more kinds of beings than laypeople and precept-keepers. People have relationships with nonresident superiors such as government officials and with those outside the human community. Some of these beings are offered festal meals, others receive regular small offerings. Still others are fed only "on demand," when they have made their needs known by causing misfortunes.

Offerings

The other major food offering, besides meals, is *som to*. According to Cushing *som to* is "rice offered to idols" (1914:255); however, his missionary bias makes this less than accurate. *Som to* are offerings made to a number of different beings. People generally offer them daily to the household Buddha image. Other beings receive *som to* offerings on *Wan Sin*. Some households make *som to* offerings on every *Wan Sin*; however, most do so only on the full and dark moon *Wan Sin*.

A *som to* offering is a small box made of banana leaf. This can be a simple box or an elaborate container with serrated edges. Minimally it contains cooked rice, removed from the pot before anyone has taken any for a meal. Usually the daily offering to the household's Buddha image has some sort of sweet added to it or a piece of fruit. Household *som to* offerings are particularly elaborate at the end of *Waa,* when people put in a number of kinds of sweets and fruits. Some of these sweets come from offerings made to old people when people come to pay respect and ask forgiveness, *khan taw*. (I discuss *khan taw* in detail below.) When people place *som to* offerings, they may put a lighted candle with them. If the people placing the *som to* offerings know the words, they request the beings to watch over and protect their households.

The temple, houses, cadastral spirit, and heart of the village, described in the previous chapter, all receive *som to* offerings. In the temple compound, offerings are presented to the Buddha image, the *tao tang ha*, chedis, and reliquaries. Both the cadastral spirit, *Tsao Mūong*, and the heart of the village, *Tsaū Waan*, receive *som to* offerings. Women of the household place the *som to* offerings around the house. Offerings are made to the spirit owner of the house, the granary, the land, the gates, the kitchen and firepots, the heads of stairs, and generalized ancestors. Other areas such as the well or other water sources also receive *som to* offerings. At the beginning and end of *Waa*, people make offerings to a wide range of spirits, including those associated with the rice fields. Finally, old people who sleep overnight in the temple during *Waa* also receive *som to* offerings. These are not for the old people; rather, they act as intermediaries and offer them to the Buddha image in either the resthouse or the temple (*see* table 4.1).

Tsao Müong receive *som to* offerings and are fed meals as part of the ongoing relationship between the *Tsao* and his followers. The *Tsao Müong* is one of a number of spirits with which people enter into contractual relationships. People make bargains with spirits; in return for a particular favor, the person will make an offering. Offerings are made after the favor occurs. If the spirit does not perform his part of the bargain, people do not make the offering. The relationship with the *Tsao Müong* is long-enduring and defines community membership. Other relationships may be individual and short term as with a lord of a particular hill field cultivated for a single year. Relationships with spirits may be collective and relatively enduring as expressed by offerings made to a dam spirit by all the people whose fields use water from that dam. Individuals may make particular bargains with the *Tsao Müong*, for example, for help in finding a lost water buffalo (see Durrenberger 1980).

There is a large number of other spirits, most of which do not receive regular offerings of any kind. These include spirits that result from violent or accidental deaths, hungry ghosts, which are spirits of people who failed to make merit through generosity, various tree spirits, *phi lu*, a monster who devours human flesh, and others. People do not enter into regular relationships with these. The traditional doctor, *sara*, may diagnose a person's illness as a consequence of an offense to a particular spirit, in which case an offering will be made as part of a cure. Hungry ghosts receive some attention from old people when they sleep at the temple. Typically old people set aside the first spoonful of rice and curry from their lunch to be offered to these spirits.

Paying Respect, Asking for Forgiveness—*khan taw*

The class of beings that receives regular offerings includes both humans and nonhumans. Some beings that receive offerings are also those to whom people pay respect and from whom they ask forgiveness, *khan taw*. However, people do not *khan taw* all beings that receive offerings, nor do they make offerings to all beings that they *khan taw* (see table).

TABLE 4.1

Beings That Receive *Som To* Offerings and To Whom People *Khan Taw*

Beings	to whom people ask for forgiveness and pay respect (*khan taw*)	to whom people make offerings (*som to*)
Possessing Power		
Tsao Mūong		X
Tsaū Waan		X
Tsao Ye/Tsao Hūūn		X
Tsao Naam/Tsao Tin		X
subdistrict headman	X	
village headman	X	
big men	X	
Power from Restraint		
Buddha and Buddha images	X	X
Buddha's teachings	X	
objects associated with the Buddha	X	X
monks	X	X[1]
nuns	X	
teachers	X	
old people	X	X[1]
Ancestors		
parents		
generalized ancestors	X	X
relatives' reliquaries		X

[1] See text for explanation.

People do not *khan taw* these beings with the same frequency. People pay respect to and ask forgiveness from the Buddha, his teachings, and the monks twice during each temple service. In addition people *khan taw* monks, novices, *mae khao*, old people, their parents, and local government officials at least twice a year, at New Year and at the end of *Waa*. People may also *khan taw* old people a third time near the full moon day of the third lunar month when they offer *khao yak ku*, a sweet made of sticky rice, brown sugar, peanuts, and coconut. Villagers do not *khan taw* the *Tsao Mūong* since they do not interact with him. However, *phu mūong* regularly *khan taw* him when they place the *som to* offerings. People may also *khan taw* various religious objects when they make a special trip to see them.

When people *khan taw* they dress up in their good clothes and bring offerings for the person or object. These offerings vary with the class of person or object. Typically people offer sweets, candles, and matches to old people, nuns, and monks. These items are then used to make *som to* offerings. People may also offer items that can actually be consumed, such as tins of sweetened condensed milk, fish, or instant noodles or clothing for their parents and grandparents. When people *khan taw* monks they may bring special offerings for the monks' personal use, such as soap, detergent, or fish sauce in addition to the standard offerings. Buddha images and other religious objects receive *som to* offerings.

To *khan taw* a person, people place their offerings on a tray. The oldest male or—if there is no male in the group—female raises the tray and offers it to the person they have come to *khan taw*. The recipient chants a blessing while the people being blessed sit respectfully with their hands folded. The content of the blessing varies with the person giving it and the people receiving it. Parents have a special blessing for their children when they come to *khan taw*. Some people are known for their elaborate blessings. Old people recite blessings quickly in low voices and it is difficult for Shan to understand them.

Blessings play an important role in paying respect and asking for forgiveness, as the monk explains:

> We monks and laypeople are able to pay respect to and ask
> for forgiveness from the Buddha, the Dharma, the monkhood,

the two lords—father and mother—and to another one, the important people to whom we are grateful. So we have already reached the time when we can pay respect and ask for forgiveness. Because of this one action, asking for forgiveness, we are able to go request and receive blessings from grandfathers and grandmothers, fathers and mothers, and also old fathers and elderly mothers, fathers and mothers, religious people, and people who have great age. This blessing is another reason for going to pay respect and ask for forgiveness. All the children and grandchildren and nephews and nieces, older siblings, younger siblings, people who know each other and those who remember and think of those blessings from grandfathers and grandmothers, fathers and mothers, and the monks at every temple—temples in the south, temples in the north; fathers and mothers, siblings in the south; villages in the south, villages in the north, villages in the west, villages in the east, villages in the north, villages in the south. So they go pay respect and ask for forgiveness like this. Because of this they ask for forgiveness and pay respect together.

Let them request and receive blessings, words which the
old fathers, elderly mothers recite. Let us be able to have the
blessing, "stay healthy and happy and let whatever we do
succeed." This is another reason we ask for forgiveness and
pay respect. Elders and parents give blessings to their
children and grandchildren so that they may escape danger.
They give blessings to those who come. (Sermon delivered by
the abbot of Mawk Tsam Pe temple on October 9, 1984, on
the day of leaving the rains retreat)

In this sermon fragment the abbot of the Mawk Tsam Pe temple makes the connection between paying respect and asking for forgiveness and receiving blessings. He also explains why people want or need blessings: they allow the recipient to escape from danger.

At New Year's and the end of *Waa*, people go to *khan taw* in other villages. As a group, people *khan taw* the monks at the temple and the village headman. Individuals may go to *khan taw* their older relatives in those communities and nuns at the temple. Monks also *khan taw* their ordainers, subdistrict, district, and provincial monks, and monks who have been in the order longer than they have been.

Paying respect and asking for forgiveness maintains one's relationships with more powerful beings. It cancels offenses committed intentionally or not and restores the general protective and nurturing relationship between more and less powerful persons. After people *khan taw*, the more powerful person gives a blessing, which is an expression of that person's protection.

People *khan taw* their parents, the Buddha, his relics, monks, novices, nuns, old people, the village and subdistrict headmen, and locally powerful people. People who have learned a skill *khan taw* their teacher whenever they use the skill they have learned. The caretakers of the *Tsao Mūong khan taw* him. People offer *som to* to the Buddha, his relics, old people as intermediaries, generalized ancestors, and assorted spirits associated with the house and its compound. Monks do not receive *som to* offerings; however, they receive daily *som* offerings of cooked rice and curries. *Som* in both usages refers to food offerings; Cushing (1914:255) defines it as "cooked rice, food for a priest."

Generally beings that receive some sort of offerings are beings people also *khan taw* (see table 4.1). Humans that people *khan taw* include precept-keepers, parents, and powerful local people. Beings that receive regular offerings are guardian spirits of all sorts, including the *Tsao Mūong* and spirits associated with households, and beings associated with Buddhism. Beings associated with Buddhism form a subset of precept-keepers or embodiments of the precepts such as the Buddha's teachings.

Government officials whom people *khan taw* can be classed with the assorted *tsao* and guardian spirits that receive *som to* offerings. In the pre-Thai period government officials were *tsao* or lower ranking titled officials. Beings with the title "*Tsao*" are owners or controllers of property or events. Thus government officials, *Tsao Mūong*, and other spirit owners of places are the same kind of beings.

KINDS OF BEINGS

There are three types of powerful beings: those who have achieved power through restraint and keeping precepts; those who simply have power; and parents and ancestors. Precept-keepers and powerful beings are powerful for all humans while parents and ancestors are powerful only for their immediate descendants. Parents and ancestors share characteristics of the other two powerful groups. For their children, they simply have power; however, when they become elders, they are also precept-keepers. Because of this I place parents and ancestors in a separate category (see table 4.1 [p.72]). I discuss parents and ancestors in more detail in the next chapter and in chapter 7.

Those who have power from restraint are grouped in terms of the number of precepts they keep, and within these groups their seniority is based on the length of time they have kept them. Monks, who keep 227 precepts, rank higher than novices, who keep only 10. A monk who has been in the order for ten rains retreats, *Waa*, ranks higher than a monk who has been in it for nine. Relative age in the order and not chronological age makes a difference. A novice who has been a novice for ten years ranks higher than "younger" novices but lower than a recently ordained monk. The lower position of *mae khao* comes directly from the fact that they keep only eight precepts. However, the status of *mae khao* is ambiguous and gender in general is a basic distinction.

Elders rank lower than those who continually keep eight or more precepts. Distinctions within this group are based on both gender and age. Men spend *Wan Sin* day and night in the temple building itself, while women stay in adjacent resthouses. Age is also important but this is chronological age and not the length of time they have been elders. Nonrelatives are more apt to *khan taw* older temple sleepers than younger ones. Length of time may enter into this as older people are likely to have spent a larger number of rains retreats sleeping at the temple. This is more plausible for women since they begin to sleep at the temple at an earlier age than men. Still, nonrelatives are more likely to *khan taw* chronologically old people than a younger woman who has been sleeping at the temple for a long period of time.

Knowledge is also a factor although it is confounded with age and gender. The traditional doctor, *sara*, and layreader, *tsale*, are both knowledgeable and have more prestige than other men in the elder category. Other men have *tsale* skills but unless they are elders their prestige is the same as other non–temple sleepers. Being an elder is a prerequisite for being a practicing *sara*. Women are not excluded from either of these two roles; they are just very unlikely to acquire the necessary skills.

Gender is an important distinction and one that follows directly from differential capacities for power. Men in general have a greater capacity for power, whether derived from restraint or possession, than women. As with precept-keepers, non–precept-keepers are divided into groups based on gender and age.

Beings that simply have power are classed in terms of the extent of their power as it is publicly demonstrated through their ability to get things done, the size of their following, and the area under their control. These beings rank lower, at least theoretically, than those who have power through restraint. The king is the peak of these "temporal" powers and he ranks lower than monks. However, there is considerable ambiguity here. The power of precept-keepers is also evaluated in terms of their effectiveness. Charismatic monks are judged in terms of the projects they can successfully inspire (Bhumiratana 1969). The respect for elders based on their age comes partly from the judgment that their age is a result of their power. The king's power is reinforced and justified in terms of his Buddhist practices, which include generosity, precept-keeping, and restraint. The power of both kings and cadastral spirits is reinforced and made benign and reliable through the practice of restraint.

Powerful beings are not necessarily benign and reliable. There are many powerful beings in the universe and one cannot maintain relationships with all of them. Without some sort of relationship with the powerful, one is fair game. Hence, people establish relationships with some powerful others so they will be able to maintain their own well-being in a dangerous universe. Paying respect and asking for forgiveness restores relationships and returns blessings, both of which help protect the person.

In the next chapter, I discuss the nature of power, how it operates, what one must do to gain access to it, and how this structures interactions with powerful others, and I return to the idea of parents and ancestors as powerful beings.

CHAPTER 5

The Nature of Power

Power (*haeng, takho*) is a basic, unquestioned part of the universe. It simply exists. It is not equally distributed throughout the universe; some beings have great power, others have little. Power is morally neutral. It is inherently neither good nor bad. Beings who have power decide how they will use it.

All beings in the universe are ranked in terms of relative power. The five Buddhas—the three previous Buddhas, Gautama Buddha of this world period, and Arimettiya, the next Buddha—have the greatest power, while beings in the lowest hells have the least. Humans generally rank somewhere in the middle. In this system humans and spirits are essentially the same; they are born, can feel pain and pleasure, and must die. Both humans and spirits are ranked in terms of power. The major difference between spirits and humans is that humans are always visible to spirits and other humans, while spirits can decide whether they want humans to see them.

THE NATURE OF POWER

Cushing (1888:200) gives the words *haeng* and *tankho* as translations for the English term *power. Haeng* is also given as the translation for *strength* (241) and *force* (147). Cushing does not elaborate on the definitions of *haeng* and *tankho* to specify what sort of strength or force they imply. He translates *haeng* as "to be strong, to be violent; n. strength, force" (1914:637) and *tankho* as "power," derived from the Burmese, with *haeng* given as its Shan equivalent (1914:269). In the Maehongson Shan dialect *tankho* becomes *takho*.

Shan understanding of power, *takho* or *haeng*, draws on a number of interconnected propositions about the nature of the universe and the way it works. Understanding what power means for Shan requires understanding something about the assumptions that underlie its working. The existence of power and related propositions are taken for granted. Power can be gained or lost. Once achieved, power can be shared and bestowed on one's followers. Powerful others protect their followers and this protection gives their followers power.

Power implies protection. If one has access to power one is protected; if one is protected, one has the power or freedom to do as one chooses (see Hanks 1962 for a discussion of power in similar terms for the Central Thai). Shan express this mutual implication of power and protection in the terms they use to describe the results of invoking powerful beings or using powerful objects. The most common expression used is "*he*," which Cushing (1914:657) defines as "to prevent, hinder, thwart, to put up a barrier." It is used in everyday speech to mean shade or protect as in *he tin* (candle), protecting a candle from the wind by placing one's hand near the flame. The temple lay reader, *tsale*, I spoke with described the function of the cadastral spirit, *Tsao Mūong*, as protecting the village by creating a barrier that keeps out dangers of all kinds—robbers, bad spirits, floods, fires—and preventing fights at village festivals. The traditional doctor, *sara*, described the function of some tattoos as "*he yoika*," making a barrier against illnesses (*yoika*), and others as "*he phi he phū*," making a barrier against spirits (*phi* and *phū*).

This conception of power is not limited to ritual specialists. An old lady, in explaining the power of a particular text, said it built a barrier around wherever it was read and used the term *he*. These barriers are seen as quite strong. The same old lady removed a piece of paper with verses from the Buddhist scriptures (*katha*) encoded on it (*ang*) when she learned that its strength was such that in addition to keeping out evil it also prevented good fortune from entering her house.

Power-protection takes the form of barriers (*he*) that ward off misfortune. Strong tattoos that protect from gunshot and knife wounds by surrounding the tattoo bearer's body with a protective barrier are called *pik*, to close off (Cushing 1914:396). A man with a large number of these closing-off tattoos is free to behave as he likes, robbing and stealing without fear of retaliatory violence, provided he follows the food restrictions that go with his tattoos and he does not break the Buddhist precept he agreed to keep. The power of these tattoos frees men from the consequences of their actions; they need not fear anyone and, instead, cause fear in others. However, men with these tattoos are likely to be unlucky, since the protective barrier also prevents good fortune and wealth from entering. The traditional doctor said that in the past he had made these tattoos for soldiers but now he is reluctant to do more because the powerful closing-off tattoos made the bearer quick-tempered. The subdistrict officer (*kamnan*) asked him to stop providing soldiers with these tattoos because the soldiers were making too much trouble drinking and fighting.

Villages and households are protected by similar barriers. The annual "repairing the village" (*mae*, repair; *waan*, village) ceremony closes off the village, drives dangerous beings out, and creates a barrier preventing these from reentering the village. An alternative name for this ceremony is *pik waan*, to close off the village. If members of a household suffer a series of misfortunes or there is an unexpected death, the householders may decide they need to renew the barriers against misfortune and danger. To do this they may either invite monks to chant in the house and sprinkle sacralized water throughout (*suut moon hūūn*) or request the *sara* to "repair the house" (*mae hūūn*) by burning *ang* in the house and at the corners of the house compound and sprinkling sacralized water and milled rice throughout the house.

At the end of sermons, powerful beings, especially the Buddha and his disciples, are invoked to give protection, *he pan*, to the listeners from a series of misfortunes. These include danger from the five enemies—fire, flood, drought, famine, and government officials; from rebirth in the hells; from illness; and from fire, evil spirits, and human enemies; and *khaw*, misfortune in general (see Durrenberger 1980, 1983). Blessings include the hope that people will be noticed by good government officials and escape the attention of bad ones (Tannenbaum and Durrenberger 1988) (see Chapter 6).

Power-protection does not cause good things to happen; it passively prevents bad things from happening. Beings with power are described as shading their followers. The traditional doctor, *sara*, used a metaphor of shade to describe power. He said the Buddha had great power, *takho yaū* (large), and it is:

> a large sphere of protection, spirits cannot enter the sphere. It is this protection which allows people who respect the Buddha to be healthy [*yuu lii kin waan*]. It is like having an umbrella when it is hot and sunny. [The umbrella] keeps people from getting a cold. Without it you would get sick.

The *sara* also described his relationship with powerful beings in similar terms, that their power shades him, *hom hao*. In curing he calls on the power of the five Buddhas to build a barrier around the sick person and protect him or her from further dangers.

A monk in a funeral sermon for an old man described the old man's power as having "shaded me and all the laypeople." He characterized this power as being like a large shady tree providing protection and coolness for a large number of beings. He developed this metaphor, extending it to people who, though powerful, do not choose to protect others, likening them to large trees without branches or leaves, which cannot shade others; people without power are like small trees that cannot offer any shade.

Power implies protection, and protection, power. If people are protected, they have the freedom to behave as they please without fear of the consequences. While power as protection appears as a passive force, beings who are protected have considerable power, since they are freed from the consequences of their behavior. Being freed from the consequences of their actions makes powerful beings extremely dangerous. Beings such as the cadastral spirit, *Tsao Mนong*, whose function is protective, and others whose power comes from the practice of restraint, are more reliable and less dangerous (see below). Nevertheless, powerful beings protect only those with whom they have ongoing relationships.

RELATIONS WITH POWERFUL BEINGS

Because the world is populated with powerful beings, many of which are more powerful than any given human, it is necessary to enter into some kind of relationship with them to insure one's protection. But powerful beings are dangerous: they can easily be offended and cause harm. Villagers know this as part of existential reality. Offended spirits cause illnesses; offended government officials create real problems for villagers.

Beings with power-protection have the potential to withhold it, leaving the person exposed to dangers from other beings. Consequently, powerful beings need to be treated circumspectly and the greater the being's power-protection the greater the restraint in behavior. One way people cope with this power differential is by limiting their dealings with powerful beings. Villagers rarely interact with government officials or with monks. One woman explained that she was afraid of unknowingly offending a monk through the use of incorrect, less polite language. Consequently she avoided talking with monks. Another method of dealing with powerful beings is through established intermediaries. Villagers make offerings for the *Tsao Mūong* but it is the caretaker, *phu mūong*, who is actually responsible for placing the offerings and making requests to the *Tsao Mūong*. Ordinary villagers do not interact with the *Tsao Mūong*. The village headman or subdistrict officer serves a similar intermediary function with government officials.

The potential for offense also accounts for the practice of paying respect to and asking for forgiveness from powerful others. A monk in a sermon explains what happens when people *khan taw*:

> When we *khan taw* that which should not have happened is gone. We are able to forgive, give each other forgiveness when we together are freed from the causes of the sin [*apet*] in deeds, the sin in words, the sin in thoughts. We say that we intend in our hearts to do so and all that is gone—whether we meant to do wrong or did not mean to. . . . Laypeople, when you come to *khan taw*, then it is finished and they [the offenses] disappear. (Abbot, Mawk Tsam Pe temple; October 17, 1984; sermon delivered when villagers came to *khan taw*)

He then lists the five acts that cannot be cancelled: killing your father, your mother, or a monk, drawing the blood of a Buddha, and causing a schism in the religion. He continues, saying, "these are the only ones which cannot be cancelled, which you cannot undo." A little later, speaking for all the monks, he adds,

> Tonight, the monks which the laypeople offended, whether they know it or not; whether they intended it or not; whether

they did it or not, they invite every one of us monks, those
with few *Waa* or many *Waa*, who are young in *Waa* or old in
Waa, to release the laypeople from the offenses. Do not
punish them with spears or thorns; do not let these touch the
laypeople—all of those who came or did not come, from
every house, everyone little or big [without or with power],
young or old, female or male, male and female sponsors of
ordinations, mister or miss, all of them, including the little
people and the large people, the new people and the old
people. Do not punish any of them. Let them be freed from
having offended in word, having offended in thought, having
offended in deed, these three offenses. Let it be like the moon
which changes, the stars which change, like the full moon. Let
it be like the full moon that is not covered with clouds or
anything. Do not let them have any of these sins. Let them
escape from, be released from, their misdeeds. Let it be new
for everyone. Let it be as I say. (Abbot, Mawk Tsam Pe
temple; October 17, 1984; sermon delivered when villagers
came to *khan taw*)

Here the abbot gives the rationale for *khan taw*. Asking for
forgiveness cancels the offense—making it as if it did not
happen. Since powerful beings can be offended, this is the
means to cancel the offense.

One enters into a relationship with a more powerful other
by making offerings, and then maintains it with regular
offerings, acts of *khan taw*, and being mindful of and grateful
for past favors. In return the powerful other protects and
nurtures his or her followers. Making regular offerings and acts
of *khan taw* is the means to maintain relationships with
powerful others. The beings discussed in the previous chapter
are the ones that are locally powerful and with whom the
villagers have regular relationships.

Relationships between two beings of unequal power are
expressed ideally in terms of *kung*. English-speaking Shan gloss
the word as "gratitude," but gratitude refers to what one should
feel towards powerful beings because of help they have given.
Cushing (1914:38) translates it as "a good or bad quality, an
attribute; honor." Davis, in his discussion of Northern Thai
metaphysics, provides a better account. He states, "The word
guna [the Pali form of Shan *kung*] does not only denote the
physical components of the body. When used in compound

form together with the word *punna* (merit) it means kindness, beneficence, or a favor for which the recipient should show gratitude" (1984:150). He elaborates this in his discussion of a soul-calling ceremony for a water buffalo: "The purpose of the ceremony is to show gratitude to the animal 'to know its *punna* and *guna*' (*huu bun huu kun man*). In addition to denoting the primal qualities or physical elements of the body, *guna* means merit, beneficence, and favour—the fact of creating a situation of indebtedness. But it also means sorcery, and in a more general sense, evil power" (1984:165). Davis provides a good sense of the complexity and ambiguity of *kung*. Beings with *kung* have power and consequently are potentially dangerous.

Shan talk about five great *kung*, those of the Buddha, his teachings, monks, teachers, and parents. Other beings said to have *kung* are the cadastral spirit, the heart of the village, the king, and generalized ancestor spirits. Lower ranking temporal powers such as local government officials and some of the guardian beings around the house are not spoken of as having *kung*.

Beings with *kung* are expected to act benevolently towards their followers. Dependents can be seen as sheltering in the shade of the powerful. Many people recite a nightly prayer invoking the *kung* of the Buddha, teachers, parents, and the *Tsao Mūong,* and requesting them to establish a protective barrier to ward off misfortune. Recipients of protective benevolence from superiors should remain mindful of and grateful for the protection they receive. Failure to do so separates one from this protection.

The traditional spirit doctor, *sara*, talking in general about his ability to be an effective doctor, said that he makes offerings in gratitude, *kung*, to the Buddha, the Buddha's teachings, his teachers, his parents, and the cadastral spirit. He said,

> I ask for their help so others do not harm [me]. It is like remembering and thinking of them [the beings with *kung*] so they do not forget me. I am happy and grateful for their protection. When there is danger their *kung* shades me, it makes a barrier and drives the evil away. It protects me from evil. Before I go to sleep I think of their *kung*. The power from making offerings goes with me. I cannot see it but the evil spirits do and they flee.

These relationships are given behavioral expression when people *khan taw*. *Kung* expresses the nature of the relationship. People who have received favors should be grateful for and mindful of the benefits they have received. By continuing to be grateful for past favors they obligate the more powerful other to continue with the relationship. Receiving and continuing to receive favors is contingent on behaving properly and being grateful. However, if one behaves properly one has a claim to continue to receive favors.

For any individual, the mortals with the greatest *kung* are one's parents. A monk in Mawk Tsam Pe was complaining that people *khan taw* in other villages before coming to *khan taw* at the temple. He thought that people ought to *khan taw* their temple first since, in his view, the monks are most important. I asked him about parents, saying that people told me parents' *kung* was greatest. The monk backed down and said that people should *khan taw* their parents first, that they have the greatest *kung* for an individual, more than monks or officials.

People tell stories about the power of their grandparents' *kung*. People like to have teeth from their grandparents, which they wear as amulets. Two different people told me the following story about the power of these amulets. A trader has teeth from his grandparents on his amulet chain. One day he stops, hangs his chain and his carrying bag on a tree, and makes camp for the night. The next morning he leaves, forgetting his bag and amulet chain. An hour or so down the road, he realizes he has left his bag and amulets and goes back for them. On the way back he stops people, asking them if they've seen his bag. No one has seen the bag, only two old people sitting underneath a tree. When he gets back to his campsite, his bag and amulets are there. The storytellers explained that the old people were his grandparents, protecting his property. Because the trader remembered his grandparents' *kung* and was grateful to them, they guarded his bag.

People receive the most from their parents—birth, nurturing, education, and support until maturity. Because of the great number of favors one has received it is practically impossible to repay the debt that one owes one's parents. The extent of the debt is so great that an awareness of it and gratitude for the favors received is enough to evoke continuing parental protection even after they are dead. Parents', generalized ancestors', and relatives' reliquaries are all sources of protection, and people either *khan taw* or make offerings to them. Other relationships with less depth are more fragile and less assured.

ACCESS TO POWER

The essence of power is its ability to protect and to ward off the consequences of behavior. One can either develop one's own capacity for power or rely on the power of amulets, tattoos, and other beings. The primary means of developing one's capacity for power is through the practice of restraint and withdrawal from everyday activities.

Capacity for Power

Like power itself, the capacity for power is unevenly distributed. Underlying the ability to practice restraint and achieve power is maleness. Women have less aptitude and ability to acquire power simply because they are female. This is another basic assumption about the nature of the universe, one related to the assumption that all beings are ranked in terms of power. According to the *sara*, men in comparison with women have greater power (*phong yaū*) (Cushing 1914:451 gives "glory" as a translation for *phong*, a Burmese derived word; in everyday usage it is another synonym for *power*). A novice expressed this fact another way, saying "Men are tall (*sung*), women are short (*tem*); men are right, women are left." He continued saying "the left side also has power."

In this system, by definition, women have less capacity for power-protection than men. Women have power but it is different from that of men. If women come into contact with powerful objects they can drain the power from those objects. This destructive capacity is concentrated in female genitalia and in objects that come into contact with either female genitalia or genital excretions. Women have the capacity to unroll the protective barrier that surrounds a person who has powerful antibullet tattoos (Tannenbaum 1987). While women are destructive of concentrations of power-protection, they have some capacity for it or they would not be able to survive.

As a consequence of this natural ability, women are rarely interested in becoming *sara,* or in things associated with power. Women cannot become monks but it is possible—just unlikely—for them to acquire some power through tattoos, amulets, and knowledge. Tattoos are used primarily by men. Women may receive some of the less-powerful tattoos as part of a cure or as preventive medicine. However, women cannot receive the two most powerful tattoos. Women are rarely tattooed, not because it is forbidden, but because they are not much interested in it.

The antibullet and knife tattoos are popular among soldiers, especially those in the various revolutionary armies fighting in Burma. These armies often have women soldiers. Women soldiers are likely to have the same antibullet and knife tattoos as their male counterparts. The tattoos men and women receive are identical, but their effectiveness differs. A tattooed woman is protected from bullets fired by either men or women. However, a tattooed man is not protected from bullets fired by women. The traditional doctor explained that the women's bullets have the capacity to unroll the protective barrier generated by tattoos. Men can simulate the effect by tying a strip of cloth from a woman's skirt around their gun barrels.

Most tattooers are male. The *sara* said that women could not be tattooers, but after considering it he said that they could tattoo, but only other women. A tattooing monk disagreed, saying that tattoos that protect against bullet and knife wounds are best made by women because their tattoos protect against objects from both men and women. While the *sara* did not agree, he put forth a parallel argument about the effectiveness of tattoos done in Maehongson Province. He said, "Consider the '*mae*' of Maehongson, which means 'mother' and makes Maehongson a female province. Since it is a female country the tattoos done here are effective in both male and female countries. Those done in male countries lose their effectiveness when their bearers enter a female country." The *sara*'s discussion of female countries raises the question of the nature of "female," whether it resides in the women's genitals or is more general. My questions about whether women could tattoo evoked this answer: while it is plausible in the Shan cultural framework, it is not conventional. This was the only time I heard about female as opposed to male countries. The conventional understanding is that female nature is something that resides in mature women's genitals.

Power through Restraint

In developing one's capacity for power, honesty, reliability, and honor become central. In one sermon a monk talked about the reliability of protection and shade in his metaphor based on a large flowering tree. The importance of honesty and reliability set people seeking power through restraint apart from other powerful people and the everyday population. People can both develop their own capacity for power and rely on the protection of powerful others. There is no contradiction between these two methods, although developing one's own capacity for power places restrictions on one's behavior.

For the explicit discussion and explanation of this aspect of power, I rely primarily on two local Mawk Tsam Pe experts: a traditional doctor, *sara*, skilled in treating illnesses and tattooing, and a meditation monk also skilled in tattooing. These local experts were the most articulate about power and what it means, since their skills rely on it. While these two men elaborated on an understanding of power that is broadly shared, their techniques for gaining power are particular to their circumstances. Their interest in power is for self-development and helping others. Both the tattooing monk and the *sara* are Shan equivalents of the "upper path" doctors, *ahtelan hsaya*, Spiro discusses for Burma (1967:23).

The experts used two concepts in their discussions of power: keeping Buddhist precepts (*sin*) and honesty (*kati* or *settsa*). In order to acquire power, a person must keep precepts and be honest. These concepts are interrelated. For a person to have power he must also have *kati* and *settsa*. Cushing states that both of these terms derive from Pali with *kati* meaning "a promise, word pledged" and *settsa* meaning "truth as opposed to falsehood" (1914:8 and 226). The *sara* explaining this to me said: "If I do not keep the precepts, *sin*, then I do not have *kati* and am not able to cure—the spirits are not frightened." Later he said: "If I keep the precepts and have *kati* then I have the benefits [*akyo*] from them and without precepts and *kati* I would have nothing." The tattooing monk discussed the capacity for power in similar terms although he used the term *settsa* for the *sara*'s *kati*.

Having the precepts means keeping at least the five precepts incumbent on laypeople. One class of powerful beings are those that steadfastly keep the precepts. People who study Buddhism normally interpret precept-keeping as the practice of Buddhist morality (Spiro 1982). It is one of three ways of merit-making, more difficult than generosity (*tana*) but easier than meditation (*phawana*). However, this is only one possible interpretation of precept-keeping. Shan understand precept-keeping as the practice of restraint and withdrawal (Tannenbaum 1987, 1989, 1991).

Powerful tattoos assume precept-keeping as the practice of restraint, rather than morality. People receiving powerful tattoos are required to keep one precept at all times. If the person fails to keep the promised precept, the tattoo will not work and, depending on the tattoo, the person will become physically or mentally ill. Typically the person observes the precept to refrain from improper sexual behavior, usually interpreted as refraining from adultery. By keeping this precept, a man with tattoos that protect him from gunshot wounds or knife cuts can rob and kill with impunity. Keeping this one precept does not imply any commitment to morality or proper behavior; often, in fact, it suggests a commitment to a life of crime. (I examine the precepts morality, restraint, and Buddhism in detail in Chapter 6.)

One gains power to the extent that one is able to withdraw from everyday activities. In the process of everyday living, Shan villagers generally recognize the impossibility of keeping even the five precepts (to refrain from killing, stealing, improper sexual behavior, lying and intoxication). In the abstract, people recognize the value of honesty and not lying, but in practice they cannot avoid lying. Rather than arguing with their children, parents cajole them with promises of nonexistent rewards or threaten them, saying that a crazy person will come get them if they do not stop crying. Sometimes it is strategically better to lie and even a "white" lie breaks the precept. It is impossible to avoid killing since an accidental death of an insect is still a killing. Borrowing something without explicit permission is classified as stealing. Men find it difficult to refuse a drink of whiskey and the strict interpretation of the precept requires refraining from all intoxicants, not merely avoiding intoxication.

Only when people are old, or in a special status such as the monkhood, does it become possible to keep precepts. Once people who are in positions to keep precepts begin to do so, they acquire the power to give blessings. The more precepts they keep, and the longer the time they have kept them, the greater their power.

A number of beings derive their power from precept-keeping. First and most important are the Buddhas. Buddhas have given up all attachment to wealth, worldly powers, and sensual pleasures and through meditation have given up attachment to their "selves." They exemplify the peak of power that can be obtained through withdrawal and restraint. Next come forest monks, those that regularly practice austerities in addition to the 227 rules incumbent on monks. Next are regular monks, followed by novices (who keep ten precepts), *mae khao* (who keep eight), and old people (who keep eight precepts on fortnightly holy days, *Wan Sin*, during the rains retreat and keep five precepts the rest of the time). *Sara* are members of this last group. All of these people have sufficient power to give blessings. They are singled out as recipients of offerings and those to whom people *khan taw*.

Other people may continually keep one or more precepts, something necessary to continue to empower their tattoos, but insufficient for them to give blessings to others (Tannenbaum 1987). Most everyday people simply try in general to keep the precepts as best they can and keep the five precepts on major holy days.

Honesty and precept-keeping are related. To get power from precept-keeping one must truly keep the precepts. This entails being an honorable person. The tattooing monk stressed the importance of keeping one's word: if one makes an appointment and fails to keep it, he maintained, then one does not have *settsa* and does not have power. People who derive their power from precept-keeping are honorable and have integrity, not just in their work but in all their interactions. The longer they keep precepts and are honorable, the greater their power. The *sara* explained it to me in the following way:

> *Kati* means not to lie and deceive; I get it from keeping precepts [*sin*] and it makes medicines work. It means doing what you say you will. If you have *kati* and sleep at the temple [overnight during *Waa*] it means you really keep the precepts. *Takho* [power] comes from *kati*, actually keeping precepts. If a person has *kati*, [a person] who really keeps precepts, then bad people will not bother him, he can travel around and be safe. [A person with] *kati* does not get drunk and steal things. People who drink will be ashamed and back off from him, so will bad spirits—as long as he has precepts and holds on to [*kam*] them. If a person has *kati* then his actions benefit [*akyo*] him, he has benefits. If he does not have *kati* he does not have benefits.

The *sara*'s discussion highlights the relationship between precept-keeping and power-protection. When one keeps precepts and is honest, evil spirits and bad people are either frightened or ashamed and do not bother him. Precept-keeping protects the *sara* and those that rely on him. Since power and protection mutually imply each other, precept-keeping or restraint is one method of acquiring power.

Honor is important not only because it allows experts to acquire power but also because the public observance of the precepts being honorably kept is important in people's selection of a curer. Additionally, failure to observe the precepts weakens a *sara*'s power and causes him to be ill. On another occasion the *sara* elaborated on this point, saying:

> If you see me drunk, then you would not believe [*yum yam*] in my ability to cure. If I fail to keep the precepts [*kam sin*], then I will not be healthy. People will not search me out to cure them. People will not believe in me or my ability and I will not have much power [*takho*]; my power [*takho*] will be weak. . . . If a person wants to be a *sara*, he needs to act like one, to be one truly. If a person learns to be a *sara* and does not behave like one then he will get sick.

Men developing their capacity for power also rely on the power and protection of other powerful beings. Honor is also important for invoking the power of one's teachers and the lineage of teachers. Specialists gain access to the power of their teachers and, for *sara*, the Buddhas, through offering *phŭŭn poy*. *Phŭŭn poy* are offerings to teachers to request their aid in making projects successful.

The offering to the Buddha presented at the opening of the *Awk Waa* festival as well as the one for the lay reader are both *phūūn poy*. The content differs slightly when one is offered to a traditional doctor. In addition to the regular offerings of milled rice, tea, tobacco, and betel, the *sara*'s *phūūn poy* has four small umbrellas, four small pennants, and a piece of red cloth rolled around a piece of white cloth. The people consulting the traditional doctor prepare the basic *phūūn poy* and the *sara* adds these extra items.

People requesting skilled help offer a *phūūn poy* to the specialist who in turn offers it to his teachers calling on them and their lineage (*say*) of teachers to aid him in this endeavor and to assure a successful outcome. *Sara* call on the power of the Buddhas as the originators of their knowledge and on the lineage of their teachers to watch over procedures and to protect both the *sara* and their patients. Through this offering the specialist draws on power greater than his own.

Having a teacher is essential. *Katha*, verses from the Buddhist scriptures, have a power of their own either as relics of the Buddha or as embodying the Buddha's knowledge and power. However, unless one learns them from a teacher this power is limited. The power is less in the words than in the teachers who provide them. Teachers and the lineage of teachers are important sources of power. Another reason that honesty, *kati* and *settsa*, is so important is that it allows one to invoke the power of one's teachers and the Buddhas. Without this augmented power, one's cures and tattoos would not be as effective.

Power is the same no matter how one acquires it. However, one's capacity for it and how one achieves it is not the same for all classes of beings—men differ from women, and precept-keepers and practicers of restraint from those who rely on the power of others. One dimension of power is that obtained through the practice of restraint. This power allows the *sara* to tattoo and cure, the monk to tattoo, and precept-keepers in general to give blessings. Those beings who acquire power through restraint are more likely to use it for good; the practice of restraint constrains the ways they can use their power. Those who gain power through other means are less constrained and they may choose to use their power for good or ill.

Relying on More Powerful Others

Beings have different capacities for power: those with greater capacities for power are able to seek it through withdrawal and restraint, while others with less capacity rely on the power of amulets or tattoos or become dependent on more powerful others.

People can gain power by relying on powerful others as lesser officials rely on greater ones or by relying on the power of tattoos and amulets (Tannenbaum 1987). With these methods of gaining power, reliability and honesty are not important. The monk in his sermon recognized this when he talked about powerful beings who are not reliable. Some tattoos and amulets give great protection and, as a result, free their bearers from the consequences of their behavior. Men with powerful antibullet and antiknife tattoos are protected from retaliatory violence and are free to steal or kill without fear of the consequences.

So far I have discussed tattoos in various contexts as they point to gender roles, power as protection, and the importance of precept-keeping as restraint. In this section I analyze tattoos to show what they do and why they work.

Shan medicinal tattoos are not decorations like the Shan "pants" tattoos. Shan think of them much as we think of vaccinations against various diseases. There are three general classes of tattoos: those that act on others, causing them to like or fear the bearer, *atsun*; those that act on the bearer, increasing his skill with words, *yapeya*; and those that create a barrier around the person, preventing animals from biting, knives from cutting, and bullets from entering the body, *kat* or *pik* tattoos. *Atsun* and *yapeya* tattoos tend to be done in red, while *kat* tattoos tend to be done in blue-black.

Verses from the Buddha's teachings, *katha*, are either written out or encoded in diagrams, *ang*, in all three kinds of tattoos. The particular *katha* used depends on the function of the tattoo. The monk or traditional doctor also recites appropriate *katha*, blowing them onto the tattoo while he is making it.

Tattoos vary in strength. Weaker tattoos do not have food restrictions and do not require keeping a precept. Weaker *atsun* tattoos cause beings to be well-disposed towards the bearer while stronger ones cause beings to fear the bearer. Similarly, weak *yapeya* tattoos cause others to believe the bearer's words while strong ones cause others to be intimidated by the bearer's speech. Women cannot receive the strongest *atsun* and *yapeya* tattoos. This distinction is transformed with *kat* tattoos. Strong *kat* tattoos free people from fear, and being freed from fear, they are able to behave as they like.

Strong tattoos of any kind require following food restrictions and keeping a precept. Foods are restricted because they are said to disagree with the medicine in the tattoos. Typically these foods include anything served at a funeral, the placenta of cows and water buffalo, and the white squash. Eating any of these foods causes the power of the tattoo to fade and the person to become physically weak.

The consequences of breaking the precept vary with the strength of the tattoo; the more powerful the tattoo, the worse the consequences of breaking the precept. These consequences range from the tattoo losing its power to the tattooed person going incurably insane. Tattoos have power because they draw on the power of the tattooer and, through the tattooer, on the lineage of teachers and on the power of the Buddhas and his teachings. This power is maintained by the keeping of a precept.

Tattoos provide protection. The *atsun* and *yapeya* tattoos cause people to like the bearers and believe what they say. Typically traders or people who have to travel get these tattoos. Causing beings to be predisposed to help the bearer reduces the danger of traveling into new areas or through jungles or mountainous areas inhabited by wild animals or dangerous spirits. The *kat* tattoos, which close off the person or surround him with a protective barrier, are similarly protective. The more powerful the tattoo the more the protection changes into intimidation.

MISUSE OF POWER

The concept of power as protection is expressed in both speech and action. Power publicly discussed in sermons or by the traditional doctor is benign. Powerful beings shade, protect, and nurture their followers. The powerful beings that villagers regularly interact with are fairly reliable and benign. However, power is essentially neutral. It can be used for good or evil, depending on the person wielding it. One indication of the abuse of power is given in blessings that ask for protection from the five enemies, including government officials, and specifically from bad officials.

Protection *as* power, the ability to act without fearing the consequences of one's actions, is expressed in stories about the misuse of tattoos. The *sara* told a story about a man who lived in Mawk Tsam Pe a short period of time and had a large number of tattoos, which caused him to speak well and others to like and want to help him. One day he announced he was going to Maehongson Town and that he was willing to run errands for people and buy whatever they needed. People took advantage of his offer and trusted him with two to three thousand *baht*, approximately U.S. $150 and a considerable sum in local terms. The man left for Town and never came back. People do not know what happened to him but assume that he absconded with the money. His ability to convince people to entrust their money to him is attributed to his tattoos.

The abbot of the Mawk Tsam Pe temple provided the following commentary about two possible uses of the powerful antibullet and antiknife tattoos. He said:

> Two types of people get these tattoos. One kind considers that he is now so well protected from bullets and knife wounds that he is free to go out and fight with people. He does not fear anything and is thus free to be wicked. Others will use their tattoos like a fence which keeps water buffaloes out of their fields. They get the tattoos, become impervious to weapons, and others, seeing the tattoos and knowing they cannot be harmed, will leave them alone.

A person chooses to use his tattoos and power for good or bad purposes. Power is effective regardless of how the person chooses to use it. There are stories about Ne Win, Burma's military dictator, and Mao Tse-Tung both possessing great power and using it effectively for bad purposes. Misuse of power is said to eventually catch up with a person. According to the storyteller, when Ne Win uses up his power and dies, he will fall into hell.

People's direct experience with actively dangerous and powerful humans is relatively rare. Thongmakhsan has little that would attract powerful outsiders. Since the late nineteenth century in the time of Tsao Kolan (Wilson 1985), the area has been relatively peaceful. Old people experienced the Japanese presence during World War II and had to respond to Japanese demands for labor to build the airport and roads. However, this was merely an extension of normal government activities.

Locally powerful men occur throughout Southeast Asia; in Central Thai, these are *nak leeng*, "a rogue, gangster, hoodlum, thug" (Haas 1964:261). They are not necessarily bad and can become local leaders (see L. Hanks 1972, Sharp and Hanks 1978) or be co-opted into the government (Trocki 1987). Occasionally local men appear who are powerful and use their power to the detriment of the local people. When one of these men appears, he makes the world a hazardous and uncomfortable place, thus reinforcing Shan perceptions of the universe as dangerous.

For some time before May 1988, people in Thongmakhsan were suffering from the presence of one such man. In May 1988, police killed him in a shoot-out near his family's rice swidden field hut. By the time I arrived in August, his death was still a topic of conversation. People told me their versions of life while this man stayed in Thongmakhsan, of the police shooting, and of their relief at his death.

I did not know this man: when I lived in Thongmakhsan in 1979 he was in prison in Bangkok and while I was in Mawk Tsam Pe in 1984 he had not yet been released. In 1979, I was told he was in prison because he robbed a trader. In 1988, people told me that he had been in prison because he raped a village woman. I do not know which account is true. The family of this woman was one of the more enthusiastic tellers of this man's downfall and they had a copy of the magazine that published pictures of the shoot-out.

People were glad that the man was dead. Shan characterize a bad person as one who adds only his weight to the earth. One woman telling me of his death said "the earth sprang back up like this" and used her hand to show approximately six inches. While he was alive people were afraid. They were careful to return from their fields before dark. Women were reluctant to go anywhere by themselves.

Most of his activities took place outside the village, although he stole minor things such as clothing from villagers.

He began attacking Western tourists and this led to his downfall. He raped and robbed a Western tourist and she was able to provide sufficient information for a sketch of the man and of his knife. This made it possible for the police to identify him. The man was back in Thongmakhsan because he was sick with malaria. While in Thongmakhsan, he robbed a man doing contract labor preparing an irrigated field for a villager and raped his wife. The woman identified the man who attacked her as the one in the police sketch.

The man was staying in the rice swidden field hut with his younger brother and sister-in-law. The police came during the night and attacked at dawn. Only the man was killed. In his bag the police found 2,000 *baht*, 184 *kyat*, and approximately U.S. $200, and a list of those he had robbed and how much he had gotten. A villager who saw the list reported that the total was around 60,000 *baht*. The police gave the *baht* and *kyat* back to the man's family to use for his funeral.

People talking about the police raid said that if the man had not been sick, the police would not have been able to attack him. They thought of the man as powerful and clever, and thought only his illness made him vulnerable. They saw the list of his victims as the man's recognition that he was going to die so that his family would understand what he had done.

People in Thongmakhsan knew what this man had done and that he was a dangerous person. They did nothing on their own to defeat him. The man's family had bad relations with most of the village and people were not afraid of alienating that family by taking direct action against one of its members. Rather, given his success as a robber and a rapist, they had substantial evidence of his power and judged that what they could do as villagers would not defeat him. Instead they relied on the superior power of the police and cooperated with the police when they came to attack the man, keeping the plan secret from the man's immediate family.

This man and his power came up in a conversation I had with the *sara* in Mawk Tsam Pe about the Buddha and the power of Buddhism. The *sara* was explaining that the Buddha and his teachings made it possible for people to live together, and that without them it was impossible. I said that this was like the man in Thongmakhsan. He agreed and went on to say "[the man] was a heretic [*tikthi*]; he was taught about the Buddha and how to behave but he didn't. He was taught and didn't believe. He listened to and followed the teachings of bad spirits [*phi am lii*]." The *sara* suggested that the man's power came from the bad spirits. People in Thongmakhsan did not talk about the source of this man's power. His success was sufficient evidence that he had power and was dangerous. His power protected him from anything that the villagers could do to retaliate. Instead they had to rely on more powerful others—the police—to defeat him.

CHAPTER 6

Shan Buddhist Sermons

Before discussing the place of Buddhism in the worldview centered on power-protection it is necessary to show what people know about Buddhism per se. This is not the canonical Buddhism of religious scholars but rather the everyday Buddhism of the villagers. In order to understand this Buddhism in locally relevant village terms, ethnographically, we must understand it as the people do. The most frequent and direct access Shan villagers have to Buddhist doctrine is through the teachings, *tara*, of the monks.

Monks express their understanding of Buddhism in their sermons. They present Buddhist concepts and interpret them in terms relevant to the villagers. Their sermons illustrate and explicate Shan concepts of the universe, its structure, its operation, the nature of the beings that inhabit it, and the relationships among them.

I first provide a brief account of the range of sermons, where they come from, and how they are structured, and follow this with an account of the universe elaborated in the sermons. Finally, I compare this universe with that developed in previous chapters. For this discussion I draw on Tannenbaum and Durrenberger (1987).

THE SERMONS

The sermons discussed here were delivered by Shan monks at festivals in Maehongson Province during 1976–1977 and 1984–1985. Durrenberger recorded and translated the 1976–1977 sermons while I collected the 1984–1985 ones. The 19 translated sermons are a portion of the larger body of sermons we recorded.

The 19 sermons come from the following events: 7 from funerals and funeral-related events; 4 from festivals held after the end of the rains retreat, *Waa*; 2 sermons delivered on the day of leaving *Waa*, *Awk Waa*, the full moon day of the eleventh lunar month; 1 from Makhapuja Day, the full moon day of the third lunar month; 2 short sermons given during *khao kam*, a special retreat (Thai, *Pariwat*); 1 ordination sermon; 1 sermon delivered when villagers came to *khan taw* monks; and 1 given when the villagers came to request the abbot to remain as the abbot for another six months. Nine different monks delivered the sermons: the abbot of the temple at Mawk Tsam Pe, where I lived, delivered 6; three other monks delivered 2 each; while the rest delivered 1 each. This collection covers the range of special events for which monks are invited to give sermons. They do not include regular *Wan Sin* sermons normally delivered on full and dark moon days, most often during *Waa*. The sermons vary in length, from five or ten minutes to forty minutes; in translation, the shortest is six pages, and the longest forty pages.

By Shan standards, some of the monks give better sermons than others and some monks are more experienced and more knowledgeable than others. One educated Shan from the Shan States, who listened to recordings of many of the sermons, commented that all were unsophisticated. Villagers recognize different monks as able to preach more or less well, and monks who give good sermons are locally esteemed and sought out to give sermons at festivals.

These sermons are extemporaneous creations by the monks at the time of the event. Monks have access to books about Buddhism and have heard other sermons so they know what a sermon should be. They are free to vary their sermons but only within the constraints of the sermon form and the appropriate topic for the occasion.

Sermons share a basic form. They begin with an invocation in Pali, minimally *"Namo tassa"* (I pay homage) (see Chapter 2) but perhaps more depending on the event; then a listing of sponsors at events that have sponsors; then the main topic, which varies with the occasion of the sermon; and finally a blessing. The blessing at the end is delivered very quickly, at a speed almost unintelligible to lay listeners.

Stylistically, the language differs from everyday speech. Monks repeat phrases and use long catch phrases, such as *taka hao khao* for the shorter *taka*, both meaning "laypeople" or the longer *khuso woon kung namoon* for "merit" instead of *khuso*. They also use couplets, for example, household/granary, *hɯɯn ye*, for house or village, and irrigated fields, *waan naa*, for village. Monks also use Pali words and passages. Neither the couplets nor the Pali passages occur in everyday speech.

Monks share many rhetorical methods. The audience favors storytelling, though not all monks tell stories. Stories include those about the consequences of attachment, the reason why monks' robes are made in patches, the benefits of ordaining sons, the importance of offering motivated solely by the desire to offer, and the immediate consequences of making offerings. Monks also develop the points of their sermons by giving the Pali terms and translating and elaborating on them in Shan in an oral hermeneutics, in the original sense of textual elaboration in the aid of translation. A monk may do both of these in a single sermon.

Sermons typically explain the event, why people celebrate it, and what its origins are. Another theme is the difficulty of the event, especially in the robes offering, *kathing*, and the ordination ceremony, since both require a minimum number of monks and sponsors with sufficient money and interest to make the offerings. Another common theme is the benefits from the ceremony and sermon, for laypeople, for the dead, and for the monks. Monks are likely to develop a number of these themes in any one sermon.

The theme of the sermon depends on the occasion. Funeral and funeral-related sermons focus on the inevitability of birth, old age, illness, and death, and how to escape these. On more festive occasions, the sermons are focused on generosity and its benefits.

The structural and rhetorical similarity suggests that monks share ideas of what a sermon is and how it is structured. They also share ideas of what content is appropriate to particular events. In sermons delivered by different monks for the same occasion, such as a funeral or the robes offering, the monks discuss similar points. This makes it possible to treat the sermons together as a composite.

THE UNIVERSE OF THE SERMONS

The most systematic information comes from funeral and funeral-related sermons. In these, monks describe the structure and operation of the universe. The universe is layered into three separate worlds: the hells, the earth, and the heavens. Each of these is further divided into a number of layers. The three worlds are populated with ghosts, hungry ghosts, animals, people, and spirits, including those that live in the heavens. Life in the heavens is sometimes described; its happiness is greater than that of this earth. In all the sermons I heard, the suffering in the hells was never described. Nor did the monks tell stories about evildoers suffering the consequences of their bad actions. This differs from Northern and Central Thai accounts where some sermons focus on the suffering that results from misdeeds (Reynolds and Reynolds 1982).

The universe operates according to the laws of *aniktsa*, *tukkha*, and *anatta*. These Pali terms are discussed and explained in Shan. They are used to account for the facts of birth, suffering, old age, and death, and to show the inevitability of death once there is birth. As one monk said,

> Because we are the kind that is born, when we have birth then there is old age suffering. Because we have birth it causes old age, which sticks in the heart. When sickness is born then *marana*, which means death, comes along with it. When there is sickness, sickness is the cause and death is the result. These things follow one another. Since it happens like this, what can we people do? There is no one who can compete against the world, resist the world. (Abbot, Wat Hoo Wiang, Maehongson Town; February 10, 1985; sermon at a monk's funeral)

Suffering is either given as *tukkha*, which is part of the everyday Shan vocabulary, or in its Shan form as hardship and suffering, *khan tsaū yaap tsaū* (to be distressed, annoyed, harassed in mind [*tsaū*]; to be distressed in mind [Cushing 1914:92 and 527]). The immediate cause of suffering is *karma* (Shan, *kam*), the consequences of a person's deeds in this and past lives. One's past behavior determines the quality of his present life (see below). However, the ultimate cause of suffering is a consequence of the laws of *aniktsa* and *anatta*.

The standard translation of *aniktsa* into Shan is *am man am me* (instability and unfixedness). Because nothing is fixed and unchanging and because people are attached to objects and persons, these change and cause suffering, *tukkha*.

> The Lord Buddha gave us *aniktsa*, it is not fixed or stable. It is always changing. One moment better; one moment fat, next moment thin; one moment old, next moment young; one moment love each other, next moment hate. This is impermanence. . . . Change arrives and change always stays. And this is called *aniktsa* nature. (Abbot, Wat Pang Mu; January 16, 1985; funeral sermon)

Anatta is usually translated as "no self." Humphreys, in *A Popular Dictionary of Buddhism* (1984), explains it as "The essentially Buddhist doctrine of non-ego" (32). The Thai monk Phra Khantipalo gives the standard "no self" translation for *anatta* (1973:74; see also Rahula 1962:51–66). Shan do not understand this term in the same way.

> The Lord Buddha preached about the knowledge of this *anatta* because all living beings are only *anatta*. *Anatta* is that which I myself, the bodies of spirits, the bodies of people, the bodies of animals, the bodies of brahma spirits truly have. We think that they are fixed [*man kūm*] because we have them like this. The Lord Buddha preached that is *anatta*. "*Anatta*" in our Shan words means that it cannot be controlled, it is not controllable [*am up pūng lay*]. Because it cannot be controlled [*am mii tsang up tsang pūng*] and so it can be destroyed. From this comes impermanence [*aniktsa*]. Because of this we must accept sickness and destruction. Difficulty [*khan tsaū*] and hardship [*yaap yang*] comes, this is *tukkha*. So if we think clearly, truly, we can see that from *anatta* comes *tukkha*, comes *aniktsa*, comes *tukkha*. (Visiting monk from Shan State; February 9, 1985; sermon during a merit-making ceremony for a monk who had died)

This sermon fragment neatly outlines the relationships among *anatta*, *tukkha*, and *aniktsa*. The causal sequence runs from *anatta*, the inability to control, which results in impermanence; lack of control and impermanence cause suffering.

In sermons *anatta* is interpreted as not being able to control or have authority over, *am up pūng lay*. This is always explained in terms of people's inability to control their own body, and emphasizes that it is wrong to call the body "ours."

> Laypeople, that is what the Lord Buddha preached and it is really the truth. It means in Shan words, we call this "*anatta*," not in charge of, not controllable [*am up am pūng lay*]. It cannot be like that because we are not in charge. . . . Monks and laypeople, all of us die and leave. Because of what? Because we are not in charge [*am up pūng lay*]. Because of the great law of *anatta*. We are not in charge and cannot control it. Our bodies want to become old and so they age. If we say, "do not grow old," if it wants to grow old, it grows old. If we say, "do not die," if it wants to die, it dies. Because of this we must accept old age and death. It is like this. We are not in charge. This is *anatta*. (Visiting monk from Shan State; February 9, 1985; sermon during a merit-making ceremony for a monk who had died)

A second monk made the same point, saying:

> If this body is really ours and we say, "sight do not grow dim," then our sight will not grow dim. If we say, "teeth do not fall out," they do not fall out. We brush two or three times a day and the teeth still fall out. We say, "ears do not go deaf" and they do not go deaf, they really listen to our words. If the body is truly ours then why doesn't it listen to our words? Because it is not truly ours. We just force it to belong to us. It is ours by force. (Abbot, Wat Pang Mu; January 16, 1985; funeral sermon)

Lack of control, *anatta*, causes change, *aniktsa*, which causes suffering, *tukkha*. The inability to control the world means it changes. Change is a direct consequence of the lack of control, hence *anatta* and *aniktsa* are often confounded or collapsed together as "change." "*Anatta* in our Shan words means that it cannot be controlled, it is not controllable. Because it cannot be controlled so it can be destroyed. From this comes impermanence [*aniktsa*]. Because of this we must accept sickness and destruction. Difficulty and hardship come, this is *tukkha*" (visiting monk from the Shan States; February 9, 1985; merit-making for a dead monk).

Spiro (1982:85) reports that Burmans understand *anatta* in a similar way: "Here is the comment of the most sophisticated Buddhist in the village: 'Everything changes from moment to moment. As a human being I do not wish to die, to be blind, to get old, etc., but I must. I have no power to prevent them. This is *anatta*.'" However, his analysis of Burmese Buddhism and its place in Burmese religion differs from mine.

Most funeral-related sermons begin with the Pali phrase "*Sape sankhara aniktsa, sape sankhara tukkha, sape thamma anatta*," which the monks then may explain in Shan. They often talk about the inevitability of change, that this is *anatta*, and that we cannot control it. The Shan woman helping me transcribe and translate the sermons explained this phrase as, "Our body doesn't belong to us, we are not able to control it—like with toothache, we cannot tell it to stop, it's not in our own control."

I had conversations with other monks. When the topic of *anatta* came up one monk explained it as "the body is not ours" (*too am tsa pen khaung hao*). On another occasion the same monk said: "*Anatta* is 'body is not ours'; it's not ours to control or direct or scold. We are not able to scold our body, saying, 'don't get old, teeth don't fall out.' We are able to say this but our body does not obey us." Later on in the same conversation he said that when you finger beads, you should say "*aniktsa, tukkha, anatta*." And with *aniktsa* you should say "unstable and not fixed," while with *anatta* you should say "body—eyes, ears, touch—is not ours." Another monk gave the same "body is not ours" analysis.

Suffering allows one to search for the causes of suffering and extinguish them. Permanence is not good; one would remain as one is and there would be no escape from the cycle of rebirth and redeath. If one were in control, there would be no change, without change there would be no suffering, without suffering, no knowledge, and without knowledge, no escape.

The only thing that is stable is merit.

> It is like this, laypeople, there is only one kind which remains in this world. . . . If we are able to practice generosity, keep precepts, meditate—merit of all kinds or even only one kind; if we have a little property we are able to do a little, if we have a lot we can do a lot. If we have a lot of time we can store up precept-keeping and meditation for a long time. If we do not have time or have only a little time, then we are able to do only a little. Whatever [merit] we have been able to store

up. Merit from generosity, generosity merit, can be the property of everyone. When you die it will go along with you, it will go wherever you are born, wherever you die, whenever. That merit from generosity will stick with you, whether you go to stay in a bright place [rebirth in one of the heavens] or in a dark place [rebirth in one of the hells], the merit will stick with you wherever you go. It is like our shadow. (Abbot from Wat Hoo Wiang, Maehongson Town; February 10, 1985; funeral sermon for a monk)

Merit, from whatever source, is permanent. People can convert a small amount of property into merit through generosity, *tana*. Precept-keeping and meditation are also ways to acquire a store of merit, although this is seen as more difficult than the practice of generosity. Earlier in this sermon, the abbot talked about how generosity is a prerequisite for precept-keeping and precept-keeping a prerequisite for meditation. Even if people have neither the time nor the ability to keep precepts or meditate, the path of merit-making through generosity is open to them. Offerings convert uncontrollable— hence unstable—material objects into merit, which the monks describe as the only thing that is unchanging.

KINDS OF BEINGS

The kinds of beings discussed in the sermons include many of the ones discussed in Chapter 2, based on places and the beings associated with them. The nature of the beings and the relationships among them are also described in the sermons. The worlds are populated with a number of kinds of beings. Both good and bad spirits are mentioned and assumed to exist. Good spirits live in the worlds above the earth, which are sometimes referred to as *sawan*, the Thai word for "heaven," but more often simply as *mūong phi*, country of spirits. These include beings described as *phi*, regular spirits, and *phi sang*, Brahma spirits, which inhabit the upper levels of the heavens of sensual pleasures. Spirits have some interest in human affairs. In a sermon about offering robes at the end of the rains retreat, the monk listed as one of the benefits to the laypeople making the offering that the spirits write down the names of the people offering the robes in a golden book and are happy for and have love for them. Bad spirits also exist, sometimes referred to directly as hungry ghosts, at other times as spirits, *phi*, which want to kill or harass people.

Buddhas exist, but are rare. It is because the Buddha discovered the way the universe operated, and taught it to the people, that it is possible to escape from it to nirvana. The Buddha is the ultimate referral and justification in the sermons. The monks say they teach what the Buddha taught, that what they teach comes from the *tara*, the teachings of the Buddha, and that they are substitutes for the Buddha.

The Buddha's teachings make it possible for people to live together. Without the teachings, people would quarrel and bad people would predominate. If people practice the Buddha's teachings, the countryside is peaceful and prosperous. The Buddha's teachings have an autonomous existence; they are one of the three "gems" of Buddhism and have power of their own. During the decline of the religion, people forget these teachings and each Buddha must rediscover the truth about the way the universe operates. The Buddha's teachings correspond to gravity in our cosmology; prior to our understanding, gravity operated, although we were unaware of it.

Associated with the Buddha are a range of powerful disciples who had special skills and powers. These disciples are usually mentioned in the blessings, when the monk invokes their characteristics and wishes them for the laypeople, as "let the laypeople have wisdom as wide as that as of Lord Saripuktara [one of the two chief disciples of the Buddha, regarded as second only to the Buddha in 'turning the Wheel of Law' (Humphreys 1984:169)]." Other disciples appear as characters in some of the stories the monks tell to illustrate various points:

> We people, is there anyone who can avoid old age, sickness, old age, and death? Not even Lord Mokkalan ["one of the Buddha's chief disciples, being renowned for his supernormal powers" (Humphreys 1984:129)] with his great power [*phong takho*]. How powerful was he? There is land under the surface, 84,000 *yotsana* deep [according to Cushing (1914:341) a *yotsana* is thirteen and a half English miles]. If he had the idea to use his power and take the top and make it the bottom and the bottom top, he could do this. Even he still had to enter *panupatitesa anupatites nippana*. Lord Mokkalan still had to reach *parinippan*, still had to pass

away. (Abbot, Wat Thong Kong Mu; January 17, 1985; sermon on the offering of a memorial flag)

After the Buddha and his disciples comes the monkhood. In an ordination sermon, one monk argues that the merit from sponsoring an ordination is of the greatest order:

> So wise men say that all other kinds of works of merit cannot compare with the ordination of novices and monks. The work of ordaining novices and monks is strong merit. Its merit is the strongest. Why is this? For the religion [*sasana*] of our Lord Buddha to persist—if there are no monks, then it cannot continue. It is for this reason we have monks. . . . Wise men wrote that the merit from this is great—as if the whole earth was the paper to write the merit on, using the water of the oceans as ink to write it, and using the mountain supporting the earth as a pen. Using the land as paper, the water of the oceans as ink, the great oceans may be dried up, but the merit of ordaining monks will not. . . . Why is the merit so great? The religion of our Lord Buddha is able to remain because of the work of ordaining novices and ordaining monks. (Abbot, Wat Pha Nawn, Maehongson Town; February 2, 1985; ordination sermon)

The only precept-keepers not mentioned specifically in any sermon are the *mae khao*.

The audience for the sermons is primarily the laypeople, and they as well as other kinds of humans are often mentioned in the sermons. In their sermons monks explain that it is practicing the religion and recognizing obligations that makes people human. People, by practicing generosity, *tana*, keeping precepts, *sila*, and meditating, *phawana*, make the world a better place, a cooler place to live. And through their practice, they improve their situation, eventually being able to escape the cycle of birth, death, and rebirth to reach nirvana.

If we are not mindful of the teachings, "when we are born as people, we are people in name only. We will be the kind of people who do not recognize obligations, we will be people who are hungry ghosts. People who do not recognize obligations are like hungry ghosts or like other kinds of people that are not people. People who do not recognize obligations are like people who are wild animals" (Abbot, Wat Pha Nawn, Maehongson Town; January 15, 1985; sermon at merit-making ceremony for a dead man). Another monk, talking about *karma,* described the consequences of having a child who had accumulated much demerit: "Whatever child frequently falls into jail or goes to court, he leads his parents to the courthouse and judge. You have to be careful of children like that, careful. He is the child of a plant. A plant which after it blossoms, dies" (Abbot, Wat Pang Mu; January 16, 1985; funeral sermon). This same monk, in another sermon, talking about the suffering associated with death, said:

> Some have not yet died and others are longing for them to die. We have people like this; there are a lot like this. Why do others long for their deaths? Wherever they stay, they do not add anything except their weight. Their words make peoples' blood boil. They behave like this. They stay in a village and it is not good. They stay in a village and it is not good and they do what we do not like. Others say a person who is not good is like a dog with a rotten head. (Abbot, Wat Pang Mu; January 14, 1985; sermon at a merit-making ceremony for a dead man)

Such people contrast with those who practice the religion, recognize obligations, and cooperate to make offerings.

> People who understand the teachings of the Lord Buddha and understand about *karma* also understand that dying is the same as not dying. They understand this because they have done a lot of good deeds, like this layperson, Grandfather Phan. This person was good. Others who have died were good, because they have done a lot of good deeds. They used to go before others, making a path of goodness. They led their siblings and fellow villagers on the good path. They led others to compete in goodness and in following the good path. . . . While he stayed in the world of people [alive], he led us to do like this—to build a road, a temple, a rest house, a hospital, or a school. They led others to build things for the public good. When those die, it is like they are not dead. People remember them and always think of them. They have died but it is like they are not dead. (Abbot, Wat Pang Mu; January 14, 1985; merit-making ceremony)

Later in the funeral sermon for this old man, the same monk elaborated on what it was to be a good person:

Some people have a large body. Besides having a large body, they are also old. Not only that, they also keep precepts and have the teachings and have hearts with love, kindness, joy, and equanimity. They have these four virtues for all people. This is the same as the large tree which has flowers, which is full of leaves, people rely on it for coolness. Crows also rely on it for coolness. (Abbot, Wat Pang Mu; January 16, 1985; funeral sermon)

Another monk, eulogizing another old man, said: "when he stayed in the country of people, he was a man who was excellent, a person who knew what was low and high. In the past he was able to offer, keep precepts, and meditate. He was a good person, a person who advised others to do good deeds. He sponsored novices and monks for their ordinations, he did large amounts of meritorious work" (Abbot, Wat Pha Nawn, Maehongson Town; January 15, 1985; merit-making ceremony).

People know how to behave well because their parents and others teach them and they listen: "When we are good it is because our mothers are also good and our teachers are good. The people who teach us are also good. Because of that we are rich. So we offer and share" (Abbot, Wat Pang Mu; January 16, 1985; funeral sermon).

In the sermons, monks differentiate among a number of kinds of laypeople. There are the main sponsors of the events, *ngao*, the foundation of the event; sponsors of monks and novices, *mae awk paw awk*, literally, mothers of leaving lay life and fathers of leaving lay life; people who keep precepts; people who have knowledge; and elders, people whose age is greater than our own. These last three are those whom people *khan taw*.

Differences among people depend on *karma*. As one monk put it:

We people, each of us, are not identical with others although some people are similar. In what way are people not alike? We call these differences *karma*. . . . We can compare the characteristics of their birth years and their merit. They are not the same. They are not comparable. For some children, if the younger sibling is beautiful, the middle child is not beautiful. The character of their *karma* is not comparable. They are not the same in this. If it is not *karma*, then if they have had the same mother and father, they must be completely identical. The children must be completely the same. If beautiful, they must all be beautiful; if rich, they must be the same; if straightforward, they must be all straightforward; and the same for wisdom, if one is sharp, they must all be sharp. But because of *karma*, one person has good wisdom, another does not; one person is female, another male; one person is beautiful, another ugly; one person is straightforward and honest, another is crooked. Because of *karma—karma* which we have made and stored in our earlier lives. . . . The Lord Buddha said like this: we are born because of *karma*; what happens, happens with our *karma*. It is a consequence of our deeds—what we have done, what we have said, what we have thought. (Abbot, Wat Pang Mu; January 14, 1985; merit-making ceremony)

Actions have both immediate and future consequences. If people perform good actions, or merely have the intention of doing them, then good consequences result. In sermons, generosity, *tana*, and intention, *tseitana*, are the two crucial factors that determine one's merit or one's benefits.

In one sermon, a monk tells the story of a poor man who realizes that his poverty is a consequence of his past failure to make offerings. He wishes he could make a large ceremony, and the intention to do so immediately improves his luck in selling firewood. He then makes a sand pagoda and offers his lunch rice to the Buddha, the teaching, and the monkhood, using two crows in a tree as the monks. Because of this, he is reborn as a king and has many more opportunities to make merit. His intention and small offering are rewarded.

While acts have consequences, it is possible to cancel adverse consequences by asking for forgiveness and paying respect to powerful others. This was discussed in the sermon delivered when villagers came to *khan taw* the monks. It is also possible to circumvent the consequences of one's actions. In an ordination sermon, a monk told the story of a woman who had sponsored her son's ordination as a novice. She had made a lot of merit but also some demerit.

She died; her bad deeds stuck with her, so she was stuck in hell. She fell into hell. In her heart she put aside the reddish orange flames and her thoughts came to the robes, the robes of her son. She thought the robes and the flames were the same. The fires of hell were extinguished. The fires of hell disappeared. Those who were the monsters that guard hell, all became beautiful people. Those who were birds with small and crooked mouths [hungry ghosts] all changed into *hangsa* [Brahma] birds and all of them ascended straight away into heaven. (Abbot, Wat Pha Nawn; Maehongson Town; February 2, 1985; ordination sermon)

BLESSINGS

Regardless of the kind of human being or one's *karma*, people attending an event, helping at an event, or sponsoring an event are included in the blessing at the end of the sermon. Blessings request in the polite imperative that the audience escape a wide range of dangers and receive a multitude of benefits.

Let it be like I say. Whatever you [the audience] want or wish for, let it be completely fulfilled. Do not let it come to a bad end, do not let it stick fast. Do not let the people become black hearted or dull or stubborn. Do not let illness and pain come into their bodies. Let them go away from their bodies and minds, away from their houses. All spells [*athat*] from spirits, spells from people, people who intend evil, spirits who intend evil, send them away; let them go ten thousand times as far as one can see, one hundred thousand times as far as one can see, one hundred twenty thousand *yotsanas* away. Do not allow officials to harass them; do not allow spirits to harass them. When spirits see the people, let the spirits have love and kindness for them. Let people have love and kindness for them. When lord officials see them, let the lord officials have loving kindness, strong and great love for everyone, small or large, young or old, female or male, all of them. (Abbot, Wat Mawk Tsam Pe; October 17, 1984; sermon delivered when villagers came to *khan taw*)

Blessings are an important part of any temple service. Monks chant blessings in return for offerings. The monk who gives the sermon ends it with a blessing. These are the same sort of blessings that people receive when they *khan taw*; however, monks' blessings are likely to be more elaborate than those of laypeople. While the blessing is recited quickly so that Shan often do not understand the content, the intent of the blessings is widely understood.

When you ask people what the blessing does, they say it keeps them healthy and happy. This is the same response that they give when asked about what their tattoos do for them (Tannenbaum 1987). The phrase "*yuu lii kin waan*," staying happy and healthy, is the minimal blessing. Being protected means that one can stay healthy and happy. The protection means that beings who might wish to cause a person problems refrain from doing so. Protection also guarantees that what a person does will succeed since nothing will hinder its completion. Staying happy and healthy sums up the intent of the blessings.

The person giving a blessing requests that the audience be protected from misfortune and danger. Some monks provide a long list of the misfortunes and dangers, including those from the five enemies, from rebirth in the hells, and from illness, dangers from fire, water, evil spirits, and human enemies, and also *khaw*, generally misfortune (see Durrenberger 1980b, 1981b). Besides sending dangers away, the blessings also request a range of positive benefits including prosperity, good rebirths, getting whatever one wishes for, wisdom, knowledge, power, and reaching nirvana quickly. While other people's blessings may not include the range of items that appear in monks' blessings, they generally request the same things—that misfortune avoids the recipient and that good things do not.

These blessings are compatible with power-protection and the way more powerful beings protect and nurture their followers. The power of the blessing is that it serves to protect the receiver, driving away misfortune, often requesting that it go "ten thousand times, one hundred thousand times farther than the eye can see." Like tattoos or amulets (Tannenbaum 1987), these blessings ward off misfortune and motivate powerful beings to have compassion for the recipient. This blessing by the Mawk Tsam Pe abbot, after people came to pay respect and ask for forgiveness from the monks, shows this compassion:

> Laypeople, whichever side you turn, wherever you walk, wherever you come from, wherever you go, let others love you equal to the love, the love the mother wasp has for her children, equal to the way the hen protects her eggs, love the way the wasp is jealous for her young, love like heart's blood,

like the *winyan* in the heart. Let whoever sees you, let them love you like parents. (Abbot, Wat Mawk Tsam Pe; October 17, 1984; sermon delivered when villagers came to *khan taw*)

Blessings invoke the power-protection of more powerful beings so that the recipient gains access to greater, more effective, protection.

These beings act in ways congruent with the logic of power-protection. Blessings invoke the protection of more powerful others who then protect the recipients of the blessing. An intermediary whose own power is sufficient invokes the aid of these powerful beings and, through the intermediary, the recipients are protected. Rather than relying on the protection of a single powerful being—the person giving the blessing—the recipient is brought to the attention of all powerful beings and can now rely on their aid. The recipient relies on his or her relationship with the blesser and, through him or her, the power of the other beings.

MONKS AND THE COMMUNITY

Monks often discuss the relationship between the laypeople and the temple, particularly at events directed toward the monkhood—ordinations, requesting the monk to stay in the temple, and paying respect and asking for forgiveness from the monks. One abbot discussed their mutual obligations in the sermon he gave when the community invited the monks to remain at the temple. Laypeople have the obligation to support the monks, to provide them with food, shelter, clothing, and medicine. The monks have the obligation to give sermons and teach the laypeople. The monastery and the laypeople form a single community, something the mutual forgiving of offenses, on both the lay and monastic sides, suggests.

Having monks and a temple provides benefits for the community. Monks provide laypeople the opportunity to make offerings, hence, merit. The benefits are not completely one-sided. When the community offers *kathing* robes, both the people offering and the monks accepting robes receive benefits. Having received a *kathing* robe, a monk receives a number of dispensations to engage in behavior that would otherwise breach minor monastic rules. Monks give blessings and send *metta*, love, to the community. The monks, by practicing the Buddha's teachings, help make the community a peaceful, cool place to live.

Monks recognize the difficulty laypeople have in collecting the goods to make offerings and making arrangements for a sufficient number of monks for ceremonies. Events that require minimum numbers of monks (ordinations, offering *kathing* robes, and *khao kam*) are recognized as particularly difficult and rare. One monk described the coming together of the minimum number of monks and the laypeople with both sufficient funds and the intention of offering *kathing* robes as being as unlikely as one needle, falling from the sky, landing on the point of a needle standing on the ground.

People have the obligation to continue the customs that their parents and grandparents followed. The account the monks give for the existence of a custom or ceremony is that it was established either by the Buddha or in the Buddha's time. There is continuity between what happened in the Buddha's time and events happening in the present. In the ordination sermon, the monk talks about continuing in the line, *say*, that the Buddha established. Monks, parents, and teachers are transmitters of this heritage.

The relationship between monks and laypeople and among laypeople is implicitly hierarchic but reciprocal. There are obligations and responsibilities on both sides. People should be respectful towards those who are above them, that is, those with greater knowledge or greater restraint, precept-keepers, or those of greater age and with greater power. These are all people with power greater than their own. This includes parents, teachers, monks, and officials. The laypeople's primary obligation is to treat them with respect. Failure to do so has negative consequences, so people *khan taw* such superiors. The potential for offense is not one-sided. In his sermon, the Mawk Tsam Pe abbot recognized the potential for monks to offend against laypeople and requested the laypeople to forgive the monks any offenses. In general, powerful others have the duty to instruct, nurture, and protect the less powerful other. People should be mindful of and grateful for these favors, and treat the other with respect.

Monks play a particularly important role in the relationship of the living with the dead. Without monks, merit could not reach the dead. Once during a sermon delivered when a memorial flag was offered for a dead man, and once during a sermon delivered during the merit-making ceremony for all those who had died in the previous year, different monks told the same story about why people make offerings to monks to send merit to the dead. The story tells of a rich couple who were heartbroken when their son died. They buried him but, because they could not forget their son, they built a shed and had a servant take food and drink every day to the cemetery. One day, because of flooding, the servant could not reach the cemetery. As he started back, he saw a monk, and decided to offer the food and drink to the monk. That night the son appeared in his father's dream and berated his father, saying he had been dead a year but he had been able to receive food only that day. The rich man accused his servant of not delivering the food and drink. The servant was able to convince the man that he had taken food every day, but that the day before, due to flooding, he had offered the food to a monk. The rich man went to ask the Buddha why it happened this way. The Buddha told him to make offerings to the monks and then pour water to share the merit.

> The Buddha spoke like this and the rich man did as he heard. He prepared food, prepared flowers, prepared rice, water, food, and flowers. Afterwards he poured the water, sharing the merit with the Lord Buddha. The Lord Buddha shared this merit, sending it to reach the son who had fallen into a poor place, staying in the cemetery. As soon as the merit reached him, his condition improved, he rose to enjoy himself in the country of the spirits. His spirit rose to enjoy itself in the country of spirits. (Abbot, Wat Thong Kong Mu; January 17, 1985; memorial flag offering)

The living do not need monks to confer merit; it follows automatically from intentions and actions. Nonetheless, people prefer to make offerings to the monks and receive blessings from the monks. Since monks keep precepts, their blessings and the merit from offering to monks are seen as especially good.

In sermons, monks discuss the full range of beings in the universe, from the Buddhas as the most powerful to those in the hells as the least powerful. Monks emphasize beings that use their power properly, nurturing and protecting their followers, and those that behave properly, showing their gratitude and respect to those more powerful. Those that do not are held up as bad examples, as the kind of being one does not want to become. Monks recognize that people suffer from bad actions, as is indicated in the stories where people are in the hells, but they do not focus on the suffering but teach how to avoid it.

Monks do not explicitly discuss the negative side of power. The abuse of power is recognized in the blessings when they ask that the lay audience be protected from dangers, including those posed by government officials and spirits and people with evil intentions. Monks, as well as traditional doctors, characterize the universe and powerful beings in positive terms. The positive elements are stressed as ways of dealing with those negative aspects that Shan assume exist and do not need to be described.

SERMONS AND POWER-PROTECTION

Shan monks do not explicitly discuss power and protection as underlying the nature of the universe. If anything, they assert that the underlying nature of the universe is given by the operation of the laws of *aniktsa, tukkha, anatta,* and *karma.* Yet there is ample evidence that the universe described in the sermons operates in terms of power and protection and that *karma* does not actually operate as universally as described in sermons.

The most direct evidence comes from the blessings given at the ends of sermons. Monks discuss power in the same terms as laypeople. Either powerful beings are asked to protect and shade people from dangers, or the monk, speaking as a powerful being in his own right, requests that the laypeople be protected from dangers. The power that people have is expressed in similar terms.

Sermons assume that the universe is hierarchically organized—from the hells to the heavens—and that beings are similarly ranked. In funeral sermons birth as a spirit is described as better than birth as a human, as a human better than as an animal, and as an animal better than in the hells. One of the rewards of generosity is rebirth in the heavens.

However, the system of ranking is not explained. The best discussion of the hierarchy comes from the sermon that a monk gave when people came to *khan taw* the monks.

> I will preach about *khan taw* because we also do this to those with great age. These are one kind which we *khan taw*. People who have knowledge of the teachings, who study and teach; people who have power and protection [*wuthi*] from age, from keeping precepts, and people who keep the precepts, know the Dharma, and have great age. What do we do? We *khan taw* them which results in a good blessing, an excellent blessing. (Abbot, Wat Mawk Tsam Pe; October 17, 1984; sermon when the community paid respect to the monks)

The explanation for why people should *khan taw* people rests on offense and giving offense. Improper actions of inferiors give offense to superiors so children pay respect to and ask forgiveness from their parents, people with less knowledge seek forgiveness from those with more knowledge, people who do not keep precepts from those that do, and so on.

The law of *karma* gives moral and ethical justification for human differences. Monks argue that one's *karma* is a consequence of one's own actions and only one's actions. A contradiction with morally neutral power is only apparent, since the act of *khan taw* cancels out the consequences of one's offenses. The monk who gave the ordination sermon talked first about how good and bad deeds do not cancel each other out, and then continued with his story about a woman who had her son ordained as a novice, died, and, because of bad deeds, went to hell. When she thought of her son's robes, she immediately went into the heavens.

As the story illustrates, objects associated with the Buddha and the Buddhist religion have a power of their own, separate from and greater than that of *karma*. This is congruent with the logic of power-protection, that beings acquire power through austerity and restraint. The Buddha is powerful because he is the ultimate precept-keeper; he gave up everything in this world. The Buddha functions as a "super" being, more powerful than other beings because of his extreme withdrawal. Because of this, things associated with the Buddha have the power to override *karma*.

Power-protection controls events and actions, and causes *karma*. Consequently if there is enough power-protection, it can override the result of actions, that is, *karma*. With this caveat, there is nothing incompatible between the laws of *aniktsa*, *tukkha*, *anatta*, and *karma* and the assumption of power and protection. Having power and protection can limit the amount of one's suffering by giving one greater control, and access to power and protection can be justified in karmic terms. The fact that living in the world causes suffering because people are attached to things and they have no control over changes does not affect the assumption of power and protection. There is a certain resonance between the "fact" that change causes suffering and the nature of morally neutral power and protection. Both focus on the issue of control and change. Having power means being able to ward off change and to protect oneself and one's followers from the negative consequences of actions. Change is negative; being alive means that one changes from healthy energetic youth to tired old age and decay. Yet it is inevitable: even the Buddha and his most powerful disciples had to die. Power can only ward off change but not defeat it. As one monk in a funeral sermon phrased it: "Who can compete against the world? Who can defeat the world?"

CHAPTER 7

Power-Protection and the Life Cycle

So far I have argued that power-protection is an underlying axiom in Shan worldview. I have supported this argument with analyses of tattoos, kinds of beings, and relationships with powerful others. In Chapter 6, I showed how power-protection underlies the ideas and concepts Shan monks present in sermons. Here I examine the place of power-protection in the Shan life cycle, and show how it functions to define relationships and how these change through time.

LIFE CYCLE AND POWER-PROTECTION

In Shan cosmology one is reborn many times, but once born one continues through the life cycle in a linear fashion. A life is divided into several segments: child, young adult, adult, and elder. Whether the transitions between the stages are marked with ceremonies or not, each stage has different behavioral expectations and status that separate it from both the preceding and following states. These differences are related to the amount of power-protection people have and their ability to extend that protection to others.

Here I describe the ceremonies, status, and behaviors associated with each stage and discuss changing capacities for power-protection as one moves through the life cycle.

Birth and Children

Today, ideally, people have two children, a boy and a girl. Inheritance is bilateral with each full sibling inheriting an equal share of the parents' wealth. Given the limited size of irrigated fields, birth control is popular. The willingness to use birth control is strengthened by an adequate health care system; if a child is born it is likely to survive to adulthood. People do not

123

prefer sons over daughters. If a couple has two children of the same sex they might have a third, hoping for a child of the other sex.

There is little ceremony associated with pregnancy and childbirth. In the recent past children were born at home, but now most women in the area go to the hospital in Maehongson Town. After birth, most ceremonies and activities are directed towards the mother. She follows a number of food restrictions both for her own protection and for that of her child. She lies by the fire for up to two weeks and receives herbal steam baths prepared by her husband.

Hanks (1963) argues that this lying by the fire is a rite of passage for Central Thai women that parallels a man's ordination (see below). This is not so for Shan. Lying by the fire entails some food restrictions and sexual abstinence. After giving birth a woman is weak; this restraint is said to restore the woman's strength and health. Whatever power-protection she acquires it is only sufficient to make her healthy, not to allow her to protect others.

The first month bathing ceremony, *ap* (bathing) *lɯɯn* (month), marks the child's formal entry into the social world. The ceremony is said to help make the child civilized. If a child behaves wildly, being generally disobedient, others may inquire whether or not the child has undergone the *ap lɯɯn* ceremony. Based on the child's behavior, they suspect not; if the child had, he or she would be better behaved. However, the ceremony is optional. In Thongmakhsan, I know of only one instance when it was held and that was for the son of the schoolteacher. In the larger wealthier village of Mawk Tsam Pe, it was standard practice.

The *ap lɯɯn* ceremony indicates different behavioral expectations for boys and girls. The gender of the child affects both the scheduling of the ceremony and some of the events in it. The "month" is an approximation: for girls, the ceremony is held less than thirty days after birth; for boys more than thirty days. If the ceremony for a girl is delayed, she is thought likely to be somewhat wild, given to visiting and travelling far from home. These are desirable characteristics in boys, and their ceremony is held later; if it were held sooner, they would be less likely to have these attributes. (For the Northern Thai, the logic for the bathing ceremony is the same except that the timing is reversed; girls are bathed after a full month, boys after less than a month [see Davis 1984:53].) A boy, before he is bathed, will have his head shaved; a girl will not. This is said to foreshadow the boy's eventual ordination. It is also a consequence of the boy's potential for wilder behavior; if it is not done the boy will be disobedient.

The ceremony involves bathing the child in water that has been boiled with medicinal plants and cooled. Pieces of jewelry or silver coins may also be placed in the water, and they become the property of the child. A woman who has successfully raised children is chosen to do the bathing. After the child is bathed, elders one by one give a blessing, stroking the child's wrist with white string, and then tying the white strings around the child's wrists. After this, the participants are given a meal. After the meal the sponsors request and receive a blessing from the elders and the ceremony is over.

There are no other ceremonies for children as children. Small children are likely to have white strings tied around their wrists at all times. However, there is no ceremony attached to this; the child's parents just ask one of their older relatives to give the blessing.

The blessings and protection transferred through the string help strengthen and maintain the children's health. As small children, they may also receive protective tattoos, especially those that cause others to have compassion for the bearer or protect against evil spirits. Many adults who have some of these tattoos told me they received them when they were children and that, while they did not want to be tattooed, their parents had it done to them. They usually did not know much about the tattoos except that they were to keep them healthy. Children often wear protective amulets on cords around their necks. These amulets are often coins with the image of the king, said to draw on the *kung* of the king.

Normally a mother does not do much agricultural work during a child's first year but stays home and takes care of the child. Parents, close relatives, or grandparents take care of small children up to the age of three or four. Children play within the house compound of their caretaker and are not allowed out of it unattended.

Small children are humored and indulged. They are said not to understand much; as a consequence there is little point in expecting them to learn how to behave properly. Nonetheless, they are taught basic behaviors, judged important. As they learn to speak, they are trained to use polite forms to grandparents and other elders. Small children are trained to share their sweets with anyone who asks but especially with smaller children; they are taught that to be *tsaū kot*, greedy ("to be crooked, cunning in dealing with others" [Cushing 1914:198]) is bad and they are encouraged to share and be *tsaū sū* ("straightforward, upright" [Cushing 1914:199]). By the time a child is three or four, the *tsaū kot* sign, a curved index finger, is enough to make a child share with others. Adults discourage children from being too demanding by telling them not to behave like a lord (*het tsao*). This training is the same for both boys and girls.

There are differences in how people evaluate male and female sexual features, and these are taught to the children. Girls around the age of two to three are taught not to expose their genitals because they are dirty and smelly. Small boys who go around naked may have jokes made about the size of their penises, but these do not have the inherently negative connotations conveyed by the remarks about the girls' genitals. This establishes early on the basic distinction between males and females, and small girls are made aware of the disgusting if not yet dangerous nature of female genitalia.

Adults tease children to embarrass them into obedience or into behaving in ways adults judge appropriate. A small child attached to his mother may be given to someone else while the mother pretends to leave, or the mother may hold another child. The first child may be reduced to tears, picked up by his mother, and soothed, and the teasing is begun again. Adults tend to laugh at children's inappropriate tears or temper tantrums.

Because small children understand little of how the world operates or what maintaining a relationship with powerful others entails, behaviors appropriate in such contexts are not expected of them. They are likely to go along when people from their households go to *khan taw,* but they only go through the motions.

The transition from humored child to obedient child is not always an easy one, as the rules that structure the child's universe radically change. Children start school around the age of six or seven. By this time they are thought to be able to understand what adults tell them and they are expected to do as they are told. This transition is not marked and children may experience this change at different ages depending on the composition of their household. If there are younger siblings it may occur earlier; if one is the only or last child, later.

Once this phase is weathered, children become semi-autonomous, capable of taking care of themselves, at least within the community. They may play with other children in the neighborhood, and are no longer restricted to the house compound. Now they rarely have their wrists tied, unless it is part of treating an illness.

School age children do not participate in agricultural production, but they contribute to their households. Girls do more chores around the house; they carry water and sweep the house. Both boys and girls are expected to wash their own clothes, help take care of younger siblings, and run errands for their parents and older siblings.

Children, male or female, do not have much power-protection. Small children have almost no power; this is marked by the fact that they almost always have their wrists tied. They must rely on their parents to care for and protect them.

Children can be useful, ordered about and sent on errands because they have little power-protection and have little capacity for offense. They rely on the power-protection of their parents and older siblings. Running errands is part of the return they make for this care and protection. It is a way of expressing their gratitude for their care. Certainly children may not recognize their obligations nor see the chores they perform as repaying their obligations to more powerful protective others. Often enough there is both a carrot (money to buy a sweet) and a stick (threats should they not do as they are told).

While parents conceptualize this relationship in these ideal terms, they also recognize that children do not always meet the ideal. In one sermon a monk described ungrateful children as children of plants. By the time one is a young adult, one does know that gratitude for power-protection is expressed through service.

Adolescents—*bao and sao*

Typically children begin working regularly a year or two after they finish school. The actual age depends on the person's interest in starting to work and the household's condition. If the household has few adult workers a child may begin working at an earlier age than a child in another household well supplied with workers. There is a period of a year or so when the children go to work but are not yet considered skilled enough for their labor to count as a full person for exchange labor. Once this training period is over, their labor is treated as equivalent to any other adult worker's.

Children finish village elementary school around the age of thirteen or fourteen. If they pursue education beyond sixth grade, they must attend the school in Maehongson Town. Going to school in Town delays the start of agricultural work. In Mawk Tsam Pe some of the children finish high school and pursue further education to become schoolteachers or nurses. In Thongmakhsan, few children finish high school and those who do gradually settle back into village agricultural work.

During this period, children take over many of the basic household chores. Boys have more freedom than girls, and girls have more household responsibilities. One reason for this difference is that boys are likely to have been ordained, usually as novices, after they have finished elementary school. A boy's ordination is seen as a rite of passage marking his transition from child to young man, *bao*.

There is no analogous ceremony for girls. There was some discussion of young adult women becoming *mae khao* for a brief period, analogous to the young men's ordinations. Young women do this in Burma and nowadays to some extent in Thailand. However, no one in Maehongson had done so. A girl is recognized as a young woman, *sao*, when she develops the physical markers of sexual maturity.

The ordination festival, *poy sang long*, is a large-scale celebration. Usually a village as a whole will decide to hold the ceremony every five or six years. The boys are older than the four- or five-year-old ordinands of Burma. All the boys between the age of ten or eleven and twenty who have not yet been ordained are likely to participate. Shan normally ordain as novices. According to the Thai Ministry of Religion the minimal age for novices is twelve, but Shan will include slightly younger boys. It is possible to hold smaller-scale celebrations or even no celebration at all. The ordination may not be celebrated if the parents are poor or if it is held in conjunction with a funeral for a parent or grandparent. A boy can be ordained a number of times, but goes through the large-scale celebration only once.

When planning an ordination, the parents and son have to decide on a sponsor. Parents may sponsor their sons, a group of relatives may join together to sponsor a boy, or someone else may sponsor him. This differs from Thai Lue, among whom parents prefer that others at least help cosponsor their sons, and Central Thai, where parents prefer to sponsor their sons (Moerman 1966). Potentially the sponsor may form a parent-child relationship with the ordinand. The boy refers to his sponsors as *paw* or *mae kham*, ordination father or mother. Minimally, he has the obligation to help at their funerals. Whether the relationship develops into anything more depends on both sides. A wealthy man may look to sponsor ordinations to increase his following; those that he sponsors can rely on him for financial support. A wealthy cattle trader in Huay Pha has sponsored a number of ordinations and provides his "sons" with access to irrigated fields at low rents. In other cases there may be little relationship between the sponsor and the ordinand.

Shan celebrate the ceremony differently from other Thai groups; an annual *poy sang long* is held in Maehongson Town during the school summer vacation and it has become a major tourist attraction. The pre-ordinands are dressed up as princes, paralleling the lifestyle of Siddhartha before he became an ascetic.

The boys who will be ordained may spend a few days at the temple to learn the words they will have to use to request their ordinations. Prior to being dressed up as princes, they have their heads and eyebrows shaved as they will have to be during their stay as novices. During the pre-ordination events, the boys are carried on people's shoulders and shaded with golden umbrellas. The men who carry the pre-ordinands are *kapi* (someone who helps a monk in "anything which is not lawful for him to do" [Cushing 1914:13], for example, handling money) *sang long*. These men are often recruited as a group from another community; they are paid for their efforts in both money and liquor.

Pre-ordination events include taking the novices-to-be to the *Tsao Mūong* altar where they are presented to the cadastral spirit and *khan taw*. The *Tsao Mūong* is also informed about their impending change of status from boys to novices. The major activities are the visiting of the pre-ordinands from house to house, reciting a blessing and being given small offerings, and the procession preceding the ordination. During this procession the pre-ordinands may be captured and held "hostage" by the men carrying them. They are usually released in exchange for some liquor.

The ceremony itself is performed in the *kyawng*. A large number of monks and novices are invited for the event. The ceremony is usually held in the afternoon after the monks, novices, and invited guests have received a meal. The monks sit on the elevated area; the monk leading the ceremony directs the "princes." The boys begin by asking for forgiveness and paying respect to their parents, and they receive their robes. They request and receive the five precepts and then request the ten precepts for novices. Monks, fathers, and older brothers help the pre-ordinands remove their princely clothing and don their robes. The pre-novices then receive the ten precepts and become novices. This may be followed by a sermon, which instructs the novices about their proper behavior or elaborates on the benefits accruing to the parents and sponsors for ordaining their sons. Offerings are presented to all the monks, novices, and new novices; together they chant a blessing for receiving gifts and chant for sharing merit. At the conclusion of the ceremony, sponsors, parents of the novices, and any elders pour water to share merit. The ceremony is over.

There are two rhetorical justifications for ordination: as a rite of passage, transforming an unripe male into a ripe one ready for adult life, and as a way for sons to repay the debt they owe their parents for raising them. The rite of passage rhetoric is consistent with the morally neutral power-protection analysis. Through ordination and the period of restraint and withdrawal, men acquire power for the rest of their lay lives. Men have different capacities for power: the power of some is so limited that they are never even ordained; others may be able to stay in the temple only a few weeks; still others may remain in the temple for years. While in the temple men have access to knowledge, which provides another source of power. The rite of passage rhetoric and the logic of power should be sufficient to account for ordination; why, then, is there a second rhetoric of repaying a debt to one's parents?

Children owe a nonrepayable debt to their mothers, who undergo the difficulties of pregnancy, the pains of childbirth, and the sacrifices involved in rearing children. This debt and the relationship it entails mean that if a child is mindful of his obligations to his mother, then the mother returns protection. The debt one owes one's mother is the greatest and, consequently, one's mother is the greatest source of power-protection.

The most powerful amulets are those one has from one's mother. A strip from the skirt one's mother wore while giving birth is the most powerful protective amulet. The cloth can be tied around the head or upper arm, or worn on a chain around the neck. Both men and women can use this amulet, but typically, as with all powerful things, only men do so. Normally, a strip of cloth from a woman's skirt destroys power-protection. No man is about to tie a piece of a skirt around his head, the highest and thus most powerful part of his body where the most powerful tattoos are placed; doing so would destroy his power. The only other use of a woman's skirt is to tie a strip from one around a gun barrel so bullets from it will unroll the protective barrier established by tattoos and amulets.

There is a basic contradiction between the protective power of the skirt one's mother wore while giving birth and the destructive power of skirts in general. The difference is between women in general and one's mother. Mothers have power. Power is attributed to parents, not because of their withdrawal from the world nor the reality of their temporal power, but because they behave the way powerful beings behave.

Since parents confer benefits, and protect and nurture their children, children are in an inferior dependent relationship with them. Children take shelter and refuge in the power of their parents. Sons seek ordination to acquire power and to establish themselves as autonomous powerful beings. They cannot do so if they are under a heavy obligation to their parents. The only way to escape this heavy obligation is to repay it, if only partially. There is a strong rhetoric that the debt one owes one's parents is not completely repayable. Ordination in this context serves two purposes: the boy is able to acquire power for himself and, since ordination is such a meritorious act and he shares this merit with his parents, he is able to partially repay the debt he owes them.

The lesser obligation a boy owes to his parents and the power acquired while a novice or a monk serves him well when he leaves the temple. Young men are semiautonomous; they do their share of household agricultural labor but they are likely to seek ways to earn money on their own. They use the money to buy liquor, travel, and go to festivals in surrounding communities. They often go visiting at night and are seldom at home. Generally they are less responsive to parental control.

Because of the power gained from being novices or monks, men are more autonomous than women. Autonomy is an expression of power; powerful beings are in control of events and through this control can escape the consequences of their actions. From the perspective of nonpowerful beings, this control is the freedom to be out of control; the powerful being is beyond social control and social expectations. Drinking and the fighting associated with the loss of control through intoxication are ways in which young men demonstrate and test their power (see Durrenberger 1983). Other people see this loss of control as a real danger: when a fight begins most people run and hide while other men try to separate the fighters. In general intoxication and fighting are considered bad, but it is appropriate for young nonmarried men to drink, and fighting is always a possibility when men are drunk. Young adult men have the opportunity to test their power at funerals and festivals throughout the area.

In the past, to be considered adult and worthy of women's interest, men had to be tattooed from the waist to the knee. These are the tattooed pants that were common among Shan, Tai Lue, and Burmans (Scott 1896). This practice has died out and only men in their sixties or older have these tattoos. Undergoing the tattooing process was a sign of a man's power and his ability to endure pain.

These behaviors contrast sharply with those of young adult women. Women do not drink, go out visiting at night, or travel much outside their villages. Like young adult males, they do go to festivals in surrounding villages, but women do so only in groups of other young women. Ideally these women are not assertive, but rather they should do what needs to be done without being told—rising early to cook rice, carrying water, doing household chores, and participating in household agricultural work. They do not have the power-protection necessary to engage in travel or tests of power like the young adult men. They are unable to repay their obligations to their parents; consequently, they behave like respectful dependents, preparing food for their parents, seeing to their comfort, and looking after them in old age.

Woman have no analogous means to acquire power-protection for their own autonomy or to repay the debt they owe their parents. Theoretically they could acquire some through becoming *mae khao*, "nuns," for a short period. Since this does not occur in Maehongson, the implications of this for women's ability to acquire power-protection or repay their debt to parents were unelaborated. Minimally it would be less than that of becoming a monk or novice since a woman would keep fewer precepts, and so even if she became a nun her ability to repay her debt to her parents would be less than a man's.

Courtship and romance are considered proper and normal for young adults. A standard topic of Shan conversation is food, and what one ate at a previous meal. There are a series of rhyming couplets related to courtship that are attached to certain foods. Common ones are *kin phak khio nawn kaw liao* (eat gathered greens, sleep by oneself); *kin mak phak khay hak tsong maa* (eat squash curry, want to love, will you come?); and *kin nūa muu nawn tsawm su* (eat pork, sleep with you). Older people in their fifties know these couplets; when they were young they carried on courting conversations using these rhymes. Now young adults know a few of these, but they do not use them when courting.

Young adult men and women have numerous opportunities to meet. Except for irrigated field preparation done by men and rice transplanting by women, there is little division of labor in agricultural work. Young adult men and women are part of the exchange labor teams. At night men go visiting at young women's houses.

During festivals and festival preparations, they can meet young adults from other villages. Festival preparation, where women stay up all night cooking rice, provides an opportunity for talking. At the *lamwong* young men from the host village and other visitors have a chance to interact with the *lamwong* dancers and other young women who are dancing. *Lamwong* dancers are often requested to dance at other villages' festivals. At other festivals where food preparation goes on all night, young people have the chance to sit and talk. During these events, the young adults may sit up talking and singing in an area slightly removed from adult supervision.

Adults

The process of establishing one's adult status begins with marriage. People are concerned that boys not marry before they are in the draft lottery at twenty, since two years of military service at low pay is a hardship for a young couple. Women marry at a younger age. One woman in Thongmakhsan married when she was thirteen or fourteen but she said she was already mature. Normally women marry when they are around eighteen.

Nonrelated young adult men and women are usually not alone with each other. If they are, the Shan assumption is that it is for sex. Minimally, having sexual relations is enough to establish a marriage. However, this is not considered the appropriate way to marry.

When a couple decides to get married, they approach their parents and ask for permission to do so. If the parents agree, they negotiate the price of goods given by the groom's family to the bride's family. This includes gold jewelry, usually a gold chain of one *baht* weight, worth around 2,500 *baht* (U.S. $100), which becomes the property of the bride; clothing for the bride; and a sum of money for the bride's parents. For marriages where the bride and groom are from the same area this amount is low, between 400 and 1,000 *baht* (U.S. $16 to $40). If the groom is from elsewhere, the amount is much higher. A wedding in Mawk Tsam Pe in 1988 involved a groom from Bangkok, the amount being 10,000 *baht* (U.S. $400), although this is much lower than the reported rate in Bangkok of 100,000 *baht* (U.S. $4,000). Ideally the money is used to provide the couple with household goods, although this is up to the bride's parents. The Bangkok groom also gave his bride a gold chain that weighed two *baht*, and agreed to send her to a school where she could learn sewing. The bride's family pays for the cost of the wedding ceremony.

This "bride price" is said to recompense the woman's parents for the cost of raising her. The rhetoric is the same used in speaking of sons' ordinations. Here money is made equivalent to merit in order to repay the parental debt. Structurally the payment marks the end of the daughter's deep obligations to her parents; the focus of her obligations changes from her parents to her husband. There is little effective difference in the power and control of resources between Shan husbands and wives; both are needed to have a functioning and successful household. The power and control may be different in wealthier households or where husbands have made much greater bride payments.

If the parents do not agree to the wedding, or if the amount of money demanded is more than the groom can pay, the couple may elope. Four of the five weddings in Thongmakhsan during 1978–1979 began with elopements; people said this was a consequence of the high price of gold at the time. The eloping couple goes to stay with relatives. After a period of time the parents are reconciled to the situation, and marriage negotiations and a wedding ceremony take place, although usually on a smaller scale than for nonelopement ceremonies.

As with any important undertaking, the couple consult an expert to select an auspicious day and time for the wedding. Weddings do not take place during the three months of *Waa* or the second lunar month, *lŭun kam*, which should also be a period of restraint. Outside these periods, any time is potentially a good time for a wedding ceremony. Once the date and time are determined, both the bride's and groom's sides invite elders, often including the village headman, and friends on both sides.

The wedding takes place in the bride's household. Friends of the bride and her relatives assemble at that house. If the groom is from another village, he and his family and friends will come in minibuses provided by the groom. If he is from the same village, the groom's side will come in a procession to the bride's house. When the procession reaches the bride's house, children block the gate, preventing the groom's group from entering the house compound. Someone on the groom's side pays each child one or two *baht* so they can proceed. Their path is again blocked at the head of the stairs into the house. Here it is men and women on the bride's side who have to be bribed to let the groom's group enter. The amount is small, about 50 *baht* (U.S. $2.00). Once the groom's side enters the house, it is invited to sit down. The bride remains in the inner sleeping room of the house with her friends. These friends also have to be bribed to let the bride out, usually for a sum of between 100 and 200 *baht* (U.S. $4.00 to $8.00).

Once the bride is lured out, the jewelry and money for the bride's parents are presented. The bride usually wears the suit of clothing provided by the groom. Then the wedding proper occurs. The wedding ceremony parallels the first month bathing ceremony, *ap lŭun*. Parents and grandparents of the couple do the initial wrist tying followed by others with the ability to give blessings. The groom's right wrist is tied to the bride's left wrist with white strings. Here the groom's wrist is tied before the bride's. If the person simply ties the wrists separately, the groom's right wrist is tied first, then the left; the bride's left and then right. Often the person tying the wrists gives the couple of gift of money by first tying a rolled-up bill to the white string. Bills of 10 and 20 *baht* (U.S. $0.40 to $0.80) are common, although the headman or subdistrict officer usually gives 100 *baht* (U.S. $4.00). After people who have the ability to give blessings finish tying the new couple's wrists, friends of the couple may also do so. However, they will just tie the wrists without reciting a blessing or stroking the recipient's arm with the string.

The ceremony and the blessings publicly acknowledge the new couple and their place in the community. The wrist-tying and the blessings strengthen the couple's power and well-being, which helps to insure the success of the marriage and the couple's endeavors.

After the wrist-tying is completed, all the guests are provided with food, prepared and paid for by the bride's side. This may be a meal of rice and curries but is often *khao sen*, a popular noodle dish. Male guests drink liquor, provided by the groom's side. If the couple is poor, the guests may be given a sweet, or a sweetened drink like milk tea or soybean milk, instead of a meal.

If the wedding takes place in the bride's village, the new couple may go to the groom's village after the ceremony. In the second village, elders and friends may also tie the couple's wrists and there is another festal meal.

The newlywed couple joins one of the parental households, typically the woman's, but this is open to negotiation and depends on which household needs the labor or whether the new husband or wife is the last child at home. Soon after the wedding, they may go *khan taw* any elders who were unable to attend the wedding.

The new couple remains in the parental household for three or four years. They work with the rest of the household members in producing rice but are likely to make their own cash crop gardens, using the income for their own purposes. At some point the couple will establish their own household. This depends on the parental household's wealth, whether there are any other people able to work and take care of the parents, people's health, premarital agreements as to how long to the new couple would stay with the parental house, and how well the new in-laws get along.

Once the couple establishes their own household, they become full members of the community, responsible for making contributions to village festivals, cooperating with villagewide work projects, and attending village meetings. They receive the respect accorded to male and female household heads.

Taking up residence in a new house is not marked by any ceremony directed at announcing the formation of a new unit in the village. Constructing the house requires little ceremony beyond selecting an auspicious day to do so and placing the appropriate offerings in the hole for the first house post, *sao mangkala* (see Chapter 3; this differs from other Thai groups [see Turton, 1978]). Erecting the house is often done with cooperative labor and, like any other cooperative labor event, the sponsor provides a festal meal. However, this occurs whenever a house is built and not only for a couple's new house. Similarly anyone who has finished a new house may invite monks in to chant to bless the house.

Village people who do not marry never achieve full adult status. They remain dependents in their parents' households. If a married couple remains in the parental home as their parents get older and can no longer direct the work, they gradually take over the running of the household and become the heads of the household.

This period is one of increasing responsibility and work for the couple. As their responsibilities increase, there is little time or money for going to festivals as they did as young adults. Because of their responsibilities for their children they are increasingly concerned with worldly matters and there is little opportunity for acquiring power through the practice of restraint.

During this period, the evidence for the power-protection of the household heads comes from their ability to provision the household and to live at the village's standard of living, and from their responsible behavior. To gain the respect of the village, they must contribute to village festivals and take part in villagewide work projects. The man may spend some money on liquor and drink during festivals, but he should not drink much more than this. The woman should work willingly, helping to prepare and serve food at village festivals. Together they should provide for their children and help take care of their parents as they age and need help. Ideally they should have enough money to sponsor their son's ordination as a novice, although there is no stigma if they cannot do so. This is more a period of demonstrating one's ability and capacity for effective behavior, a consequence of power-protection, than a period to accumulate or test power-protection.

This is the ideal. In Thongmakhsan, as in other villages, there are men who drink more than people consider appropriate; there are women who do not help with festival preparations; and there are households that do not even try to live up to the community's standard. People who deviate from the ideal do not receive respect.

Elders or Temple Sleepers—*kon nawn kyawng*

One becomes an elder with the capacity to give blessings when one first enters *Waa*, the rains retreat. Entering *Waa* means sleeping overnight at the temple on holy days, *Wan Sin*, during this period. There are twelve *Wan Sin* during this three-month period. One should spend at least the full and dark moon days and the last day, the full moon day of the eleventh month, at the temple. The last *Wan Sin* is important because one leaves *Waa* on the following morning. Large villages like Mawk Tsam Pe regularly serve a festal meal to the old people on the day after the full moon, when they leave *Waa*.

To become an elder, one simply chooses to do so. Women tend to do so at an earlier age than men. When one sleeps at the temple, one keeps eight precepts, with the implication that temple sleepers keep the five everyday precepts at all other times. This is more difficult for men since they hunt, fish, and drink liquor. Women may begin sleeping at the temple in their late thirties, while men begin to do so in their early fifties. People expect those in their sixties to be temple sleepers; those who have not done so will begin then.

People also expect that temple sleepers will have little interest in sexual activity. One Thongmakhsan man of the proper age to sleep at the temple had not begun to do so because of his reluctance to give up sex; he had recently married a young woman. Sexual activity for young men and women is both normal and proper but as one gets older one's interest in sex should decline. Less interest in sexual activity along with less interest in hunting or drinking is a mark of declining involvement in the world and of increasing restraint. The older one gets, the more restraint one can practice, and hence, the greater one's ability to acquire power-protection through temple sleeping and precept-keeping.

There is also an economic factor in determining when people will begin to sleep at the temple. The more well-to-do one's household, the more likely that one may begin to sleep at the temple at an early age. It is better to be less involved in agricultural production because in farming one cannot avoid killing small animals or insects. There is also the sense that in actively producing goods one remains too attached or committed to worldly things and that this does not fit well with temple sleeping. Temple sleepers are less likely to engage heavily in agricultural or other productive work. Sufficient wealth and a healthy household frees potential elders from worry about subsistence and allows them to take up temple sleeping when they want to.

To sleep at the temple all one needs is a water container, mat, pillow, blanket, and towel. If people can afford one they also buy a small individual mosquito net; this is practically a necessity since the temple grounds tend to be infested with mosquitoes and temple sleepers may not kill them.

Preparations for sleeping in the temple begin the night before *Wan Sin*, as the old people collect the candles, incense, matches, and popped rice, and prepare flowers and an offering for the temple. In the morning each prepares a lunch, a pitcher of water, and a small bottle to hold the water to pour during the chant to share merit. The mat, blanket, pillow, and mosquito net are rolled up and tied together. Someone from the household carries the old person's supplies to the temple.

Temple sleepers go to the temple and participate in the regular temple service. They are distinguished from other laypeople because they wear a towel or cloth draped over one shoulder and always pour water during the chanting to share merit. They receive the five precepts along with the rest of the audience. Once the regular service is over, people not sleeping at the temple hurry out. An old man requests the eight precepts from a monk who has come over to give the precepts. The rest of the monks and/or novices go about their regular business. The old people receive the precepts. They remain in the temple to meditate or to tell their beads. Meditating and fingering the 108-bead "rosary" are said to be equivalent. When fingering their beads, people may mentally recite a number of phrases. Some recite the Triple Gem—the Buddha, his teachings, and the monks, or suffering, impermanence, and inability to control. Spiro (1982:33, n.4) states that Burmese often recite the ten virtues of the Buddha.

If the temple compound has a rest house, the women temple sleepers will spend the day and night there, and the men in the temple building. If there is no rest house, then both men and women will spend their time at the temple itself. There are rest houses in most temple compounds.

After the women finish meditating they go to the rest house. In the rest house the women arrange their bedding and meditate again. There is no formal organization to these activities. Meditation or telling the beads is brief; it lasts only as long as one has the ability to meditate or until one finishes fingering the beads. One meditates again before lunch, after lunch, in the middle of the afternoon, before going to bed, and again in the middle of the night.

There is usually tea to drink and pickled tea to chew. Either the temple caretaker or, if the temple has them, nuns prepare tea and take it to the rest houses. In the temple, the temple caretaker provides the tea.

People eat lunch at 11:00; one of the eight precepts is not to eat solid food after noon. People sit in circles of six to eight and share the curries they brought for lunch. People try to bring good food to share, often including a sweet of some sort. Curries are passed to the other circles, if there is a lot of a dish and the other circle does not have any of it. People offer their first spoonful of rice and curry to hungry ghosts, spirits of those who failed to offer to the temple; these offerings are the only food these spirits receive. Someone from one's household, usually a child, comes to remove the dishes and leftovers from the temple and rest house.

In the late afternoon, people may bathe. If there is water at the temple area, they will bathe there or go home to bathe. In the evening, people may listen to tapes of sermons or go into the temple to listen to a *tsale* reading a book about Buddhism. Once or twice during *Waa* the village or a household may sponsor a special reading and invite the temple sleepers to come listen. The sponsors usually prepare soybean milk or milk tea to offer the temple sleepers in the evening. In the morning they may provide a festal meal for the temple sleepers and the monks, novices, and nuns.

Normally the temple sleepers go to bed early. Around 8:00, people put up their mosquito nets and begin going to bed. They get up in the morning around 5:00. Someone from their house comes to collect the bedding and brings a *som to* offering. The old person gives the person who brought the offering a blessing. The offering is placed on the Buddha altar in the rest house or in the temple. The female temple sleepers go into the temple to join the male temple sleepers. They all receive the five precepts and then go home to eat and resume regular life.

When one sleeps at the temple, one is said not to have children or grandchildren, husband or wife, or any fields. Sleeping at the temple is time out from one's regular activities and worries. Mostly people sit, talk quietly among themselves, or, after lunch, nap. People hold tightly to the precepts during this time. One woman said that they cannot even pull up plants; to do so would be to break the precept about killing. Temple sleepers walk quietly and mindfully; there is little joking, and no loud talk.

The general expectation for temple sleepers is that they will behave honorably. Behaving honorably means keeping the five precepts and being slow to anger. There is gossip about temple sleepers who do not keep the five precepts and those who begin to do so only because of their age and other peoples' expectations rather than their own desire. In Thongmakhsan, one man, who is both a temple sleeper and the village's most skilled traditional doctor, drinks. People discuss his behavior, saying he sets a bad example and that it is just not right. There were rumors that he also wanted to divorce his wife and marry a younger woman. Because he is a traditional doctor, his failure to follow behavioral expectations is more censured than if he were simply a temple sleeper. Still people gossip about what they perceive as temple sleepers' failure to keep the five precepts.

Being a temple sleeper is a regular phase of the life cycle; it marks the beginning of one's withdrawal from worldly concerns. This is appropriate behavior for older people. Just as young adults are expected to want to pursue pleasure, older people are expected to be less interested. Young people go to festivals at night to dance, play games, and court. Old people go to festivals to listen to the *tsale* reading and make merit.

A healthy old age is interpreted as a mark of merit and power. Old temple sleepers stay home and wait for others to come *khan taw*, they do not go to *khan taw* others. Younger temple sleepers will go *khan taw* after their children have asked for forgiveness and paid respect to them. The longer one has slept at the temple and the greater one's age, the greater one's power-protection and the more likely people other than immediate relatives will *khan taw*.

There is some local variation in this pattern, based on the size of the village. In the small village of Thongmakhsan people *khan taw* all the temple sleepers; in the larger village of Mawk Tsam Pe, with many more temple sleepers, people go to their close relatives and other respected elders.

There is a limit on the relationship between old age and evidence of power-protection. When old people become senile and are no longer capable of sleeping at the temple, their ability to protect others is gone. Only close relatives, children, and grandchildren are likely to *khan taw,* because the old people are parents or grandparents, but not because they are powerful.

What marks a powerful old person is a healthy old age with children and grandchildren and at least some resources so the person does not have to work. These are visible consequences of power and merit. People in villages know the circumstances of everyone and can interpret them in terms of power. These interpretations determine whether one goes to *khan taw* a particular old person who is not a close relative. These difference are also expressed in terms of the funerals performed once old people die.

CHAPTER 8

Death and Power-Protection

Distinctions among kinds of people based on power-protection continue at death. Powerful people and precept-keepers have more elaborate funerals and eleventh-month merit-making ceremonies, *khotsa*, than others. For people continually keeping eight or more precepts, these ceremonies must be held at different places and times from those for laypeople. Just as monks eat with other monks and not with other precept-keepers or laypeople, so monks are cremated at a particular monastic place and their *khotsa* are prepared before the *khotsa* for laypeople.

When and how one dies provides information about one's capacity for power-protection. A violent death, a dramatic and unexpected loss of power-protection, contrasts sharply with the more gradual fading of power-protection usual when an old person dies. This difference in how one dies is marked by different kinds of funerals and merit-making ceremonies for those who die violent deaths and for those who die more peacefully. The type of death is reflected in the spirit formed at the death; a violent death results in a particularly virulent spirit, a monk's death in no spirit. How one dies reflects one's power-protection and *karma* in this life and has implications for the quality of one's next life.

People die when they use up their power-protection and their *karma*. In a funeral sermon, a monk explained that people cannot know when they will die, how they will die, where they will die, and whether they will have a good or bad rebirth. All of these depend on merit. The monk went on to explain:

> Whoever makes lots of merit, they are bright and clear. When they die, they are able to die well. When they live, they are able to live well. . . . People say to us, may you come well, stay well, depart well; may you have these three. If we have these three kinds of good things we will not suffer a long

time. We will die and not suffer or stay in this life and not suffer much. (Abbot, Wat Pang Mu; January 14, 1985; merit-making ceremony)

A grandmother, commenting on the process of death for the oldest man in Mawk Tsam Pe, said, "His death is drawn out because of *bap* (Northern Thai, demerit). If there wasn't *bap*, then the death would be easy. The *bap* has to be from a past life because in this life he was a good man."

Bad deaths result from bad deeds in this and previous lives. The *sara* said that people who misuse powerful tattoos will die violent deaths. Those that die without much pain, at an old age, surrounded by their relatives, are ones with much merit in both this and previous lives and a goodly amount of power-protection.

Karma, the consequences of actions both good and bad, determines how one dies. People appeal to *karma* to explain the overall pattern of peoples' lives, something unknowable until one's life span is practically over. *Karma*, merit, and power-protection are not contradictory explanatory principles. All are used to explain length and quality of life and type of death.

In everyday conversations people who are about thirty say they have reached the noon of their life. This gives an idealized life span of sixty years; to die at or around the age of sixty is somehow appropriate. Nevertheless, many people live longer than this sixty-year span, others much shorter.

A serious illness initiates a series of actions associated with death that ends in the merit-making ceremony, *khotsa*, performed in the first half of the eleventh lunar month for all the persons who died in the community that year. The first stage is a death watch. Once people hear the news that someone is seriously ill, they visit that person's house. Other members of the household receive the guests and serve tea and pickled tea. A person may go through a number of death watches depending on how frequently he or she falls seriously ill. As a person begins to recover the visits stop. As it becomes increasingly clear that the person is going to die, more and more visitors come.

As a person nears death, close relatives and children pay final respect. These relatives should not cry, as their grief keeps the person's spirit from departing. During the final moments, people encourage the person to go ahead and die, not to linger, and crying relatives are scolded for hindering the person's death. The dying person should prepare for death, separating from the living and the concerns of the living and focusing on the next life. Proper mental preparation means that when the person dies, the spirit will not be shocked at its new state and will not attempt to carry on activities of the living as do unprepared spirits. These unprepared spirits are dangerous to the living regardless of their intentions when they interact with the living.

FUNERALS AND *KHOTSA*

After a death, the dead person's house is a center of activity. People come to help make the coffin, contribute rice and other foods, help prepare them to feed the people, and gamble. Funerals typically are held on the third day after the death. During this period, people are at the dead person's house day and night. This is deemed necessary because the spirit of the dead person is still around the house and is dangerous. At night, the survivors hold ceremonies to make merit for the dead; they either invite monks to chant the *apitham* verses, or ask a *tsale*, a layman versed in reading Shan, to read Buddhist texts out loud. Inviting monks is more expensive, since it requires a larger money contribution for the monks and better quality food. After merit-making is finished, guests are served a sweet drink such as soybean milk or sweetened tea. During the ceremony, food preparation and gambling continue. Since it is important that there be human activity at all hours of the day and night before the funeral, gambling is considered to be particularly appropriate at funerals. Many people come to gamble and the excitement and interest help keep people awake through the night. The police are much less likely to enforce laws against gambling during funerals.

On the day of the funeral, people from the area come for the ceremony. The coffin is brought out of the house and set in a palanquin preparatory to being taken to the place where it will be cremated. A meal, usually lunch, is served to the people at the dead person's house. Food is taken to the temple for the monks. After the meal the monks come to the funeral house and lead the procession to the cremation place. The cremation place, *pa* (forest or jungle) *hio*, is outside the village proper, away from any houses. There the monks receive offerings placed on the coffin and they chant. A monk may be invited to deliver a sermon at the cremation place. If the funeral is large, the sermon may be delivered at the temple prior to the cremation. People place wood on the pyre. The coffin is opened; a coconut is opened over the face of the deceased so that it may be washed a last time with the coconut water. Relatives of the dead person may come to view the body for the last time. The pyre is lighted and most people return home. A few men remain to make sure the fire burns out. As people return home, they stop to wash their hands and faces with *naam makhawn*, water that has been boiled with auspicious plants, to remove traces of the death.

During the ceremonies at the cremation place people should not cry or obviously grieve. If they do, the spirit of the dead person will not leave, causing a dangerous spirit to remain in the area. People who are upset at the death do not attend the cremation. Small children, pregnant women, and those who are sick also do not attend the cremation since they are considered weak and vulnerable to spirit attack.

The funeral concludes the next morning with the offering of a small memorial flag, *tam khawn*, made the evening of the cremation. A *tsale* may be invited to read at the house after the *tam khawn* is made. Monks may be invited to the house to receive their morning meal. If this is the case, other guests also come and receive a meal. Otherwise, the flag is just taken to the temple and offered.

A day or two after the cremation, relatives collect the unburned bones and some of the ashes. If the person died a nonviolent death in old age, these are placed in a reliquary, either in the wall surrounding the temple compound or in an *umang*, a small chedi. A picture of the dead person may be attached to either place. Children and grandchildren place *som to* offerings at the *umang* of their parents, grandparents, and other close relatives.

The last ceremony associated with death is the merit-making for the dead, *khotsa*, during the first half of the eleventh lunar month. Relatives of those who have died usually sponsor one collective *khotsa* for all the village laypeople who have died that year, including children, if the parents want to participate, and those who died violent deaths.

The day before the ceremony people come to help prepare the food that will be offered to the monks and provided for the guests. The night before the ceremony people come from the surrounding areas to listen to a *tsale* read from Buddhist texts and to gamble. After the reading is over, a sweet is served.

The next day the ceremony is offered. In the morning, the relatives of each dead person offer a memorial flag, *tam khawn*. If the relatives can afford it, they offer a large one, about five feet long, hung on a tall pole and erected in front of the temple. If not they offer a small one, similar to the one offered the day after the funeral, placed inside the temple near the altar.

Monks receive a meal and offerings; guests receive a meal. Usually the ceremony is carried out in the early afternoon, and monks and guests receive lunch. If the ceremony is small and the sponsors poor, the ceremony may be performed in the morning. This requires a less elaborate meal and fewer people are likely to attend.

Each household that has had a person die prepares an offering with rice and sweets, similar to the regular *som to* offerings. This is the offering for the dead person, *kawk* (container) *kon* (person) *tay* (dead). The offerings are presented, one to a monk. After the sermon, the monks pour water into *kawk kon tay* to share the merit made at the festival with each dead person. The dead are said to wait until this festival to collect the merit and then are free to be reborn.

STATUS AND TREATMENT AFTER DEATH

Distinctions among living people are maintained at death. The elaborateness of ceremonies, whether there is a dangerous spirit, and where one is cremated all depend on the power of the dead and how they died. Children, because they have little power, receive unelaborated funerals, while more powerful persons such as monks or wealthy old people receive elaborate ceremonies.

Children

The funeral for a small child is a simple affair. The ceremony is performed soon after the death. If, as is likely now, the child dies in the hospital, the parents may have the hospital take responsibility for the funeral. It is expensive to have the funeral performed in Maehongson Town, where the hospital is located, and very difficult to have the body moved from Town to the village.

In the recent past, children were buried in a cemetery separate from adults. The spirits of the children were said to remain around the cemetery, but were not dangerous. The children's spirits may tug at the clothing of passersby but cannot hurt them. People described these spirits as more playful than annoying.

A child's parents may or may not help sponsor the *khotsa* for those who died in the past year. The wealthier the parents are, the more likely they are to participate. Whether they participate also depends on the age of the child; the older the child, the more likely they are to participate, regardless of wealth.

Violent Death

Violent deaths are associated with a sudden loss of power. Dying a bad death automatically lowers one's status. While alive one might have had considerable power-protection but its sudden loss means that one really did not have control over events and, hence, did not really have power.

Violent or accidental deaths or deaths in childbirth are all classed as bad deaths; the person is described as dying bathed in blood. When a bad death occurs, the funeral is performed as soon as possible. The funeral for the man killed by the police was held the next day. The body was not brought into the village but was cremated in the hill field where he died. His family then abandoned the field.

The spirit created from a violent death is particularly dangerous. Ideally when people die, they know that death is coming and are mentally prepared for it. When someone dies a violent death, he or she is unprepared and likely to attempt to carry out plans made while living, putting those that live at risk.

Since the man killed by the police died particularly violently, his shock and anger at his sudden death was such that his spirit was likely to be angry and seek revenge. By having his funeral immediately and not bringing the body into the village, people minimized contact with the spirit. By abandoning the field, his family also minimized contact with the spirit, since spirits tend to remain near where they died or were cremated.

The soul (*winyan*) of a person who dies bathed in blood is said to be trapped in the blood, unable to find its way out. Consequently, at the *khotsa*, family members offer a model boat to provide the soul with the means to escape. The boat contains three small dolls, one to steer, one to paddle, and the third representing the person who died, dressed in male clothes if the deceased was a man, female clothes if a woman.

The family of a person who died a violent death may participate in the *khotsa* preparations along with others sponsoring the ceremony. However, when it is time to make the offerings and share merit with the dead they must do this separately. The spirits of those that die violent deaths are said to be unable to enter the temple. In a case where a man died in an automobile accident, a monk went with the family to the edge of the temple compound, received the *kawk kon tay*, the offering for the dead person, chanted, and poured water to share the merit with the dead man.

The family of the man killed by the police sponsored a separate *khotsa*. There had been another death in Thongmakhsan that year, but that person's relatives did not want to cosponsor a single ceremony for fear their son would be reborn with the man who died the violent death. People reason that those who make merit together will be reborn together.

The man's family prepared the *khotsa* at their house as normal, but the ceremony was performed along the road away from the village. In addition to the *kawk kon tay* and the model boat, the family offered a new shirt, new pants, hair cream, a comb, and other items they thought his spirit might desire. They said these offerings were to provide anything their son might desire so he would not hang around and pester the living for them.

Death in Old Age

Dying in old age prepared for death creates a spirit but, unlike those caused by violent or sudden deaths, it is not particularly dangerous.

The funeral described above is for an adult nonviolent death. The funeral for temple sleepers, especially those who have lived a long life (seventy or eighty years) is more elaborate. If the relatives can afford it, they sponsor a "tug-of-war," *tit lūūm*, funeral. Tug-of-war funerals have been described for Burmese monks and monks in Shan areas but not for laypeople (Keyes 1975, Scott 1896, Spiro 1982).

Participating in tug-of-war funerals is said to give merit. A *tsale*, lay reader, told me the following story as an explanation for tug-of-war funerals for monks. A disciple of the Buddha, Tsao Kao Pannya, a forest monk, died in the jungle. At his death an elephant organized the funeral and pulled the sledge. An angel and the spirit of a banyan tree pulled on the other side. They did this to get merit. The angel drew the sledge up the seven layers of the heavens and then brought it back to earth to let the monk be cremated. This story is not generally known and Keyes (1975) reports that he knew of no local explanation for the tug-of-war funeral.

People know what a tug-of-war funeral entails, who is eligible for one, and that they get merit from participating in the tug-of-war. Esoteric or textual explanations are not needed. The esoteric accounts are not wrong but they do not account for the whole range of phenomena. The *tsale*'s story does not explain why there are lay tug-of-war funerals. Funerals maintain the distinctions based on power-protection established while alive. Precept-keepers and those who die at home in old age with some wealth are all powerful persons. Lay and monastic tug-of-war funerals are marks of that power-protection. I discuss the differences between lay and monastic tug-of-war funerals below.

Preparations for a tug-of-war funeral last five to seven days because a sledge has to be built and decorated. The coffin is placed on this sledge and dragged to the cremation place. At some point outside the village, the tug-of-war takes place. People divide into two groups, sometimes based on the villages they come from, and perform a tug-of-war, pulling the sledge towards the cremation place or back towards the village. The battle is said to be between life, the village direction, and death, the cremation place. Death always wins.

The most elaborate lay funeral in Mawk Tsam Pe´ was held when the oldest man in the village died. It was a tug-of-war funeral taking place on the fifth day after his death. The man who had died was the father of the abbot of the temple in Naapaatsaat, a village about 11 km from Mawk Tsam Pe and 5 km north of Thongmakhsan. This abbot was one of the most respected monks in the area. On each night before the funeral, monks were invited to chant at the deceased's house. Close relatives in the village, people from Maehongson Town, and Naapaatsaat village as a group sponsored these ceremonies. One night the chanting was repeated as two groups sponsored separate ceremonies. The funeral and merit-making sermons describing what it is to be a good man, using one's power properly, referred to this man. The large-scale funeral was a consequence of the man's age, his family's wealth, and his status in the village and the surrounding area, and that of his son, the Naapaatsaat abbot.

Tug-of-war funerals can be made for either men or women. The first tug-of war funeral I saw was for an old woman in Huay Pha. My assistant, who was from the Shan State in Burma, found this remarkable; he said that where he was from this type of funeral was limited to men.

For laypeople, type of death and age are the most important criteria in determining the kind of funeral. If a person dies a violent death or is young, regardless of the household's wealth, a tug-of-war funeral is inappropriate. Wealth is important but secondary. If the deceased's family is poor, it cannot afford to sponsor a tug-of-war funeral. When an aged but poor man died, the people carrying his coffin to the burning site moved back and forth as if they were the sledge being pulled back and forth in the tug-of-war. At least for Maehongson, gender is an irrelevant criterion for tug-of-war funerals.

The unburned bones and some ashes are collected and placed in a reliquary in the temple wall or a small chedi in the temple compound. Depending on the rank of the person the chedis may be very elaborate. In Maehongson Town, behind

Kyawng Muiy Taw, are a number of large chedis containing the remains of rulers of Maehongson.

The only distinction marked at a *khotsa* for laypeople is between those who have died a normal death and those who have died a violent death. This distinction may be less stressed, as in the case where the offering for the person who died a violent death is made outside the temple compound, or more stressed, as in the separate ceremony in Thongmakhsan. This was a consequence of the particularly violent death and the fact that his family did not have a good relationship with the rest of the village.

If a large number of people have died in the past year or if the household of one person is particularly wealthy, the ceremony is likely to be large, with many temples invited and a large number of relatives from other villages attending. If few people have died or they are poor, the ceremony is smaller, with fewer monks and few relatives. The two ceremonies in Thongmakhsan were small; each household invited three temples and served breakfast. The *khotsa* in Mawk Tsam Pe the year the old man died was large, with eleven temples invited and lunch provided. It would have been larger, but the day before there was a separate *khotsa* for a monk who had died that year.

Monks, Novices, and *Mae Khao*

The funeral ceremonies of a monk, novice, or *mae khao* are more elaborate than their age or circumstances would warrant if they were laypeople. When a monk dies, he is given a tug-of-war funeral on the scale of those for elderly wealthy laypeople. The older the monk, the longer the preparations, and the greater the time between the death and the funeral. The funeral for the most senior monk in the province occurred almost a year after his death. The funeral celebration lasted a week. People and monks from all over the province attended the funeral. Novices receive tug-of-war funerals although they are twenty years of age or younger. *Mae khao* are less likely to receive tug-of-war funerals since most are fairly poor and there is less likelihood for outside sponsors, since *mae khao* keep fewer precepts and, consequently, have less merit. However, like monks and novices, they are cremated in separate places and their *khotsa* are held separately and prior to the *khotsa* for laypeople.

Monastic tug-of-war funerals for monks and novices have a number of features that are absent in lay tug-of-war funerals. These have to do with the sledge, *lɑ̄ɑm*, the setup of the cremation place, and how the funeral pyre is lit. The palanquin for a lay tug-of-war funeral is more elaborate than for a normal lay funeral. However, with a monastic funeral the palanquin and decorations are even more ornate and intricate. A lay tug-of-war *lɑ̄ɑm* has a single-layer base for the coffin and a single layer above it. The monastic *lɑ̄ɑm* has two (for novices) or more (for monks) layers below and above the coffin. With a lay tug-of-war funeral, the sledge and coffin are cremated at the regular cremation place. For a monastic funeral a special fenced-in cremation place is created. The corners of the fence and opening into the enclosure are decorated with five-tiered umbrellas and auspicious plants. The sledge with the coffin is eventually dragged into the center of the enclosure.

Over the coffin at monastic funerals is cloth held aloft by four poles (it also appears to be the custom in Northern Thailand; see Keyes 1975:53, and Kingshill 1976). The cloth may be orange, yellow, or white. If it is orange it is likely to be part of a monk's robe. According to informants at two different monastic funerals, it is *phaa thɑ̄ng khii nok*, the cloth to protect the coffin from bird droppings. When the Buddha died, he died under a banyan tree and there were many birds in the tree, so they needed the cloth to protect the Buddha's body from the bird droppings. One man added that the cloth helped protect birds and insects from the flames and so was part of keeping the first precept against killing living beings. These explanations are culturally plausible and probably derive from a Shan text that my informants knew. Their explanations are limited specifically to the cloth over the monks' coffins. However, cloths appear over a number of objects, not just monks' coffins, and so require a more general explanation. I return to the broader question of cloths above objects in the next chapter.

If the monk has a monastic rank of *Phra Khruu* or higher, the king provides the mother of fire and a representative to light the pyre. For other monks, a monk lights the fire. At lay funerals, a funeral specialist, *phawm tsanta*, lights the pyre.

Being a *phawm tsanta* is not a high status position. Ideally the pyre is lit via a Rube Goldberg arrangement of fireworks. The fireworks, although lit in the daylight, are spectacular but often fail to ignite the pyre. Fireworks may be used in lay funerals but it is rare; I saw this only once at a funeral in Maehongson Town for a man who was the relative of a government official.

The ideal funeral for monks and novices is a tug-of-war funeral. However, not all monastic funerals meet the ideal. Tug-of-war funerals are large and often rowdy with a tug-of-war taking place a number of times before the cremation. During the funeral for the oldest monk in the province, tug-of-wars took place on the days preceding the funeral but not on the day of the cremation. People explained that the committee feared the cremation would take place late, as people involved in the tug-of-war would not stop. While two of the monk's funerals I attended did not have tug-of-wars, the cremation site was set up in the same manner. People said there was not enough room, or that having the tug-of-war would cause too much trouble.

The *khotsa* for a dead monk is held separately from and prior to that for laypeople. The *khotsa* for an old monk in Mawk Tsam Pe was held on the first of the waxing moon of the eleventh lunar month, the earliest possible date. The ceremony was the same as *khotsa* for laypeople: a *kawk kon tay* was offered and the abbot of the temple poured the water to share the merit with the dead monk. However, this was the largest *khotsa* for which I have information, with twenty-one temples invited.

I have not observed a funeral of a *mae khao*. A *mae khao* in Huay Pha provided for her own funeral, having set aside money from the sale of her irrigated field for this. An informant in Thongmakhsan reported that the funeral was elaborate and done in Northern Thai style, but commented that this was unusual. The *mae khao* was cremated in a place where neither monks nor laypeople were cremated, and her *khotsa* was also held separately.

There is a straightforward relationship between prestige at time of death and the kind of funeral one receives. Bad deaths and monastic deaths define the range of funerals. A bad death funeral is held almost immediately, while a monk's funeral may be delayed for months. The eleventh-month merit-making ceremonies, *khotsa*, in these two cases are offered separately from those whose lives and deaths marked them as more ordinary beings. However, the reasons for the separate offerings are distinct. People who die bad deaths are judged to have had little power, at least for good, and, like heretic spirits or spirits of those who failed to make offerings to the temple, are said to be unable to come up into the temple. Here it is the low prestige of the person, indicated by the kind of death, that prevents the offering in the temple. A violent death of a person judged powerful for evil makes it likely that his *khotsa* will be held completely separately.

With monks' deaths, this is reversed. It is the high prestige of the monk that prevents the merit-making ceremony being performed with that for laypeople. Monks are powerful beings, usually for good. Their prestige as precept-keepers and the power this implies overrides age in determining the type of funeral.

Funerals for people whose prestige falls between these extremes depend on the age at death and the household's wealth. Children receive minimal funerals and *khotsa,* and are cremated in a separate place. Their lack of power distinguishes them from other people and this distinction is marked by their different treatment at death. Most deaths fall in the middle range. Since long life, like wealth, is taken to be a marker of both merit and power, the older and wealthier the person, the more elaborate the funeral and *khotsa*. Death does not dissolve differences in power-protection among persons. Different funerals, places of cremation, and *khotsa* underscore these distinctions.

SPIRITS AND ANCESTORS

Immediately after death a spirit is formed. The type of spirit depends on the person and how he or she died. A child's death creates a harmless spirit. The more sudden and violent the death the more dangerous the spirit. A violent or accidental death results in a spirit, *phi tay hong*, who remains to haunt and harass the living. In a violent death, since the death is sudden, the person is concerned with regular day-to-day affairs, and the spirit will try to complete plans made before death. Bad death spirits cause injury to living persons simply by coming into contact with them. While some bad death spirits may actively seek to harm living persons, others, by their nature, cause harm without intending to do so. *Phi tay hong* are said never to disappear. The most dangerous ones are those that result when one dies bathed in blood, from childbirth or gunshot. The spirit created when the Thongmakhsan man was killed by the police was seen as very dangerous. A Mawk Tsam Pe man who died somewhat suddenly created a spirit that remained around his house. After a number of incidents, his relatives held a ceremony to keep the spirit at bay. This spirit is potentially dangerous to the living. Ideally when people know they are going to die, they think about the next life and withdraw from involvement with the living. The resulting spirit is not particularly dangerous since it is already prepared for death. After the *khotsa* the spirits are said to disappear, except for the *phi tay hong,* who are said to remain.

Only the death of a monk does not produce a spirit.

Although a dead person is said to be reborn soon after the *khotsa*, one can still rely on the power of one's ancestors. People request teeth from their parents and grandparents as amulets, and these have protective power. In the story in Chapter 5, the spirits associated with the teeth were seen as old people. People continue to ask for protection from their dead relatives when they place *som to* offerings in the house for their great-grandparents and at the reliquaries of their near dead relatives. People can rely on the *kung* of their ancestors to help and protect them, provided they are mindful of and grateful for past benefits. Beyond this, ancestors do not play a large or active role in Shan life.

CHAPTER 9

The Bounded Nature of Space, Time, and Person

Power-protection partitions the Shan universe, dividing it into bounded units containing different amounts of power-protection. The differences in kinds of people—adults, children, males, females, householders, bandits, government officials—are a consequence of differences in one's capacity for and ability to acquire power-protection. Power-protection organizes the structures within which Shan live and interact, defining villages and, within them, identifying and delimiting such different powerful areas as houses, the temple, the cadastral spirit, and the heart of the village. Height, innerness, and internal fences serve to further delimit power and define areas of interaction within these structures. Like space, time is divided into units with particular values, times that are good or bad for general or particular activities. I examine Shan division of space, beginning with areas marked by canopies and fences, and going on to reexamine the larger units of village, temple, and household. I demonstrate that Shan construct time and person similarly as bounded units separating and containing different qualities.

SPACE

Canopies—*pik tan*

Cloth canopies over monks' biers are part of a wider phenomenon. The local explanation, that it is a cloth to keep bird droppings from the coffin, accounts only for the canopy above the bier but does not include these other instances. Canopies appear in three contexts: over the funeral bier of monks (see Chapter 8), over the cooking area when rice for a *som to long* offering is prepared, and sometimes over the area where the *tsale* reads out loud from a sacred text, *haw* (to read out loud) *lik* (book), depending on the text read.

Som to long is the large, *long*, *som to* offering. While it can be made at any time, usually villages as a whole sponsor this offering at least once during *Waa*. In Thongmakhsan this is prepared on the night before the full moon day of the tenth lunar month and offered the next morning at dawn. A *som to long* offering is also a normal part of the *poy mahatukh* celebrated along with the *Awk Waa* festival.

The *som to long* offering commemorates the rice the Buddha first ate after he decided that severe asceticism through fasting was not the path to enlightenment. While the Buddha was in his ascetic phase, he sat meditating under a tree. A woman, Sutsinta, had earlier promised an offering to the tree spirit if she had a son. After she gave birth to her child, she returned with her offering, saw the Buddha, mistook him for the tree spirit, and gave him her offering. She had prepared fifty balls of rice; the Buddha kept forty-nine and offered one to the tree.

People come to the temple the night before to prepare the *som to long* offering. As the name suggests, this is a larger scale *som to* offering so they bring a wide range of fruit, sweets, and savories. Some of the fruits, like pomelo or melons, are carved or decorated, while others are broken up for individual offerings.

Regular *som to* offerings minimally contain freshly cooked rice placed in a small banana leaf box with a sweet, savory, or piece of fruit added if these are available. Unlike normal *som to* offerings, where the rice is simply the first rice removed from the pot, rice for the *som to long* offering requires special preparation. The place, the wood, and the people doing the cooking all differ from what occurs for everyday rice preparation. Ordinarily the youngest competent woman in the house gets up early to cook the rice. The person(s) cooking *som to long* rice should take the eight precepts and dress in white. This is an ideal that occurred at only one of the three *som to long* preparations I saw in Thongmakhsan. On the other two occasions the monk had already gone to sleep when the people who would cook the rice were ready to receive the precepts. *Som to long* rice is cooked over a fire made of fragrant wood.

The rice is prepared at a waist-high table surrounded by a low bamboo fence with a cloth or Shan mulberry paper canopy above the firepot. Banana and sugarcane shoots are attached to the corners of the table. The cooking table may also be decorated with paper cutouts of animals like lions or the garuda bird.

People explained the canopy and the fence by saying that they formed a barrier, *he way*. A monk elaborated on this, saying that the fence and canopy were associated with power, *takho*, that these appear together. He also said the people cooking the rice do not actually enter the enclosure. Because of the power, the firepot is elevated on a table and does not stand on the floor as is usual. The table puts the firepot higher than women's genitals. The monk added that this was so people would not stoop while feeding the fire.

Although most offerings are good for people to eat, *som to* offerings in general are not. Cats, dogs, birds, and ants eat *som to* offerings left where they are placed. If someone eats the special *som to long* rice balls, people said he or she will become mute. Once the *som to long* rice balls have been offered, people may request one to break up and place in the corners of their irrigated fields. They said that this would help keep insects and other pests out. Regular *som to* offerings are not used this way.

A *haw lik* is any ceremony where a *tsale* reads a Shan book about Buddhism out loud. When *tsale haw lik*, the text is almost sung, allowing the *tsale* to read ahead and interpret the text. This is necessary since old Shan is written without tone marks and the *tsale* has to decide which word the writer intended. Most young people say that they do not understand what the *tsale* is reading because of the way it is sung. Old people, however, are said to understand. At a *haw lik* ceremony it is mostly old people who sit and listen; younger people may sit but they talk or otherwise pay little attention to what is being read.

Any temple festival will have a *tsale* reading in the morning as people gather in the temple, as occurred in the *Awk Waa* festival described in Chapter 2. *Haw lik* are held the night before a *khotsa* is offered, and may be held as an alternative to inviting monks to chant on the nights before a funeral. Households may also sponsor a *haw lik*, typically on a *Wan Sin* during *Waa* when they invite the temple sleepers to listen. Usually the sponsors provide a special meal for the old people the next morning. A household may also sponsor a *haw lik* because its members have been suffering from assorted misfortunes or simply to improve the prosperity of the household.

For a *haw lik* ceremony, a household needs to invite a *tsale*, select and obtain a text to be read, prepare a special area where the *tsale* reads the book, and make a sweet to offer to the guests. The *tsale* receives a *phūūn* with a money offering in it, as described in Chapter 2. Minimally the area for reading the book is a mattress for the *tsale* to sit on, with a slightly higher area where the book is placed. It may be fenced, *phaa* (fence) *ratsamat* ("lattice fence usually of bamboo constructed with rhombic intersticices, and erected by the side of a road passed by great personages" [Cushing 1914:532]), and have a cloth canopy, *pik tan*, above it.

The area prepared for the *tsale* to read depends on the type of text to be read. There are a range of books available; most temples have a number of books, and some householders own either hand copied or printed Shan texts, most produced in Burma. A household sponsoring a *haw lik* either uses a text that it owns or borrows one. Books, whether owned by the temple or by householders, are stored on or near the Buddha altar.

If the book has *katha*, powerful words said to be from the Buddha, then there will be a fenced area with a canopy above it. These texts are said to protect against misfortune or help the householders secure all kinds of property. This kind of text is likely to be read at *haw lik* ceremonies to improve the household's fortune. All the household-sponsored *haw lik* ceremonies I have seen have had this special fenced area covered with a canopy, while I have not seen this arrangement for *haw lik* associated with funerals, *khotsa*, or temple festivals.

Haw lik are performed at night. The *tsale* reads for an hour or so until he finishes a number of chapters, and there is a break where the sponsors serve a sweet. If it is held on a *Wan Sin* during *Waa*, the sweet is usually soybean milk or sweetened milk tea since the temple sleepers, keeping the eight precepts, cannot eat solid food after noon. Otherwise the sweet will be one from the regular Shan repertoire of rice desserts. After the break the reading resumes. Many people leave after the food is served with only the older people who can understand the reading staying until the end.

Fences—*phaa ratsamat*

Canopies, when they appear, are associated with fenced areas. However, fences appear without canopies. These low fences, not much higher than six inches, occur in a number of contexts. They may be used to establish separate areas within larger structures, as when the *sara* made one to use while tattooing in his room to receive guests, or where the abbot of the temple sat while other monks were chanting to open the temple, *suut* (chant) *moon* (blessing) *kyawng* (temple). They also mark temporarily important ritual spaces, as the fence surrounding the space where monks chanted to begin construction of a new chedi, the tower room adjacent to the heart of the village, where the repairing village ceremony will be held, and the temporary ordination hall, *simh*, built over water. Fences also occur around the base of a money tree (*ton* [tree] *phapa*), small sand chedis (*tsati* [chedi] *saay* [sand]), and around the *khing sang phut*, a special offering in honor of the Buddha, erected at the temple at *Awk Waa*.

The fenced-in area inside an existing structure defines a special activity area. The *sara* set up the fenced enclosure for tattooing with strong medicine, *yaa haeng,* those "which had benefits, *akyo*, especially, the great beloved [*piyaa long*] tattoo. It is a powerful attraction tattoo, causing spirits and people to like the bearer. Its protection, *kung*, was greater than all others." Once he had this set up, he did his tattooing within the enclosure. Only the tattooer and his client entered the enclosure. This created a special activity area similar to the rice cooking area for the *som to long* offering and the *haw lik* enclosure for powerful texts. These areas have limited access: usually only those with special knowledge, like *sara* or *tsale* or precept-keepers, can enter them.

Similarly, the fence creates a special ritual area where monks enter and chant but which is closed to women and most laypeople. Here the fences function similarly to the elevated areas within the temple or the buried *sima* stones, which define a permanent *simh*.

Money trees and other special offerings are also placed within these low fences. Unlike the temporary enclosures, there are no restrictions on who creates these offerings or handles them. Once made they are treated respectfully. After they are offered, the money is removed and the rest of the structure destroyed or abandoned.

Fences also mark off powerful objects, separating them from the more mundane world. A monk discovered a large footprint in a cave, which he interpreted as the footprint of an arahant since it was larger than normal and there were no other footprints near to indicate that someone had entered the cave and made the print. The monk viewed the footprint as a powerful supernatural object and he carefully placed a small fence around it.

Fences are more than boundary markers: they enclose power and distinguish powerful spaces. Canopies mark even more powerful areas. Access to these powerful spaces is restricted, typically to people with special skills or to precept-keepers. These spaces are often temporary; after the event is over, the space reverts to normal.

Phaa ratsamat fences are associated with power, and with powerful objects and places. These mark spaces in which power is contained or from which it emanates in a controlled manner. The fences around the arahant's footprint, chedis, and the rice preparation area for *som to long* all define powerful spaces; objects inside must be treated with caution and respect. The *sara* controlled the transfer of power to the tattoos inside the fenced-in area. The *tsale*'s reading of powerful texts and the monks' chanting from the tower room during the repairing the village ceremony both create and control power to construct protective barriers, around the house where the text is read and around the village, respectively.

Fences present similar height and front-back distinctions as does spatial division of the temple. Fences, height, and front-back indicate a division of space based on power that parallels the power-protection distinctions among beings. The insight that fenced areas contain power helps explain the spatial organization of Shan villages.

Village and Fields—*waan naa*

The broadest extension of the village includes all households and fields and is expressed in the couplet "*waan naa*," village and irrigated fields. Conceptually a village is surrounded by fields controlled by villagers and there is a boundary between one village's cluster of fields and another's. In reality the boundaries are not that clear since people from one village may own and work fields in another village's area.

This area is the domain of the *Tsao Mūong*; his protection includes all the people, their livestock, and their fields. Since the *Tsao Mūong* protects only those who maintain relationships with him, there are clear conceptual, if not physical, boundaries around a village's fields. People with fields in another village's area do not participate in the offerings to the cadastral spirit of that village and are not included in his protection. The cadastral spirit's protection is extended to his followers and their property, and his domain does not have any physical markers such as fences. The territorial aspect comes from the fixed location of his supporters' villages, households, and fields.

The Village—*waan*

Both the cadastral spirit, *Tsao Mūong*, and the heart of the village, *Tsaū Waan*, refer to the village as a whole. Although households as units make offerings to these beings, their domain is the community and they both function to protect all their followers.

During the annual repairing the village ceremony, the village as a unit is given concrete realization as a bounded entity closed to outsiders, at least for the duration of the ceremony. The village as a unit with territorial integrity is also marked when the village sends away misfortune, *khaw*. This ceremony is performed as needed, usually when many villagers are sick or crops are not doing well. Each household contributes a small amount of many kinds of food. The cadastral spirit's caretaker, the *phu mūong*, presides. He calls *khaw* in the community to come to the offerings, and then the offerings, now containing the *khaw,* are taken out of the village.

Villages contain a range of beings, but these are either human or spirits with whom villagers maintain relationships and who are considered relatively benign. This contrasts with the location of the cremation place, *pa hio*, where spirits of the dead are said to congregate; since these spirits are not benign, the cremation place is located on waste land outside the village.

The village is not fenced, so its conceptual unity does not have any physical manifestation (*see* figure 3.3 [p.51]). Many villages in Maehongson now have gates at the entrances into the community, but these were built as part of the King's sixtieth birthday celebration. The village is not made up of homogeneous units. Fences serve to mark areas within the community. Both the heart of the village and the cadastral spirit compound are enclosed in fences (*see* plates 3.4 [p.50] and 3.5 [p.56]). These fenced areas contain power, and are identified as areas with limited access. In addition to these, there are fenced compounds for the temple and households.

The Temple—*kyawng*

The distinction between temple and households is particularly marked. Ideally the temple compound is at the edge of the village, somewhat isolated from the lay residences (*see* plate 3.2 [p.43] and figure 3.1 [p.40]). It has its own "cadastral spirit," the *tao tang ha*, something that separates it from households and puts it on a similar conceptual level as a village. However, he ranks lower than the village cadastral spirit, indicated in his title, *tao*, which is used for officials of lower rank than *tsao*.

The temple compound is included in the *Tsao Mūong*'s domain, although monks neither make offerings to him nor participate in his feast. The *Tsao Mūong* is asked to prevent fights and maintain the peace at temple festivals. The domain of the *tao tang ha* is limited to the temple compound. Like the villagers, the *Tsao Mūong* has a supportive and protective relationship with the temple and its inhabitants.

This reflects the incorporation of the temple into the village; while it is possible, if unpleasant and dangerous, for clusters of households to have no temple, there cannot be a temple without a village or at least some laypeople to support it. Without laypeople to offer food, clothing, shelter, and medicine, the four monastic requisites, monks could not survive. Monks must have laypeople to offer food; they cannot take it on their own. At an abstract level, the temple and village are complementary, each providing the other with needed services.

Because monks continually keep 227 precepts, they are so powerful as to be another type of being. They cannot eat meals, or share an eleventh-month merit-making ceremony, *khotsa*, with laypeople. Residents of the temple compound remain in the compound, and interactions between monks and laypeople are constrained by the polite language laypeople use when addressing monks. This parallels the limited interaction with the cadastral spirit. The *Tsao Mūong* and the monks are the most powerful beings in the village.

The temple is another bounded, protected area. The *tao tang ha*, Buddha images and texts, and the monks together create this area. The temple compound serves to enclose and separate these powerful beings and objects from the rest of the community. The power of the monks is such that when a monk dies there is no dangerous spirit, and dead monks do not haunt the temple compound. Monks are not likely to be threatened by malevolent spirits because of their own power from keeping precepts, the power of Buddhist objects located in the temple compound, and the power that comes from the daily monastic chanting. There is no need for ceremonies analogous to repairing the village or house.

Households

Households are similarly protected by their Buddha images and the *Tsao hūūn tsao ye*, analogous to the *tao tang ha* and the *Tsao Mūong*. Unlike monks, householders in and of themselves have little power; they live in the world and are unable to practice the restraint that would empower them. They are both weaker than monks and exposed to more danger. Consequently, they rely on a wide range of protective devices and powerful others to maintain their households. The annual repairing the village ceremony also renews the households' protective barriers. When they have had a series of misfortunes or simply desire to improve the prosperity of the household, people may invite monks to chant or place *ang* with protective *katha* in the house, or ask the lay reader to read powerful or auspicious texts, or have the traditional doctor perform a repairing the house ceremony. All of these serve to strengthen or renew the household's protection against misfortune.

Like the village, whose broadest extension includes both households and fields, the household's domain includes both the house plot and fields. While most of the protective spirits who receive regular offerings reside in either the house or the house compound, there are spirits associated with fields who also receive offerings at the beginning and end of the rains retreat. A household's misfortunes may include crop disasters, and both humans and rice suffer from *khaw*, a wasting disease. Unlike villages with a *Tsao Mūong* or the temple with the *tao tang ha*, there is no one overarching spirit responsible for protecting households and their fields. Instead, householders enter into relationships with the particular spirits of their fields and the various spirits in the house and house compound.

These powerful beings create local protected areas, identified with the people who maintain relationships with them. These protected areas are identified by the fences that enclose them. The fences, and the sacralized string and *taa liao*, spirit shield, from the repairing the village ceremony, contain power and powerful objects that serve to create the protected area for the compound residents.

In general the universe is dangerous, filled with beings who have no reason to behave benevolently. One acquires a safe area for oneself through relationships with more powerful others. The relationships motivate powerful others to act compassionately. Powerful others nurture and protect their followers, creating a safe haven for them. Power-protection functions to create these bounded protected areas, hence the metaphors in sermons about powerful individuals being like large trees with the protected others residing in their shade. Having relationships with powerful others creates a small island of safety within this larger dangerous universe. One's safe haven is not permanent; the protective boundaries must be renewed and recharged. The need to renew boundaries is compatible with the sermon emphasis on impermanence and with the need to renew relationships with powerful others through regular *khan taw*.

These bounded areas divide the world into two parts: safe and dangerous. However, "safe" is a relative term and the safety is restricted to those who have relationship with the other whose power creates and maintains those protective barriers. Boundaries and safe areas are a consequence of power as protection, and depend on relationships with powerful others. Powerful beings create these areas, which can expand and contract depending on the relationship with the powerful other and one's own power. The safety of a bounded area can be strengthened through augmenting one's own power, protective amulets, and ceremonies to renew the boundaries.

Differences in power need to marked and maintained. If one interacts incorrectly with a powerful object or being, then one is at risk. Abandoned temple sites and chedis remain powerful even after the structures disappear. These places become imbued with power from the monks and their chanting. People cannot build houses on these sites, since they are too powerful for that purpose. If they did so, the inhabitants could not prosper. These distinctions in space and access to powerful spaces follow the same logic of limiting interaction with more powerful others. One needs to know what one is doing in dealing with powerful others or entering powerful places. This knowledge requires an appropriate level of power, which makes such interaction possible.

TIME

Units of time have qualities in much the way that bounded areas contain power. Shan divide time into bounded units based on the lunar calendar and its division into months, fortnights, and days. One identifies a day in terms of the month and its place in the waxing or waning moon period.

The lunar month is a recognized, identifiable unit of time. If a person dies at the end of a month, his or her funeral should not be carried over into the next month. A number of beings attached to the lunar months determine their qualities. These include the location of the world serpent, *naga*; kinds of beings spirits eat; and the fourteen beings that take turns as "lords of the earth," *mae kham lin*, each with a good or bad quality attached. There are some qualities, not directly related to any being, attached to particular day numbers in the waxing or waning moon periods; for example, the ninth of each period is not good for leaving or ending things (*awk am lii*). Finally, qualities are attached to a regularly changing day number. *Ngam lᾱᾱn*, a bad day, occurs when the number of the month and the number of the day match; for example, the second day of the waxing or waning period in the second lunar month is *ngam lᾱᾱn*, as is the third of the third month.

In addition to the lunar month divisions, Shan also have a seven or eight planet day week. These days are sun (day 1), moon (day 2), Mars (day 3), Mercury (day 4), Jupiter (day 5), Venus (day 6), Saturn (day 7), and Rahu (day 8). These eight days are mapped into the Western seven-day week. The planet day becomes the corresponding week day, Sunday, Monday, and so on. Rahu, the planet that obscures the sun during eclipses, is assigned to Wednesday afternoon.

Fewer beings are connected directly to the planet week. The location of *phi long*, the great spirit, changes daily. There are animals associated with each day of the week, as well as days good for planting particular kinds of crops.

The qualities associated with days of the week vary. Some days are uniformly bad (like *wan muiy*), others uniformly good (*wan thoon*), and with still others the quality is judged good or bad depending on the quality and task; for example, *wan tsum* (to immerse in water [Cushing 1914:455]) is good for working with water but not for tasks that depend on fire or dryness.

There are more kinds of bad days—nine that I know of—than any other kind. They are *wan muiy* (inauspicious); *wan pyat* (to be ended or cease [Cushing 1914:431]) or *tang kya* (to delay, hinder [Cushing 1914:78]); *wan hsum* (loss); *wan phay mai* (fire burns); *wan yawm* (decrease, decline); *wan pao wan ham* (empty, vacant [Cushing 1914:391], empty, abandoned [Cushing 1914:635]); *wan musa* (falsehood); and *wan yikara* (a kind of bad spirit). The names indicate the quality of the days and these names are universally bad—inauspicious, loss, destroyed by fire, or decrease. While these days are bad, it does not mean that people are inactive. The main restriction is that people do not begin activities on these kinds of days. If a household has planned to plant or harvest a field and they realize they have scheduled this for a bad day, they simply make a token beginning of the activity the day before and then proceed as planned. Davis (1976) reports a similar practice for the Northern Thai.

There are only three generally good days: *wan thoon* (riches, wealth); *wan phu* (to take hold of [Cushing 1914:455]), and *wan lawt* (freed or escaped). There are a number of kinds of days whose good or bad nature depends on the project being planned. *Wan tsum* is good for working with water—building dams, irrigation systems, anything connected with *naga*, the serpent, here associated with water. Months associated with either *khao* (enter or begin) or *awk* (leave) alternate and are alternatively good for moving, starting a new business, entering a new house or leaving a house, finishing something, and so on. On *awk am lii* (bad to leave), the ninth of the waxing and waning moons, it is bad to move, to hold a cremation, or to do anything related to leaving the community. *Khao am lii* (bad to enter), the tenth of the waxing and waning moons, is a time when it is bad to move into a new house or generally begin anything.

Although this lunar calendar also organizes the Buddhist calendar, Buddhism is not directly reflected in the qualities given units of time, except for the full and dark moon *Wan Sin*. People say that on full moon *Wan Sin* (the fifteenth waxing moon period) all the doors to the heavens are open and the doors to the hells are closed. Those who die on this day will necessarily be r_born in one of the heavens. The reverse is held for dark moon *Wan Sin* (the fourteenth or fifteenth waning moon period): all the doors to hell are open and all the doors to heaven are closed. People dying on this day have a rebirth in hell. (For a more detailed discussion of the Shan calendrical system, see Tannenbaum 1984b.)

PERSON

House compounds are defined and protected through the use of a sacralized white string that encircles the house. The string is charged by the monks' chants and forms a boundary and a barrier keeping misfortune out and protecting the inhabitants. The white strings used to tie peoples' wrists are similarly empowered through blessings. The parallel use of empowered white strings indicates that a Shan "person" is a similar bounded protected area.

Having one's wrist tied is somewhat unusual for Shan. Other Tai groups, especially the Northeastern Thai, perform public ceremonies on a number of occasions (see Tambiah 1970, and Inge-Heinz 1982). Only small children, newlyweds, or someone who has been ill have these strings around their wrists. Once when I was visiting Chiang Mai, a Northern Thai monk gave me a blessing, which entailed another layperson tying the white string around my wrist. When I returned to Thongmakhsan people asked if I had been sick while I was in Chiang Mai. They were responding to the white string as a sign of illness rather than as a more auspicious blessing. Since the string remains until it falls off, a healthy adult may have one. When a child's white string falls off, it is usually quickly replaced with a new one tied by a close relative such as a grandfather or grandmother.

During the first month bathing ceremony, *ap lūūn*, an infant is presented to the community and his or her ability to live is strengthened through the protection from the blessings of the elders who tied his or her wrist. With weddings, the new couple's relationship is strengthened by the blessings the two receive together. These blessings reinforce the child's or the new couple's ability as a unit to ward off misfortune and attract good fortune.

In the case of illness, wrist-tying is the last step of a ceremony to recall the person's *khawn*, life-force ("a fairy or spirit attached to a person from birth, also *khwan*" [Cushing 1914:138]). Illness may be a consequence of the *khawn* deserting the person, or the *khawn* may depart because of the illness. After the *khawn* is lured back to its body, the wrist-tying and blessing helps bind it to the body.

In other Tai groups, wrist-tying is primarily associated with returning the *khwan* ("guardian spirit, psyche" [Haas 1964:50]) to the body and strengthening the body-*khwan* connection (Tambiah 1970; Plion-Bernier 1973). What is important for Shan is the blessing rather than the *khwan* calling. These blessings are similar to those delivered at the end of monks' sermons or given when people *khan taw*. They request that misfortune be averted and that good fortune find them. They differ only in that they are focused on the individual whose wrist is being tied rather than on a larger audience. Men, women, children, and newlyweds all receive blessings, which help to establish them as units and strengthen their ability to live in the dangerous universe.

Like other bounded areas, individuals can be invaded by malevolent influences or weakened through the loss of protective powers. The remedy in all these cases is to place one's self under the power-protection of more powerful beings. This may require the help of specialists, who draw on their own power, developed through restraint, and that of their teachers and the Buddhas to protect and enhance the patient's own power-protection. Depending on the seriousness of this weakness, there are a number of possible remedies. One can have the traditional doctor prepare a special candle and offerings to repair one's astrological position, *mae kyo mae kio*; one can send the misfortune away by making a small offering, placing it on a river, and having it float away, *loy khaw loy kio*; one can make offerings to the Buddha or monks; or one can perform a combination of these (see Durrenberger 1980, 1982, for descriptions of these ceremonies). Alternatively one may renew and reestablish the relationship with the offended powerful other by making an offering and *khan taw*. These actions increase one's store of power and the protective barriers that contain the power. With these changes, the person regains health and well· being.

This protective and strengthening function of blessings parallels the protective function of tattoos, discussed in Chapter 5. Blessings are similar to tattoos and amulets, which function to keep the bearer healthy and cause assorted beings to have compassion for the individual by augmenting his or her power and strengthening the individuals' barriers against misfortune. Like tattoos, blessings depend on the power of the person who makes them. Unlike tattoos and amulets, which take a material form, blessings do not, and they cannot be weakened by exposure to the negative power of women. Tattoos and amulets protect individuals as individuals, while blessings may have a broader range including audiences at events, newlywed couples, and individuals.

Blessings, treatments, and amulets and tattoos all replicate for individuals the repairing the village and repairing the house ceremonies. They increase the power of the focus of the ceremony and strengthen the barrier that contains it.

An individual is defined in terms of power-protection, one's survival depends on or requires power-protection, and one has both an innate supply of power-protection and the potential for increasing or decreasing that supply. Throughout the life cycle one goes from an almost powerless being to one who acquires sufficient power-protection to take care of others.

Small children have little power-protection and little autonomy; they can be ordered around without taking offense. Young adult males, having returned to lay life after a period as novices or monks but not yet married, have much more power-protection and cannot be casually ordered around without offense. They assert their autonomy and power-protection through drinking and engaging in rivalries with males of similar age both within their village and in other villages (Durrenberger 1983). In the recent past, fights between young adult males from different villages were regular occurrences at village festivals. These fights are less common now because the young men know each other from attending subdistrictwide youth groups and training sessions related to agriculture and village defense. In these meetings, the young men have another, less violent arena for competition and exhibiting power. This suggests the possible development of an areal identity beyond the village (Tannenbaum 1990).

This assertive phase of power-protection does not last long, although some individuals may continue to express their power as force. Usually with marriage and the responsibilities of a family, power-protection is expressed as effectiveness both in production and in fulfilling household and village obligations. Here the focus shifts from demonstrating one's power through the ability to ward off consequences of one's own actions to protecting one's family.

The power-protection of elders is not demonstrated in activity but in withdrawal from worldly concerns and in sleeping at the temple. One's sphere of protection potentially expands from one's immediate family to all those who come to *khan taw* and receive blessings.

The ideal male development cycle goes from residing entirely in the protection of others as an infant or young child through developing one's own sphere of protection, expanding it to include one's family and eventually anyone requesting it.

For women the process is slightly different, since they seldom acquire sufficient individual power-protection to assert it through force as demonstrated in fighting or competitive drinking. Once married, they, along with their husbands, demonstrate their power-protection through their joint ability to be productive, to provide for their children, and to participate in community activities. As temple sleepers, they develop their own capacity for power-protection and can give blessings on their own. In old age, their sphere of protection expands, as does that of men, to include more than their immediate family.

The power-protection of sick people is quite limited, since sickness weakens otherwise powerful people. An old man, respected for his knowledge, was often called on to empower white string and tie his grandchildren's wrists or to blow *katha* to cure mild ailments. While he was sick with pneumonia, people no longer requested his services. Because he was ill he could not give blessings or protect others. After he recovered, people again requested his help.

Ideally, one's power peaks in old age and one is commemorated with a tug-of-war funeral. Reality intervenes and the inherently unequal distribution of power becomes clear as people reach or fail to reach a comfortable old age, and die in possession of their full faculties or senile. As old people become weak or senile, their ability to give blessings and protect others is gone. Now they must rely on their children to take care of them. People talk about the reversal of roles entailed in this "second childhood" and recognize both its difficulties and its incongruities.

While with illness and senility one's power-protection is diminished, after death one's power-protection is replenished, at least for those who have children and who die good deaths. Those who have died can still protect their descendants. After death, amulets such as teeth from parents or grandparents continue to embody protective power, regardless of the fact that the dead are considered to have been reborn.

The boundaries of individuals' power-protection are not fixed. Powerful beings can extend the boundaries of their protection widely and include many beings; those with less power have a correspondingly narrower ability to protect others, and their sphere includes fewer beings.

In sermons, monks described the power of a good man with the metaphor of a large shade tree, giving coolness to a wide range of beings; a monk may thus describe the man as having a large body (see Chapter 5). Monks end sermons with a request that their blessings reach everyone, young and old, small and large. In everyday speech, a powerful person is a *kon long*, large person. The "larger" the person, the greater the shadow cast. People can rely on the shade of the powerful person, and his shade is the extension of his power to protect his followers. The *sara* talked about the power of the Buddha as a sphere of protection that surrounded him, and said that the *sara* uses this sphere of protection to shelter and cure his patients.

Throughout the life cycle, one's sphere of power-protection expands and contracts. At village levels these spheres of protection are small. Locally powerful individuals are not particularly powerful. People in Thongmakhsan are poor and their most powerful persons do not compare well with those in other, richer, villages. Even the monks that stay in Thongmakhsan's temple are not particularly knowledgeable or powerful; recent abbots have been a monk who was ordained in order to quit his opium addiction and a retired policeman.

To find very powerful individuals one has to go beyond the village context, since villages, almost by definition, are not centers of power. Even the man in Thongmakhsan who was killed by the police was not particularly powerful and he had only a limited ability to protect others; ultimately he could not protect himself. In the modern Siamese era one looks to government officials and rich men for large spheres of power-protection.

In the pre-Siamese era, powerful people with broad spheres of protection came from elsewhere, as was the case of Tsao Kolan, a prince from Mawk Mai state. In 1865 Tsao Kolan, along with approximately one thousand followers, entered the Maehongson area. Before this, he had disputed the right of Mūong Nai officials to collect Burmese head taxes in Mawk Mai, spent some time in a Burmese prison, and escaped, going first to Mūong Mai and later to Mawk Tsam Pe. At that time Mūong Mai was a small principality ruled by an official appointed by the Chiang Mai prince. Tsao Kolan took over and the Chiang Mai appointee fled to Pai. Tsao Kolan and his followers made themselves leaders of existing Shan communities, incorporating them into his sphere of power-protection. Tsao Kolan left a son to rule Mūong Mai while he and most of his followers went to Mawk Tsam Pe, an established village with connections to Pang Mu, another large Shan village (Wilson 1985:34–35). The Northern Thai prince eventually sent an army and Tsao Kolan retreated to Mūong Mawk Mai (according to Mangrai [1965:228], he received a Burmese pardon and so could return).

At the peak of his power in this area of Maehongson, Tsao Kolan's sphere of protection encompassed a wide area and a large number of followers—large in local terms but probably small in terms of his previous sphere in Mawk Mai, to which he returned when he had the opportunity.

Power-protection operates in the same way in both small and large arenas (Tannenbaum 1990). Local people seldom have the ability to coalesce such large spheres of power-protection around them. Differences among people are relatively small, and local interactions are not hampered by the caution that wide differences create.

Places, people, and time are all bounded entities that contain qualities that affect one's ability to successfully undertake actions and achieve objectives. Having power and maintaining it provides a wide range of action and allows people to control what happens, sheltering others in their protection. Being in control is a sign of power-protection and a positive Shan value since it allows one to initiate actions that are likely to succeed and it limits the negative impact of change.

CHAPTER 10

Power-Protection and Buddhism

Power-protection is the underlying assumption of Shan worldview. Shan live in a universe structured in terms of power-protection, which implies the ability to control others' actions and responses so that one is free to behave without fear of the consequences. With it one can understand why some "Buddhist" practices are emphasized and others minimized. Generosity is important not just because it is a "Buddhist virtue" but also because it demonstrates one's power and effectiveness and provides a standard of ranking in power competition. Here I show how power-protection influences Shan understanding of the following Buddhist concepts: the Triple Gems (the Buddha, his teachings, and the monkhood); *karma*; and *anatta*, and the way this is related to the concepts of *aniktsa* and *tukkha*.

THE TRIPLE GEMS

The Buddha, his teachings, and the monkhood are the three gems of Buddhism. Each Buddha rediscovers the nature of the universe and how it operates. His discovery is preserved in his teachings and by the monks who continue to practice and teach what the Buddha has discovered.

The Buddha

The Buddha and his teachings are central to canonical Buddhism. This is a logical consequence of his rediscovery of how the universe operates and his decision to teach people how to escape the cycle of rebirth and redeath. His importance for Shan, however, goes beyond his discovery and teaching roles.

The Buddha is the most powerful being. In the process of becoming enlightened, the Buddha gave up his comfortable life, his beautiful wife, his child, and eventually, through meditation, his attachment to his self. His power derives from his restraint and detachment. He practiced restraint to an extent not normally possible, and thus has the greatest power-protection.

He, his teachings, and the monks are part of the five great *kung*. People call on the power of the Buddha to protect them. Traditional doctors invoke the Buddha to protect them and their patients. Like other powerful beings, people regularly *khan taw* the Buddha to maintain an ongoing relationship with him for their own protection.

Images, amulets, and tattoos all get their protective power from the Buddha as well as from objects associated with him, his relics, and places where he stayed or visited. Chedis, since they encapsulate a relic of the Buddha, are powerful places, as are the footprints he left behind. Images derive their power from their resemblance to the Buddha; this is demonstrated through their power to protect or the miracles associated with particular images (Reynolds 1978). Replicas derive power from their identity with the powerful object copied, so chedis may encapsulate replicas of relics and powerful images may be copied.

The Teachings

The Buddha's teachings are an important relic. Since they are his words they are one source of power. However, they are powerful in their own right since they contain the knowledge of how the world operates and, consequently, the means to control it. The power of the teachings is seen in the way texts containing them are treated. They are kept in high places, usually on or adjacent to Buddha altars. In ceremonies where they are read, they are placed in a separate fenced area with a canopy above them (see Chapter 9).

The teachings are the least powerful of the three gems. The teachings of the Buddha are often encapsulated in *katha*. While *katha* have power of their own, the words by themselves do not have great power. The power of *katha* is enhanced when one learns them from a powerful person and maintains the proper relationship with that powerful other. If one does this, when one recites the *katha*, the *katha*'s power is augmented by the power of the teacher and the lineage of teachers. The power of *katha* is enhanced by the power of the person who recites them. The same blessing has more power when a monk, as opposed to a novice, recites it. The *katha* embodied in amulets or tattoos are more or less powerful depending on the power of the person making them. Amulets empowered by forest monks, who practice meditation and strictly follow the monastic precepts, have great power.

Power-protection is embodied in and created by the actions of beings. It is they who practice restraint and empower objects such as amulets or *katha*. Objects by themselves may have some power, but that power is strengthened by the actions of beings who practice restraint. A Buddha amulet has some power but until it is chanted over the power is minimal. Places may be powerful but only because of their association with powerful beings. A place where a *simh* once was is powerful because monks chanted in it and their actions made it a powerful place.

The Monkhood

The importance of the monks for maintaining what the Buddha taught was recognized in the sermon given at an ordination ceremony. In that sermon, the monk spoke of the great merit accrued from ordaining and sponsoring ordinations since, without monks, the religion would die out (see Chapter 6).

Monks are powerful beings in their own right. By practicing austerities and withdrawing from everyday life, keeping the monastic precepts, they automatically acquire power. Through their practice of restraint, monks are powerful beings, and like powerful beings they protect their followers, the villagers who provide their support (Tannenbaum 1987, 1991). They are "tame" powers, protective and nurturing and not likely to strike out at their followers or revoke their protection.

By continuing the unbroken monastic line begun in the Buddha's time and practicing the Buddha's teachings, monks are both living relics and images of the Buddha. Monks provide laypeople the opportunity to make offerings, hence, merit. Monks give blessings and send love, *metta*, to the community. The monks, by practicing the Buddha's teachings, help make the community a peaceful and cool place to live. The temple with its monks has a "civilizing" influence on the community by encouraging people to live in accord with the Buddha's teachings.

Among Thai groups different parts of temple compounds are emphasized. For the Northern Thai the chedi is the focal point (Swearer 1976). For the Central Thai during the present dynasty, the ordination hall has become the focal point (O'Connor 1985). Among Shan neither of these is important. Rather it is the *kyawng*, the equivalent of the Central Thai *sala kanparien*, that is the focus. It is the *kyawng* as a monastic residence that is important, rather than the *kyawng* as a place for powerful Buddha images. Most Shan *kyawng* have a multitude of images on the altar area, and unless they have received an image from Central Thailand, none of the images is particularly large or dominating.

People circumambulate the *kyawng* when there is a procession or major offering. When the *kyawng* is the only building within the temple compound this is not surprising. However, when the compound contains other buildings, including a *simh*, ordination hall, and a chedi, people still circumambulate the *kyawng*. Why? What is important for Shan is the monks. The *kyawng* is where monks live. The small houses in the temple compound built as residences for monks are also *kyawng*. Unlike the Burmese, for whom "*kyawng*" can refer to a range of buildings inside a temple compound, a school, or a group of temples (Sadler 1970; Mendelson 1975), for Shan it refers to a monastic residence (Cushing 1914:79) or, by extension, to the temple compound.

O'Connor (1985, 1989) argues that relics and images play key but different roles in defining Northern and Central Thai polities. Relics are localized in chedis where they are enshrined, and sanctity, analogous to Shan power-protection, emanates from them. Images play a similar role in defining sanctity for Central Thai. For Shan, monks play a role similar to Northern Thai relics and Central Thai images.

As with the Buddha, but not with the teachings or other relics, one can maintain continuing relationships with monks. The centrality of monks in Shan Buddhism derives from their role as powerful active beings able to confer protection on those who enter into relationships with them.

KARMA

Power-protection is the cause of differences among people, a paraphrase of the monks' karmic explanation in Chapter 6. *Karma* is the result of actions and as such derives from power-protection, which determines actions.

Power-protection and *karma* are not competing explanations. Nor are power-protection and *karma* equivalent. Shan do appeal to *karma* as the ultimate explanation for the distribution of power-protection and for the consequences of misusing it. But power-protection is an active principle, causing *karma*, while *karma* is the justification for these differences in the here and now.

CONTROL AND *ANATTA*

It is difficult to make claims for anomalous interpretations of Buddhism. As people have differential capacities for understanding, so they will understand Buddhism differently. There are no wrong interpretations, merely less correct ones. In Chapter 6, I introduced Shan definitions for three of the four noble truths: no self, *anatta*; impermanence, *aniktsa*; and suffering, *tukkha*. For *aniktsa* and *tukkha*, Shan understandings parallel those of scholars, with *aniktsa* translated as "instability" and *tukkha* as "suffering." *Anatta* as "lack of control" is, however, truly anomalous. While Burmans appear to share a similar understanding of *anatta*, Spiro (1982:84–91) treats this as an essential error in their ability to understand Buddhism. By representing the Burmans' understanding as an error, it becomes plausible to ignore its anomalous character. Instead of trying to discover why Burmans, Shan, and, perhaps, others interpret *anatta* as lack of control, their understanding is dismissed and scholars judge them based on their own understanding.

Control is an important corollary of power-protection. Dying a violent death demonstrates the impotence that results from the inability to control events. Beings without this ability may be dangerous but not powerful. Witches, *phi phū*, and other nonpowerful spirits, drunks, and women all fall into the dangerous but not powerful category.

Because control is an important corollary of power-protection, the Shan translation of *anatta* as "lack of control" makes sense. To be powerful, one must also be able to protect one's self and one's dependents; without this one is not powerful. And without control one cannot protect; beings without control are not powerful, but are simply dangerous. Power *is* power-protection.

Phi Phū and Other *Phi*

People do not talk much about witches, *phi phū* (*phū* "a wizard, sorcerer, witch" [Cushing 1914:461]); one learns about them through indirect references and occasional gossip. I initially learned about *phi phū* when I was doing research in 1979–81 in Thongmakhsan. A Thongmakhsan man eloped with a woman from a nearby house; the woman's mother was very upset and suffered a stroke. People explained that her extreme reaction was a consequence of the man coming from a *phi phū* family. *Phi phū* are contagious: if a person eats an unspecified number of meals with a *phi phū*, he or she will also host a *phi phū*. The bride's mother had reason to believe her daughter would soon possess a *phi phū*.

Hosting a *phi phū* is unfortunate but not necessarily malign. People interacting with a person suspected of having a *phi phū* need to behave more circumspectly; if one angers a person who hosts a *phi phū* that anger will cause the *phi phū* to react, regardless of the host's intentions. Likewise people who have a *phi phū* need to control their emotions so this force will not be unintentionally released.

Both men and women are capable of hosting witches. A person can use *phi phū* power intentionally to cause harm. While *phi phū* are usually contracted through contagion, a person may desire to host one. In this case the person desiring a *phi phū* seeks out a person who has one and requests to share the *phi phū*. This sharing does not diminish the donor's *phi phū*. Hosting and using a *phi phū* gives one a certain attractiveness. A particularly beautiful woman is said to get her beauty from hosting a *phi phū*. An older woman who is unusually attractive to men may be said to host a *phi phū* (see Eberhardt 1988).

Once one has a *phi phū*, one cannot get rid of it. The only way to mitigate its automatic operation is by either ordaining as a Buddhist monk or novice or becoming a *mae khao*. As long as one continues to keep the precepts associated with these statuses, one has sufficient restraint and hence power-protection to prevent the automatic actions of *phi phū*; once one no longer keeps these precepts, the automatic response of the *phi phū* resumes.

Phi phū reverse many of the characteristics associated with powerful beings. Normally a powerful being protects and nurtures dependents; here, the person hosting the *phi phū* nurtures and protects it. Offending a powerful being terminates one's relationship with it; with *phi phū* there is no way to terminate the relationship. One acquires *phi phū* through sharing too many meals with another person who already has a *phi phū*. This is a reversal of the normal value of sharing meals. Powerful beings are in control of their actions and those of others. Through this they mitigate the negative consequences of change (Tannenbaum and Durrenberger 1988). Those possessing *phi phū* are not in control, rather *phi phū* react automatically to injure those who offend their hosts. Lack of control means that the being is both weak and dangerous (for a more detailed discussion of Shan witches, see Tannenbaum 1993).

Bad death spirits, *phi tay hong*, are similarly weak but dangerous. Contact with a *phi tay hong*, or any other spirit of the dead, weakens the living. A bad death spirit can actively seek to kill someone or, simply through carrying out a plan made while alive, visit someone and cause injury by its presence, without any intent to harm. Like *phi phū*, the *phi tay hong* and other spirits of the dead operate automatically; the beings have no control over the consequences of their interactions with the living. Regardless of their intent, they are harmful.

There are other spirits who have little power and whose only means of accomplishing their goals is through harming people. They cause misfortune because they want something; in return for an offering they withdraw, as does the misfortune associated with their presence. These offerings are to lure or drive the spirit away from the human domain and prevent it from causing further harm.

The power to destroy is power, but without control one is not capable of protection. Because these spirits cannot control their destructive nature, they cannot protect and they do not have much power in the Shan scheme of things. This lack of power, however, does not diminish their menace.

Drunks

Normally Shan do not fight, nor do they allow their children to fight. People, when angry, may engage in shouted arguments, but they are rarely violent. Parents may resort to force with five- or six-year-old children, when as one man said, "they don't obey and only recognize pain." But even this violence is rare.

However, men drink to get drunk and when drunk are apt to be violent. Young men, as part of their assertion of their power, flirt with drinking and the hazards associated with drunkenness and lack of control. This lack of control makes drunks a threat; their behavior is unpredictable and prone to violence. Fighting is never acceptable Shan behavior, but if one fights when drunk, then the lack of control associated with drunkenness is an acceptable excuse. Women, because they do not drink alcohol, do not have this excuse and ought never be violent.

Drinking at festivals or other celebrations creates vulnerable settings. Drinking is part of the festivities, but men are liable to get drunk and when drunk behave unpredictably. The celebration after Thongmakhsan came in second in a soccer tournament was one such setting. Many people from Thongmakhsan went to Huay Pha to watch the final game, which Thongmakhsan lost. A number of men brought liquor with them, which they drank while watching the game. After the game, the cattle trader in Huay Pha invited the team and assorted supporters back to his house, where he provided them with more liquor. Most people went back to Thongmakhsan. The women in the young adults' group decided to fix a festive meal for the team when they returned to Thongmakhsan.

When the team and their supporters came back they were in high spirits, dancing to long drum and gong music. The dancing lasted about half an hour and then the older women decided it was time for food. All proceeded calmly and the food helped sober up some of the people. After eating, most left.

A number of fairly drunken men remained. Two of them got into an argument that threatened to become violent. People separated them, hiding one in the kitchen, and when the coast was clear, hustled him home to avoid further confrontation. Once one had left, those remaining tried to convince the other to go home. He left the house supported by his brothers only to return saying he didn't want to leave. His friends tried to talk him into leaving, not through threats but cajoling him: "It's late, you're tired. Why don't you go home?" But none of these worked.

Again people tried to convince him to leave, this time stressing the fact that he was upsetting the woman, his first cousin, whose house it was. She was known to be easily upset, and getting upset made her ill. But he persisted, finally provoking the woman into a violent outburst when he said, "I don't care. If she dies, I'll pay for the funeral." The woman kicked over a water container and ran upstairs in tears. In the resulting chaos, the others were able to lead the drunken man home.

When the drunk would not leave, people remaining in the house became increasingly nervous and the atmosphere was tense. Many of those still at the house returned home. (I would have too, but I was staying at the house.) A handful of men, friends and relatives of the drunk, remained to try to cajole him into leaving. While there was no physical violence, the threat of it was palpable. The man was clearly out of control and dangerous. As with other dangerous beings when they cannot be ignored, he was treated gently, and attempts were made to lure him away. Since no one had sufficient power to deal with him through force, he had to be tolerated and placated, much as when the village sends away misfortune, *khaw*, by luring it with offerings.

Women

Women have less capacity for power-protection than do men. Their genitalia are destructive of power-protection. Any object that has been in contact with a woman's genitals or genital excretions has the capacity to remove protective barriers (Tannenbaum 1987; see also Terwiel 1979 for Central Thai; and Davis 1984 for Northern Thai). Women do not ride on the top of minibuses because that would place their genitals above men's heads and destroy their power or that of their amulets. Women's skirts, underwear, and pants are hung up to dry in low places so men will not be able to walk underneath them, thus destroying or weakening their power. Traditional doctors do not go underneath the elevated houses to avoid having anything unclean above their heads; they go underneath their own homes but avoid the areas underneath women's sleeping rooms. A strip of skirt tied to a gun barrel will give bullets fired from that gun the ability to unroll the protective barriers established by closing-off tattoos.

Through their genitals, women automatically acquire the ability to destroy power-protection. They have little control over its operation. Like those that possess *phi phū* spirits they must refrain from actions that would cause harm. In day-to-day activities women and men work, eat, and live together without women's ability to destroy power-protection being a threat. Women, like men, understand the danger associated with their genitals and accept responsibility for containing that danger. Women tease young girls so they will learn to cover their genitals, and train visiting anthropologists so that this danger is contained.

For most men, the care women take in not placing their genitals or objects that have been in contact with them higher than men's heads is sufficient. Husband and wife work together to demonstrate their power-protection through their collective ability to support their household and participate in household and community ceremonies. Only when men are in special statuses do women's destructive capacities become a real threat. *Sara* and monks, particularly, have to be careful to avoid women and objects that have been in contact with women since contact would seriously weaken their power. The greater the power, the more sensitive it is to objects that would weaken it and the greater the danger in entering powerful areas or interacting with powerful objects or beings. The care that *sara* and monks take to avoid women both protects women from dangerous contact with their power and protects their power.

Unlike drunks, women are not out of control and dangerous because of that. They have greater ability to contain their destructive powers than do assorted spirits or those that host *phi phū*. They need to remain in control and stay mindful to limit their destructive capacity, which they do through controlling where they go and where they place things. Just as power is contained and isolated through fences, women contain and isolate their destructive capacity by not entering powerful areas or spatially isolating objects that have been in contact with their genitals. Women, because they can contain and hence control their destructive nature, have the capacity for power-protection; they can and do take care of, nurture, and protect their families. Nevertheless, their ability to acquire power-protection is always limited by their nature and its automatic destructiveness.

Women's natural ability to destroy power-protection and the general principal of acquiring power through restraint, identified with precept-keeping, also provide an explanation for the nonexistence of female monks, *bhikkhuni*. They exist in Taiwan and China in Mahayana Buddhism. The historical evidence for mainland Southeast Asia is ambiguous. Mangrai (1981) states that there is Burmese inscriptional evidence for *bhikkhuni* down to the fourteenth or fifteenth century, but that it is unclear whether these were true *bhikkhuni* or merely forerunners of nuns, women keeping eight precepts. Shan explanations state that the Buddha reluctantly established a line of female monks to please his wife, but by doing so he shortened the time span of the religion (see also Van Esterik 1982a:57).

Monks speaking about the possibility of female monks said that they would have to keep more than the 227 precepts kept by male monks. The number of precepts for *bhikkhuni* varies: Mangrai (1981:26) gives 311 precepts; in sermons I heard one monk give 310 and another 311 precepts.

There are contradictions: female monks keeping more precepts than male monks would be more powerful than male monks, and women are inherently destructive of concentrations of power. I suggest that *bhikkhuni* do not exist in mainland Southeast Asia because of these contradictions.

The traditional religious role for a woman is to dress in white and keep 8 precepts, to become a *mae khao*, woman in white. Keeping 8 precepts places women at the lower continuum of power from precept-keeping and in the same range as old people, who keep 8 precepts on holy days during

Waa. Unlike novices and monks, who keep 10 and 227 precepts, respectively, they have little status in the community. Being female they cannot accumulate large quantities of power. They normally do not have access to knowledge of the chants from the Buddhist scriptures, which would provide another source of power. In Thailand in general these women do not have much prestige (Van Esterik 1982a). Shan treat them with some respect; they are one of the groups that people *khan taw* twice a year. The *mae khao* from Huay Pha were invited to Thongmakhsan's *Awk Waa* festival. Since *mae khao* are precept-keepers, they are part of the focus of the ceremony and are given offerings, albeit lesser amounts than monks and novices (see the discussion in Chapter 4).

Mae khao have withdrawn from lay life and live in the temple compound. Most are relatively poor old women, who have little wealth. Retiring to the temple to become *mae khao* does not fit with the ideal life cycle in which, in old age, one lives in relative comfort surrounded by children and grandchildren. As elders, their spheres of power-protection should be at their widest expansions. Retiring to the temple suggests that one does not have sufficient power-protection to achieve the ideal state.

The everyday status of old people tends to be higher than that of *mae khao,* even though they only keep eight precepts on *Wan Sin* during *Waa*. Their power-protection, from whatever sources, is sufficient for them to achieve the ideal elder status. They have the capacity to continue to protect and take care of the children and grandchildren. Those old women who become *mae khao* do not.

Mae khao rank lowest of all the precept-keepers in the temple compound. Living in the temple compound, they have removed themselves from family and village affairs. While they accrue power through keeping precepts, they possess little ability to protect others. *Mae khao* are like sick old people who lose the power to give blessings since their illness demonstrates their own lack of control. If the women who become *mae khao* had the power-protection necessary to control their own fortunes they would not become *mae khao*.

Retirement to the temple in old age is not a valued Shan option. Unlike men in the Northeast who reordain as monks after their wives die (Klausner 1972), Shan men seldom do so. The ideal for men as well as women is a comfortable old age as a respected elder able to take care of others rather than the seclusion and development of power monastic residence implies.

Power-protection and *anatta* were, for me, two separate pieces of the Shan puzzle. My definition of *anatta* came from sermons monks delivered, mostly at funeral-related events. My understanding of power-protection built slowly, drawing on explanations and insights from the *sara* in Mawk Tsam Pe. However, power-protection and the importance of control and the dangers associated with being out of control began to highlight control as an issue important to Shan. *Anatta* as lack of control viewed from this perspective is not anomalous or an error based on the psychological difficulty of grasping "no self," but a logical and coherent extension of Shan understanding of the nature of the universe, power, what it means, and how it operates.

Anatta, *Aniktsa*, **and** *Tukkha* **Revisited**

Power-protection implies control and with it the limitation of change and suffering. But power-protection and control do not last forever. The crucial nature of this is clear in the Shan translation of *anatta* as "lack of control" and the key role that *anatta* plays in the destruction of power-protection. One cannot control one's own body; it decays and nothing can be done about it. As one's body decays so does one's capacity for power-protection, until it is completely gone and one dies. Without power-protection, and the control it implies, there is change, *aniktsa*, and suffering, *tukkha*. Ultimately, because of *anatta*, power-protection can only ward off change but not defeat it. To repeat what a monk said in a sermon, "Who can compete against the world? Who can defeat the world?"

CHAPTER 11

Conclusions

In the introduction, I argued that to demonstrate power-protection as the central feature in Shan worldview I needed to show that it accounts for local explanations, "Buddhist" practices, and practices anomalous in "Buddhist" terms. In the previous chapters, I have done this, showing how Shan use power-protection in a wide range of contexts, including the mundane and the religious, and how it is the logic underlying practices labelled "Buddhist" and "animist," relating to spirits. In Chapter 10, I turned specifically to the issue of power-protection and Buddhism, showing how power-protection reinterprets the Buddhist triple gems, and *karma*, and how the Shan translation of *anatta* as "no control" fits with this conception of power-protection. Rather than restating those arguments here, I discuss the implications that this analysis has for the study of "Buddhist" cultures in Southeast Asia and for anthropology in general.

The central role of power-protection for Shan raises questions about power-protection in other lowland "Buddhist" cultures. There are hints throughout the ethnographic literature of similar worldviews operating in other mainland Southeast Asian lowland contexts. I first discuss evidence for power-protection in Central and Northern Thailand and Burma and go on to the question of why these indications have been ignored, suggesting that it has to do with the way anthropologists understand Buddhism and Buddhist societies. Finally I return to the issues of ethnography and anthropology raised in the introduction.

POWER-PROTECTION IN OTHER LOWLAND SETTINGS

Here I examine some of the material on Central Thai and briefly consider Northern Thai and Burman materials to show

that there are widespread indications that power-protection is
not limited to Shan.

Central Thai

I have chosen to reexamine Bang Chan, the site of the first
extended anthropological research in Thailand, for two reasons.
First, there is a wealth of materials from the project (Textor
1960; Phillips 1965; L. Hanks 1957, 1966, 1972, 1975; J.
Hanks 1963; Sharp and Hanks 1978; and others). Second, I
admire the work done by the anthropologists associated with
the project. My ability to rework their data and analyses is an
indication of the quality of the original work.

I begin with the more concrete, drawing on Textor's (1960)
analysis of "non-Buddhist supernaturals" to suggest how
power-protection provides a more ethnographically coherent
framework for them. From the concrete I turn to forms of social
interaction (Phillips 1965), and to forms of social organization
(L. Hanks 1966, 1972, 1975). My analysis becomes
increasingly inclusive to suggest how power-protection
underlies Central Thai religious, social, and political
organization. This is not an extensive reanalysis, merely a
sketch to show how power-protection illuminates the Bang
Chan materials.

Textor's (1960) work provides a wide range of practices
and objects that make sense from a power-protection
perspective. His goal is to describe and classify these "non-
Buddhist" supernatural objects in structural-functional terms
based on who interacts with the objects, who makes them, what
rewards and punishments are associated with them, their
historical derivation, and so on (see Textor 1960:13–24). He
accepts a tripartite division of religious activity into Buddhist or
moral, non-Buddhist, and Brahmanical. However, he cannot
maintain his analytical separation, and his discussion of non-
Buddhist practices necessarily includes discussions of
Brahmanical and Buddhist practices. The range of objects, their
functions, and the types of relationships people in Bang Chan
enter into with them suggest that an analysis based on power,
powerful beings, what they do, and how one interacts with them
would be more revealing.

Power implies protection and protection implies power. Powerful beings protect and nurture their dependents and in return expect respect and obedience. Control is an important corollary of power-protection and powerful beings exhibit their power through control. Textor's ghost lords with territorial jurisdiction, protective deva, three supernatural objects with territorial responsibilities, and Buddha statues all behave as powerful others protecting and taking care of their dependents (1960:236–55, 472, 487–500, 531–40). Those interacting with these beings must use respectful language, propitiate them, and be grateful to them for their protection. Textor discusses a number of powerless ghosts, those raised by doctors and sent to damage others (1960:351–67). These, like the spirits that result from violent deaths, are dangerous but not powerful.

Many of the amulets, objects, and techniques described are generally protective; if they do not make a person invulnerable, they cause people to like the user and this liking is protective. Many of these are used by *nak laeng*, Textor's "rogue-racketeers," to make them invulnerable. Textor (1960:105) recognized these men's deviancy from the Buddhist moral code, but had no way to link rogue-racketeers with other powerful beings and the need for protection in a universe where power gives people the protection to behave as they choose.

Power-protection provides a more culturally coherent way to sort Textor's "non-Buddhist supernatural objects." It underlies the three systems that Textor sees and provides the rationale for people needing protection and the logic to sort kinds of protective devices, relationships with powerful beings, and what one can do with these techniques if one is powerful.

Phillips (1965) describes Thai patterns of social relationships, how to maintain them, the kinds of interaction patterns they entail, and the ways people of Bang Chan view them. From his review of the literature, his impressionistic account, and his sentence completion data, Phillips constructs a view of the people of Bang Chan that identifies their desire for autonomy but also their respect for authority and their willingness to go along with it; their positive evaluation of equanimity and coolness; their willingness to break off relationships; their evaluation of responses of others in terms of benefits to themselves; and their negative evaluation of aggression while at the same time they fear it.

Phillips's conclusions about the value of autonomy and coolness rests partially on his discussion of the importance of control and its relationship to aggression (Phillips 1960:184–92). He relates the desire for control to fear of aggression and the importance of maintaining a neutral stance to the outside world. While fear of aggression and fear of expressing one's aggression may explain the value of control, control and aggression are not necessarily related. In a power-protection framework, control and being in control are important ways of demonstrating one's own power. Less powerful people, such as Bang Chan farmers, fear aggression because they lack the power-protection to protect themselves from it or the power to control and use aggression.

Phillips attributes the Bang Chan emphasis on autonomy and self to a Buddhist ideological orientation. This Buddhist orientation is assumed and used to interpret observations, but Phillips does not show that people of Bang Chan use Buddhism this way. The Buddhist perspective leads to the contradiction that people in Bang Chan seem to search for autonomy but are also willing to accept their own dependency, and the dependency of others on them.

Autonomy and dependency are two possible means of interaction with a dangerous universe. If one has sufficient power-protection, then the autonomous route is possible; without this, dependency and relying on the power-protection of others is necessary. If one relies on the power-protection of others one must be careful to speak correctly, do as one is told, and avoid offending the powerful other.

People accept dependency as necessary and know how to treat dependents. Capacity for power-protection changes through the life cycle. When one is small, one has little power-protection and must rely on others. As a man matures, his quest for power and autonomy becomes increasingly important. A search for autonomy and a recognition of dependency is not contradictory from a power-protection perspective. Some people are not endowed with power or the capacity for it and dependency is their only option, so those that reject being a "boss" (Phillips 1965:150) are recognizing their limits.

Taking a power-protection perspective makes sense of Phillips observation that the sentence completions he noted focused on satisfaction of psychobiological needs. Powerful beings nurture and protect their followers. Being able to do so is a sign that one is powerful, and receiving food and care are signs that one is being protected by a powerful other.

The patterns of interaction that Phillips describes also make sense in entourage terms. L. Hanks (1966, 1975) argues that entourages are the social-organizational building block for all groups in central Thailand. These groups range from farming families in Bang Chan to the Thai government (L. Hanks 1966:66). Entourages are clusters of patron-client ties, focused on the patron. The relationship is inherently hierarchical and unequal and the relationship between the client and patron determines the status of the client with other clients. A patron has resources, which attracts clients, and together the patron and clients gain what they separately could not achieve. An entourage has "no necessary goal unless it be contented living" (L. Hanks 1966:56).

Entourages are the social expression of a system based on power-protection. People cluster around a powerful being who nurtures and protects them. They need the relationship because the world is a dangerous place. Because the relationship is based on differences in power-protection, it is inherently hierarchic. The relationship between the entourage leader and his followers is that of powerful being and dependents. The leader protects and nurtures his followers; the followers are respectful, obedient, and grateful for the protection and nurturing they receive. L. Hanks (1972:80–90) suggests that families and kin are entourages and that kinship is constructed in entourage terms. Joining an entourage creates a safe area within the dangerous world. Entourages are not particularly stable as the power of the leader waxes or wanes and as the ambitions of the followers are met or not met.

Power-protection and relationships between more and less powerful beings create larger political units. Sharp and Hanks (1978) show how social groups coalesce around powerful people—those that have resources to redistribute but also have the ability to protect their dependents. Their range of examples suggests that power-protection, and the social-organizational form that results, is not limited to Buddhism.

Sharp and Hanks discuss the decline of the Moslem community near Bang Chan and the fact that only two households remain, descendants of the original leader. To describe the leader, they provide the following from Hanks's field notes:

> He was a brave and vigorous man. After the war in Saiburi, he came to Thonburi as a prisoner of war with many of his younger kinsmen. . . . While there in Thonburi, one day he could not bear to see his niece courting with the Thai people of Somdet Chao Phraya Srisurijawong the elder. . . . He had special power and he put his finger on the head of this girl and broke her head. When Somdet Chao Phraya heard about this, he had our leader seized. The Somdet wondered why he did not defend himself and noticed that the man did not seem afraid. When questioned, our leader said that he did not want to kill Thai people, even if he could. If the Somdet Chao Phraya did not believe in his power, he would demonstrate it. So he put his finger on a piece of wood and split it in order to demonstrate his power. After that the Somdet Chao Phraya released him and later gave him land for the Moslem people on his estate. (Sharp and Hanks 1978:71)

This man, because of his power, secured land for his dependents and the protection of a more powerful leader. The Moslem community coalesced around him and prospered until, sometime after he died, a plague of rats destroyed the crops.

Among the Thai settlers a *nakleng* named Chyn acted as a local police force and provided protection for people travelling to temple festivals. Eventually he became a guardian of the Bang Chan temple, recognized for his ability to control laborers and get things done. His ability to coerce and control people was attributed to his talismans (Sharp and Hanks 1978:106–9).

While Chyn's power came from personal force, the first subdistrict headman, *kamnan*, relied on his wealth and the support and protection of higher government officials, much the same way as the Moslem leader did. His power and increased wealth served to draw people to settle in his house compound and the immediate village.

The *kamnan*'s wealth and official power enabled him to organize any enterprise he deemed needed. Like Chyn the martinet, he wore an array of amulets about his neck to make him invulnerable. His authority, too, rested in part on occult powers: "The *kamnan* learned from many teachers to make holy water, expel spirits, and many other things. He could stop quarrels and prevent people from accusing each other in court. He knew love magic, too." (Hanks's notes, 7/6757; Sharp and Hanks 1978:117)

Sharp and Hanks suggest (1978:274, n.26) that the *kamnan*'s power was directed more towards benevolence, reducing friction between people, and curing, while Chyn's was manifested more in the defeat of adversaries. I suspect this difference is in how these powers are used, rather than in what they can be used for. People may be shy to argue in front of a powerful person for fear of offending, whatever the source of power.

The resources that cause people to coalesce around a particular individual are not simply material. They also include "occult" powers, which allow the entourage leader to actively protect his dependents and help guarantee the material success that allows him to nurture his followers.

Power-protection is an active principle that creates leaders and accounts for their ability to have people and polities coalesce. This "occult" or supernatural element is a real part of a person's ability to lead. Ritual power, as Wolters (1982) recognizes, is the real exercise of power and control. These leaders accomplish much, and to lead means that one has the force and charisma to exercise one's will through conquest and the creation of a polity. Being a man of prowess or a powerful being is expressed in ritual, religious, and political terms.

Power-protection focuses attention on the relationships between more or less powerful others and not on territorial aspects of polities. The strengths and weaknesses of polities formed by powerful people are those that derive from the personalized ties between leaders and followers. They are flexible, able to adjust to changing positions of power. This is attractive to ambitious local leaders where no one leader can capture and sustain a monopoly of power. (Leach 1954 and Kirsch 1973 stress this in their discussions of relationships within and between upland groups.) But this makes larger conglomerations impermanent since each leader has to demonstrate his power through success to create his own network that has no basis to endure longer than the leader.

These polities strongly resemble Greenwood's (1973) "peasant-state." There is a continuing tension between ruling centers and producer villages based on the rulers' desire to appropriate and mobilize village resources and the villages' desire to maintain their resources and autonomy. Depending on the relative strength of the center and the villages, the balance between appropriation and autonomy may shift but the relative autonomy of villages persists. This tension has been at the forefront of Tai political forms (O'Connor 1985). It results from the personal, entourage-type relations among leaders and followers and derives from the way power-protection structures relationships. Because leaders have their own followers, because relationships are personal, because one needs to demonstrate one's power through success, it is difficult to develop the basis for a more stable polity. Tai polities have dealt with the issue in different ways, with more or less success (see O'Connor 1985).

Northern Thai

There is a wide range of literature on the Northern Thai (Davis 1984; J. Potter 1976; S. Potter 1977; Kingshill 1976; Turton 1987; Irvine 1982; Rhum 1987). In all these works there are indications that power-protection operates in the Northern Thai context. Here I limit my discussion to Davis, Irvine, and Turton. The works by the Potters and Kingshill provide some reference to such things as monks teaching magic (J. Potter 1976:40), the protection of matrilineal spirits (S. Potter 1977:116), and a spirit of a monk reborn as a lizard who helped protect people in the forest (Kingshill 1976:208). These hint at a power-protection dimension but the authors do not provide sufficient information to go further.

Davis's discussion of Northern Thai in Nan provides information that can be interpreted in terms of power-protection. In discussing agricultural rites, Davis (1984:169) states, "The central theme of all Northern Thai agricultural rites is the protection of rice, people, and human settlements from the ravages of animals and the forces of nature." He emphasizes the contrast between forest and settlement rather than the protective nature of these rites and of power in general. However, power as protection makes sense of the "magical potency" he discusses and the texts that are sources of it (1984:139–40). Those owning texts must pay respect to them and ask forgiveness from them; in return the texts provide a blessing and power. Davis (1984:140) reports that the traditional doctor with whom he studied "begs Vissukamma's [the originator of magic and exorcism, 107] pardon for his transgressions and bids the deity to protect him from malevolent spirits, living enemies, the forces of Adversity [*khaw*?], and black magic." Rhum (1987) agrees with Davis and presents parallel information about the importance of texts for men's power and the importance of power for men's worth. Rhum makes an explicit statement of the protective power derived from knowledge: "By virtue of having to read Northern Thai and having read Northern Thai texts I had acquired mystical potency and protection against worldly dangers" (1987:5).

As with Shan, there are extensive ceremonies of paying respect and asking for forgiveness from elders and from spirits associated with the house and house compound (Davis 1984:133–36). The blessing Davis quotes (1984:134) is similar to those Shan elders give. Kingshill (1974) also refers to paying respect and asking for forgiveness from parents and other powerful beings who give blessings that protect those who receive them.

Irvine's (1982) dissertation on insanity and its treatment in the Northern Thai and national Thai contexts focuses on many topics that can be interpreted in a power-protection perspective. He discusses meditation as a source of mystical power, the importance of control for power (1982:206), and the importance of the spirits of teachers (1982:201–4, 206, 214–17, 220–28). In discussing tattoos, especially those he classifies as containing aggressive magic, Irvine states:

> Both of these [aggressive tattoos] are particularly valued by males whose way of life is defined in terms of aggression and violence, as with the hero/pariah category of the village tough [NT *nak leng*], who knows no law but his own and whose

strength is measured less in terms of muscular power than in terms of the potency inherent in the magic he possesses. We might add that among such men possession of powerful aggressive spells is accompanied by tattoos which assure invulnerability against spirit, man and beast. However, it would be misleading to suggest that such power is limited to such men, for it also serves as a standard of evaluation among respected community members. . . . Possession of powerful magic is indeed one factor in the emergence of leaders of dominant position. (1982:210)

Finally his whole dissertation is framed in terms of "bounded entities" and the assorted means people have to deal with perceived threats to these entities (Irvine 1982). While Irvine does not discuss what these entities contain, the threats to them all weaken their power.

Turton (1987) makes an indirect but strong argument for power-protection in his discussion of invulnerability among Northern Thai and more broadly within Southeast Asia. The objects that he discusses make people invulnerable to a range of attacking beings, and the techniques to do so include tattoos, amulets, and texts. Most involve some restrictions derived from the spirit of the teachers and the necessity of being respectful to the spirit. Davis and Irvine discuss many of the same techniques, restrictions, and applications. Invulnerability is protection and this protection is empowering.

Burman

I turn to a brief discussion of power-protection in the Burmese context to suggest that the phenomenon is not limited to Tai peoples but is part of a broader Southeast Asian pattern, something Turton (1987) suggests for invulnerability.

The universe is populated with dangerous beings, some potentially helpful to humans (Spiro 1967; Htin Aung 1962). These beings may behave erratically, making the world a dangerous place (Spiro 1967:78). Spiro (1967:75), discussing Burmese spirits, *nats*, states: "Nats are not so much harmful, as *potentially* harmful; it is not malevolence, but slight, which motivates their punitive behavior." However, if people maintain proper relations with the *nats* then they are protected from danger (Spiro 1967:53; Nash 1965b:167–82). As with Central and Northern Thai, the Burmese use a wide range of protective amulets and tattoos (Scott 1896; Spiro 1967; Nash 1965b; Htin Aung 1962). Alchemy, the search for or the creation of special powerful objects, provides another source of power (Nash 1965b:190–92; Spiro 1967, 1982:164–71; Htin Aung 1962:41–50; Scott 1896:401–6; and Mendelson 1961a, 1961b, 1963, and 1975:144–47). The unknowable nature of other beings' intentions makes it necessary to seek protection through relying on powerful others, amulets, alchemy, and tattoos.

The Buddha and objects and beings associated with him have the greatest power (Spiro 1967:278). Spiro, continuing his discussion of the power of the Buddha, states: "Anyone who recites his rosary and worships the Buddha is immune to the influence of nats [and other supernaturals], and if he recites the nine 'virtues' [*gunas*] of the Buddha he is doubly immune. As the folk saying has it, 'Anyone who regularly recites the *gunas* [of the Buddha] is like a pagoda'—i.e., nothing can harm him." Spiro (1967:271–80, and 1982) uses this to argue that while there are two religious systems in Burma, Buddhism is dominant. Nonetheless, the power of the Buddha is congruent with a system of power-protection where one derives power from restraint or from relying on more powerful others.

Associated with the Buddhas as a source of power and the use of alchemy are *gaings*, followings clustered around a *weikza*, master wizard, who possesses enormous power and has overcome death (Spiro 1982:163). *Gaing* members practice alchemy and develop their power under the guidance of their master. Members of *gaings* often seek to extend their lives until the birth of the next Buddha, Maitreya. They are often associated with millennial movements as the leaders are said to be reincarnations of powerful kings or associates of powerful kings (Spiro 1982:171–80; see Mendelson 1961a for a description of one center, also Mendelson 1961b, 1963, and 1975). *Gaings* are expressions of the search for power-protection localized around a recognized adept.

Burmese social organization appears similar to the Thai entourage. There are powerful people who draw followings around them. Nash, in discussing leadership in an Upper Burmese village, states:

> Three concepts, *pon*, *gon*, and *awza*, define relations of power, influence, and authority among villagers. *Pon*, in its secular meaning, is the power to carry out plans, to bend others to one's will, to move destiny to one's advantage. If a person has *pon*, as a corollary he necessarily has *awza*. *Awza* is the authority to command. . . . The *awza* of a man with *pon* stems from his personal powers, his marked and conspicuous abilities to succeed in the world. . . . *Pon* and *awza* are the power dimensions of social relations, *gon* is the moral content. (Nash 1965b:76)

Earlier, Nash (1965b:45–73) described Burmese family and kinship in terms that resonate with L. Hanks's (1972) discussion of Central Thai family organization as an entourage.

There are some differences in the ways that power-protection is developed among Shan, Northern and Central Thai, and Burmans. For Northern Thai, texts are important as containers of knowledge and power. Shan emphasize teachers and proper relationships with teachers over mere textual knowledge. Without a teacher, the words in the texts have limited power. The Burma case shows interesting similarities and differences. As with Tai groups, powerful men draw people to them, creating a group dependent on the leader's power to nurture and protect them. Amulets and tattoos play similar protective roles. While powerful beings protect and nurture their dependents, this protection is contingent on the dependents' proper behavior. However, the Burmese emphasis on alchemy and *gaings* focused on gaining mystical power and awaiting the appearance of the next Buddha does not appear in these other groups. Tambiah (1977) provides an account of a group in Central Thailand that appears similar to the Burmese *gaing* but this, as far as I know, is the only instance. These differences suggest different organizing principles and methods of gaining access to power-protection, but the parallels among all the cases indicate that an examination of power-protection in mainland and island Southeast Asia, as Turton's (1987) analysis suggests, would be fruitful.

These examples suggest the regional importance of power-protection. I do not claim that the particular form worked out for Shan is directly applicable to these other cases. I expect that power-protection is transformed in ways congruent with the local political, religious, and economic systems. Nevertheless, a systematic analysis of power-protection in these cases will provide useful information on local contexts and lead towards an understanding of the dynamic interrelationships among these cultures.

MULTIPLE MEANINGS OF "BUDDHIST"

Anthropological understandings of Buddhism have suffered from overly Western and single-stranded interpretations. One problem is simply historical. Western study of Buddhism brings with it the history of East-West relations and assumptions. Almond (1988) shows how the British interpreted and placed Buddhism within the Victorian understanding of religion and religious issues. For English scholars, Buddhism came to reside in texts in libraries and could only truly be understood by the scholars, not by those who claimed to be Buddhists (Almond 1988:13).

Almond goes on to argue that these scholars then placed themselves as judges and interpreters of true Buddhism:

> Buddhism developed as "something" primarily *said* in the West, delimited and designated by virtue of its ideological containment within the intellectual, political, and religious institutions of the West. Buddhism as it manifested itself in the East could only there be *seen* through the medium of what was definitively said about it elsewhere. (Almond 1988:33)

From this background come judgments about "corrupt" Buddhism, or Buddhism as a thin veneer over other practices, or judgments that people who call themselves "Buddhists" do not really understand Buddhism (Almond 1988).

One anthropological consequence has been the tendency to see many religious systems in mainland Southeast Asia, since Buddhism is understood in this framework of Western judgments. The key issue for the study of religion in mainland Southeast Asia has been explaining the religious complexity and the problem of integrating "Buddhist," animist, and "Brahmanic" practices (Keyes 1977a, 1984; Kirsch 1977, 1982; Spiro 1967, 1982; Tambiah 1970, 1976, 1984; Textor 1960). Even while the importance of studying "practical religion" (Leach 1968) was recognized, most authors still refer to the texts for ultimate justification of local practices (see the argument over the nature of gender in Thailand in Kirsch 1975, 1982, 1985; Van Esterik 1982a; and Keyes 1984).

Buddhism is a practical religion in both senses of the word. It is what one does, praxis, rather than what one believes that matters. Arguments are over particular practices, such as the way monks wear their robes or the pronunciation of the ordination ceremony, rather than over issues of doctrine. Gombrich (1984:13) states, "Strictly speaking, there is no heresy: no Buddhist can be expelled from the Order [of monks]—let alone from the wider community of Buddhists— for holding an unpopular opinion." It is also practical in the sense that what is effective is judged to be correct. The Jengtung state chronicle reports an incident in which the monkhood became corrupt through the mispronunciation of the ordination ceremony. Monks who had learned the chants correctly came to visit and their correct pronunciation of chants saved Mong Khemarattha from demons and destruction (Mangrai 1981:113–17). Evidence that the way ceremonies were pronounced was incorrect came from their inability to ward off danger, while evidence for the correctness of the visiting monks' pronunciation was its effectiveness in protecting the country.

Texts are important as the ultimate referent not for belief, but for practices. The monk in the Jengtung state chronicle who went to search for the proper pronunciation did so because his study of the texts indicated that the current practice was wrong. The Buddhist texts are the referent for practice, even if the practice said to be sanctioned by the text is not textual. Bechert (1984:153) indicates that this was the case when Burmese monks decided that their robes should cover both shoulders.

This suggests that texts, like Buddha images and amulets, are important as objects. Buddha images, amulets, and tattoos derive part of their power from the words contained in them, much the way texts are powerful objects because they contain powerful words (see above and Chapter 9). Words of powerful beings are treated as if they were powerful objects rather than speech. One sits respectfully to receive the words, and understanding is irrelevant. Shan monks and old people mumble blessings that are not understood by the audience, but this does not affect the effectiveness of the blessings (see also Tambiah

1970:195–222 for an account of this for Northeastern Thai). In fact, one does not actually have to listen to the words, but merely be in their presence while they are recited. People may chat or doze during sermons or the reading of texts, but this does not decrease their effectiveness. Words and the texts that contain them are powerful objects and the importance derives from their power and the power of the Buddha who said them rather than from their meaning.

Different segments of the "Buddhist" population make different claims about Buddhism and what is Buddhist. Jackson (1989) shows how middle- and upper-class Thai argue about political legitimation in Buddhist terms (see also Suksamran 1982). The problem is that religion is not merely a psychological system used to satisfy psychological needs, as Spiro would have it, nor is it just the opiate of the masses, as Marxists would have it. It is both of these and more. Any world religion has multiple meanings and possible interpretations, depending on who is making claims and when. The anthropological problem is to understand and contextualize these various interpretations and assertions about Buddhism rather than accepting them at face value or deciding that one interpretation is more "correct" than others (see Anderson 1978; Almond 1988).

ANTHROPOLOGICAL ANALYSES OF THERAVADA BUDDHISM

For most anthropologists, Buddhism is an unexamined concept. There is little explicit discussion of doctrine. The edited volume *Anthropological Studies in Theravada Buddhism,* while claiming to be a "first attempt to provide an empirical basis for the serious comparative study of Theravada Buddhism" (Nash 1966:xii), focuses on analyses of the role of monks and temples in communities. Most authors refer to merit and demerit, merit-making, and precept-keeping, and mention other concepts such as Buddhist virtues, the Four Noble Truths, and "no-self" in passing, but these are not analyzed.

More recent ethnographic analyses treat Buddhist concepts as unproblematic and not requiring any explication. Even ethnographers dealing ostensibly with Buddhist topics such as Bunnag (1973) and Tambiah (1970, 1976, 1984) focus primarily on social relationships and roles rather than on what

Buddhism means for the people practicing it. Authors of works on other topics similarly assert that the people are Buddhists and that Buddhism is important for understanding the people, but they do not provide any analysis (Keyes 1989; Nash 1965; L. Hanks 1962, 1972; Ishii 1986). These authors accept the standard translations of Pali terms and do not question whether the people they study understand the terms in the same way.

Spiro (1966, 1967, 1982) is one of the few anthropologists who finds this casual acceptance of Buddhism problematic. In "Buddhism and Economic Action," he (1966) raises the question of the relationship between Buddhism, local understandings of Buddhism, and actions. He frames this question in terms of *anatta*, saying:

> the key Buddhist concept of *anatta* (the nonexistence of a permanent self), taken as independent variable, is often used to explain much of the seemingly mysterious behavior of the East. At the risk of playing the parochial anthropologist I must exempt my "village" . . . from the putative explanatory net of this concept. Although almost every villager whom I interviewed had learned about *anatta*, less than 2 percent knew the meaning of this term. . . . How, then can *anatta* explain any aspect of *their* behavior? (Spiro 1966:1163)

I address Spiro's analysis of *anatta* below. What is important here is that Spiro raises the question of how people understand Buddhism, and stresses the importance of sorting out levels of understanding before one simply glosses their behavior as "Buddhist." The bulk of Spiro's (1982) ethnographic work on Burma deals with just this question: How do Burmese understand their religion and how should we understand those understandings and their relationship to Buddhism?

This concern motivates his detailed analyses of Burmese Buddhism (1982); his analysis is captured in the subtitle, "A great tradition and its Burmese vicissitudes." He assumes that Buddhism and its basic principles are well defined and well understood and the problem is to figure out where and why the Burmese deviate.

While he discusses many aspects of both scriptural and Burmese Buddhism, I focus only on his analysis of *anatta*. Spiro's most sophisticated Buddhist understands *anatta* as "no control" and confounds it with "change," much the same way as Shan monks and knowledgeable laypeople do (see Chapter 6). However, Spiro (1982) treats this as an essential error in their ability to understand Buddhism. He assumes that the definition of *anatta* as "nonself" is nonproblematic and that local practices should be interpreted through comparison with the scriptural tradition. Assuming for the moment that *anatta* as nonself is nonproblematic, there is still no justification for ignoring local understandings of Buddhism. Instead of trying to discover why Burmans, Shan, and, perhaps, others interpret *anatta* as the inability to control, their understanding is dismissed and they are judged based on a scholar's own understanding of textual Buddhism. Anthropologists are then in the uncomfortable position of trying to explain why "Buddhists" do not understand Buddhism.

However, *anatta* as nonself is problematic. *Anatta* as inability to control, particularly control one's body, is part of the scriptural tradition (Collins 1982:97). While this bolsters my argument that Shan are not heretics, it does not change the fact that Shan understand and construct *anatta* in ways that make sense in local, and not necessarily scriptural, terms. Since Buddhist terms are open to a range of understandings within the scriptures, why anthropologists restrict themselves to a narrow sense of the terms is even more puzzling.

The simplest reason for anthropologists to translate "*anatta*" as "no self" is that this is the way popular introductory texts on Buddhism translate *anatta*. Anthropologists simply accept the authority of these texts and do not worry any further about the meaning of Buddhism.

The idea that the religion of the lowland states of mainland Southeast Asia is Buddhism has the status of a cultural cliché (Lehman 1972). As a cliché one can accept this without question and, without question, one need not analyze it. Anthropologists, political scientists, and lowland intellectuals accept and assert this cliché. This acceptance of "Buddhism" has been productive: one need only look at the considerable literature on Buddhism and whether or not it is merely a thin veneer over animist practice, whether there are two religions, the relationship of Buddhism to other religious practice, and the debate on gender in Buddhist textual terms. However, these debates are inconclusive and, I suspect, irresolvable, because there is a poor match between the questions and the reality the analysts are trying to explain.

ANTHROPOLOGY, ETHNOGRAPHY, AND REALITY

The concern over deconstruction, reflexivity, and the construction of reality creates doubts about the possibility of the anthropological exercise. If the reality of our work lies merely in the way we construct it and not in the cultures or peoples we are describing, then anthropology has no existence separate from literature and textual creation.

This approach relies on the assumption that words construct the world, a modification of the Sapir-Whorf hypothesis. We cannot see reality, we merely interpret it using words to do so. Clifford, in his list of linguists who have "made inescapable the systematic and situational verbal structures that determine all representations of reality" (1985:10), curiously excludes any reference to Chomsky or posttransformational grammars. This omission is telling. Keesing's (1972) critique of ethnoscience as dependent on an outmoded linguistic model is relevant here. Keesing argues that relying on pretransformational descriptive linguistics undermined the ethnoscience program of cultural description and categorization. Rather than expressing the categorization and description mode of pretransformational linguistics, Clifford and others reflect the language-determines-thought emphasis of Sapir-Whorf. There are structures that underlie the diversity of category systems and expressions, given by the deep structure of language and the human capacity for culture (Foster 1967; Chomsky 1972; Keesing and Keesing 1971). Both approaches are limited by their failure to understand current linguistics.

Ethnoscience and the analytical textual approach have another interesting parallel. Both are methodologies in search of a question. Eliciting and describing categories is a good method as one begins to explore a cultural domain, but it provides no theory to justify the practice. Textual and verbal analyses are also good methodological approaches. While the strong form of the Sapir-Whorf hypothesis cannot be supported, there is support for the weaker form that suggests that metaphors and tropes emphasize certain connections and make others implausible (see Lakoff and Johnson 1980). Sorting out the multiple meanings of "Buddhist" is one example where such analysis is insightful. However, the textual analysts reject the reality that their techniques would be useful for understanding.

Science is the process of asking questions and pursuing answers using whatever methods and assessment criteria are appropriate to the investigation. We cannot codify discovery procedures and guarantee that the results of such procedures are "scientific." More often, as in the case of ethnoscience, the results are trivial rather than scientific (Keesing 1972). Nor should we reject the possibility of approximating the cultural reality "out there" to the best of our ability using whatever techniques and methods are available. To do so is to let anthropology become a "privileged discourse [which] indulges in esthetic or epistemological subtleties" (Clifford 1985:21).

Throughout this monograph I have argued for a return to the classical anthropological concern of ethnography. This does not entail the rejection of anthropological methods and analytical techniques developed since Malinowski and Mead. Rather, one should use those techniques to construct the best ethnography possible, wherein one demonstrates the logic that informs the people's behavior and the consequences this has for their actions. This is not the glorification of ethnography and cultural trivia. Instead it is a call for descriptively adequate accounts of cultures, that is, accounts that describe and explain cultures in their own terms. These ethnographies make it possible for anthropology to become a truly comparative discipline, one that is groping towards an understanding of what it is to be human.

BIBLIOGRAPHY

Almond, Philip C. 1988. The British Discovery of Buddhism. Cambridge: Cambridge University Press.

Anderson, B. 1978. Studies of the Thai State: State of Thai Studies. IN The Study of Thailand. 193–247. E. Ayal, ed. Papers in International Studies: Southeast Asia Series, no. 54. Ohio University.

Bechert, Heinz. 1984. "To be a Burmese is to be a Buddhist": Buddhism in Burma. IN The World of Buddhism. Heinz Bechert and Richard Gombrich, eds. 147–58. New York: Facts on File Publishers.

Bhumiratana, Amira. 1969. Four Charismatic Monks in Thailand. M.A. Thesis, University of Washington.

Chomsky, Noam. 1965. Aspects of a Theory of Syntax. Cambridge: MIT Press.

———. 1972. Language and Mind. New York: Harcourt, Brace, Jovanovich.

Clifford, James. 1985. Introduction: Partial Truths. IN Writing Culture, J. Clifford and G. Marcus, eds. 1–26. Berkeley: Univ. of California Press.

Clifford, James, and George Marcus, eds. 1985. Writing Culture. Berkeley: Univ. of California Press.

Colburn, F., ed. 1989. Everyday Forms of Resistance. Armonk, N.Y.: M. E. Sharpe.

Cushing, J. N. 1888. Handbook of the Shan Language. Rangoon: American Baptist Mission Press. Reprinted 1971, Gregg International Publishers, Westmead, England.

———. 1914. A Shan and English Dictionary. Rangoon: American Baptist Mission Press. Reprinted 1971, Gregg International Publishers, Westmead, England.

Davis, Richard. 1976. The Northern Thai Calendar and Its Uses. Anthropos 71:3–32.

———. 1984. Muang Metaphysics. Bangkok: Pandora Press.

Douglas, Mary. 1973. Natural Symbols. New York: Random House.

Durrenberger, E. Paul. 1980. Annual Non-Buddhist Religious Observances of Mae Hong Son Shan. Journal of the Siam Society 68:48–56.

———. 1981. The Southeast Asian Context of Theravada Buddhism. Anthropology 5:45–62.

———. 1982. Shan Kho: The Essence of Misfortune. Anthropos 77:16–26.

———. 1983. Shan Rocket Festival and Non-Buddhist Aspects of Shan Religion. Journal of the Siam Society 71:63–74.

Durrenberger, E. Paul, and Nicola Tannenbaum. 1983. A Diachronic Analysis of Shan Cropping Systems. Ethnos 48:177–94.

———. 1990. Analytical Perspectives on Shan Agriculture and Village Economics. Yale University Southeast Asian Studies Monograph Series, no. 37.

Eberhardt, N. 1988. Siren Song: Negotiating Gender Images in a Rural Shan Village. IN Gender, Power, and the Construction of the Moral Order, N. Eberhardt, ed. 73–92. Univ. of Wisconsin-Madison, Center for Southeast Asian Studies, Monograph 4.

Errington, Frederick, and Deborah Gewertz. 1987. Cultural Alternatives and a Feminist Anthropology. Cambridge: Cambridge Univ. Press.

Foster, George M. 1965. Peasant Society and the Image of Limited Good. American Anthropologist 67(2):293–315.

Geertz, Clifford. 1973. The Interpretation of Cultures. New York: Basic Books.

Gombrich, Richard. 1971. Precept and Practice. Oxford: Clarendon Press.

———. 1984. Introduction: The Buddhist Way. IN The World of Buddhism. Heinz Bechert and Richard Gombrich, eds. 9–15. New York: Facts on File Publishers.

Greenwood, Davydd. 1973. The Political Economy of Peasant Family Farming: Some Anthropological Perspectives on Rationality and Adapatation. Rural Development Occasional Paper, no. 2. Rural Development Committee, Center for International Studies, Cornell University, Ithaca, New York.

Haas, Mary. 1964. Thai-English Students Dictionary. Stanford: Stanford Univ. Press.

Hanks, Jane R. 1960. Reflections on the Ontology of Rite. IN Culture in History. S. Diamond ed. 298–301. New York: Columbia University Press.

———. 1963. Maternity and Its Rituals. Southeast Asia Program Data Paper, no. 51. Dept. of Asian Studies, Cornell University. Ithaca, New York.

Hanks, Lucien M. 1957. The Cosmic View of Bang Chan Villagers, Central Thailand. Proceedings of the Ninth Pacific Science Congress 3:107–13.

———. 1962. Merit and Power in the Thai Social Order. American Anthropologist 64:1247–61.

———. 1966. The Corporation and Entourage: A Comparison of Thai and American Social Organization. Catalyst 2:55–63.

———. 1972. Rice and Man. Chicago: Aldine.

———. 1975. The Thai Social Order as Entourage and Circle. IN Change and Persistence in Thai Society, G. W. Skinner and A. T. Kirsch, eds. 197–218. Ithaca: Cornell University Press.

Htin Aung, Maung. 1962. Folk Elements in Burmese Buddhism. London: Oxford Univ. Press.

Humphreys, Christmas. 1984. A Popular Dictionary of Buddhism. London: Curzon Press.

Inge-Heinz, Ruth. 1982. Tham Khwan, How to Contain the Essence of Life: A Socio-Psychological Comparison of a Thai Custom. Singapore: Singapore Univ. Press.

Irvine, Walter. 1982. The Thai-Yuan "Madman" and the "Modernizing, Developing Thai Nation" as Bounded Entities under Threat: A Study in the Reflection of a Single Image. Ph.D. dissertation, School of Oriental and African Studies, University of London.

Ishii, Yoneo. 1986. Sangha, State and Society: Thai Buddhism in History. Peter Hawkes, Transl. Monographs of the Center for Southeast Asian Studies, Kyoto University.

Jackson, Peter A. 1989. Buddhism, Legitimation, and Conflict: The Political Functions of Urban Thai Buddhism. Singapore: Institute of Southeast Asian Studies.

Keesing, Roger M. 1972. Paradigms Lost. Journal of
    Anthropological Research 28:299–332.
Keesing, Roger M., and Felix Keesing. 1971. New Perspectives
    in Cultural Anthropology. New York: Holt, Rhinehart,
    and Winston.
Keyes, C. 1971. Buddhism and National Integration in
    Thailand. Journal of Asian Studies 30:551–67.
———. 1975. Tug-of-War for Merit: Cremation of a Senior
    Monk. Journal of the Siam Society 63(1):44–66.
———. 1977a. The Golden Peninsula. New York: Macmillan.
———. 1977b. Millennialism, Theravada Buddhism, and Thai
    Society. Journal of Asian Studies 36:283–302.
———. 1984. Mother or Mistress but Never a Monk. American
    Ethnologist 11:223–41.
———. 1989. Thailand: Buddhist Kingdom as Modern Nation-
    State. Boulder, Colo.: Westview.
Khantipalo, Phra. 1983. Buddhism Explained. Bangkok:
    Mahamkut Rajavidyalaya Press.
Kingshill, K. 1976. Ku Daeng, the Red Tomb: A Village Study
    in Northern Thailand. Third revised edition. Bangkok:
    Suriyaban.
Kirsch, A. Thomas. 1973. Feasting and Social Oscillation:
    Religion and Society in Upland Southeast Asia.
    Southeast Asia Program Data Paper, no. 92. Dept. of
    Asian Studies, Cornell University, Ithaca, New York.
———. 1975. Economy, Polity, and Religion. IN Change and
    Persistence in Thai Society, G. W. Skinner and A. T.
    Kirsch, eds. 172–96. Ithaca: Cornell University Press.
———. 1977. Complexity in the Thai Religious System: An
    Interpretation. Journal of Asian Studies 36(2):241–66.
———. 1982. Buddhism, Sex Roles, and the Thai Economy. IN
    Women in Southeast Asia, P. Van Esterik, ed. 16–44.
    Occasional Paper, no. 9. DeKalb, Ill.: Northern Illinois
    Univ., Center for Southeast Asian Studies.
———. 1985. Text and Context: Buddhist Sex Roles/Culture
    of Gender Revisited. American Ethnologist 12:302–20.
Klausner, W. J. 1972. Reflections in a Log Pond. Bangkok:
    Suksit Siam.
Kuhn, Thomas S. 1962. The Structure of Scientific
    Revolutions. Chicago: Univ. of Chicago Press.

Lakoff, George, and Mark Johnson. 1980. Metaphors We Live By. Chicago: Univ. of Chicago Press.

Leach, Edmund R. 1954. Political Systems of Highland Burma. Boston: Beacon Press.

Leach, Edmund R., ed. 1968. Dialectics in Practical Religion. Cambridge: Cambridge Univ. Press.

Lehman, F. K. 1972. Doctrine, Practice, and Belief in Theravada Buddhism. Journal of Asian Studies 31:373–80.

Lévi-Strauss, Claude. 1963. Structural Anthropology. New York: Basic Books.

Mangrai, Sao Saimong. 1965. The Shan States and the British Annexation. Ithaca: Cornell University, Department of Asian Studies.

———. 1981. The Padaeng Chronicle and the Jengtung Sate Chronicle Translated. Michigan Papers on South and Southeast Asia, no. 19. Ann Arbor: Center for South and Southeast Asian Studies, University of Michigan.

Marcus, George, and Michael Fischer. 1986. Anthropology as Cultural Critique. Chicago: Univ. of Chicago Press.

Mead, Margaret. 1963. Sex and Temperament in Three Primitive Societies. New York: William Morrow and Co.

Mendelson, M. 1961a. The King of the Weaving Mountain. Journal of the Royal Central Asian Society 48:229–37.

———. 1961b. A Messianic Buddhist Association in Upper Burma. Bull. of Oriental and African Studies 34:560–80.

———. 1963. Observations on a Tour in the Region of Mt. Popa, Central Burma. France-Asie 179:786–807.

———. 1975. Sangha and State in Burma. Ithaca: Cornell University Press.

Moerman, M. 1966. Ban Ping's Temple: The Center of a "Loosely Structured" Society. IN Anthropological Studies of Theravada Buddhism, M. Nash ed. 137–74. Southeast Asian Studies, Cultural Report Series, no. 13. Yale University.

Nash, June. 1965. Living with Nats. IN Anthropological Studies
      in Theravada Buddhism. M. Nash, ed. 117–36.
      Southeast Asian Studies, Cultural Report Series, no. 13.
      Yale University.

Nash, Manning. 1965a. Ritual and Ceremonial Cycle in Upper
      Burma. IN Anthropological Studies in Theravada
      Buddhism. M. Nash, ed. 97–116. Southeast Asian
      Studies, Cultural Report Series, no. 13. Yale
      University.

———. 1965b. Golden Road to Modernity. New York: John
      Wiley and Sons, Inc.

O'Connor, Richard. 1985. Centers and Sanctity, Regions and
      Religion: Varieties of Tai Buddhism. Paper presented
      at the American Anthropological Association meetings,
      Washington, D.C. Dec. 4–8.

———. 1989. Cultural Notes on Trade and the Tai. Ritual,
      Power, and Economy: Upland-Lowland Contrasts in
      Mainland Southeast Asia, S. Russell, ed. 27–66. Center
      for Southeast Asian Studies Occasional Papers Series,
      no.14. DeKalb: Northern Illinois University.

Pfanner, David. 1965. The Buddhist Monk in Rural Burmese
      Society. IN Anthropological Studies in Theravada
      Buddhism. M. Nash, ed. 77–96. Southeast Asian
      Studies, Cultural Report Series, no. 13. Yale
      University.

Phillips, Herbert. 1965. Thai Peasant Personality. Berkeley:
      Univ. of California Press.

Piker, S. 1968. The Relationship of Belief Systems to Behavior
      in Rural Thai Society. Asian Survey 8:384–99.

Plion-Bernier, Raymond. 1973. Festivals and Ceremonies of
      Thailand. J. E. Soulier translator. Original French
      publication 1935. Bangkok: Sangwan Surasang.

Potter, Jack. 1976. Thai Peasant Social Structure. Chicago:
      Univ. of Chicago Press.

Potter, Sulamith Heins. 1977. Family Life in a Northern Thai
      Village. Berkeley: Univ. of California Press.

Rahula, Walpola. 1962. What the Buddha Taught. New York:
      Grove Press.

Reynolds, Frank. 1978. The Holy Emerald Jewel: Some Aspects of Buddhist Symbolism and Political Legitimation in Thailand and Laos. IN Religion and Legitimation of Power in Thailand, Laos, and Burma, Bardwell Smith, ed. Chambersburg, Penn.: Anima Press.

Reynolds, Frank, and Mani Reynolds, eds. and trans. 1982. The Three Worlds According to King Ruang. Berkeley Buddhist Series, no. 4. Berkeley: Asian Humanities Press.

Rhum, Michael. 1987. "Grapholatry" in Northern Thailand: The Magical Qualities of Written Words. Paper presented at the Association for Asian Studies meetings, Boston, March 1987.

Roseberry, W. 1982. Balinese Cockfights and the Seduction of Anthropology. Social Research 49(4):1013–28.

Sadler, A. W. 1970. Pagoda and Monastery: Reflections on the Social Morphology of Burmese Buddhism. Journal of Asian and African Studies 5:282–93.

Scott, Sir James [Shway Yoe]. 1896. The Burman: His Life and Notions. London: Macmillan and Co.

Scott, James C. 1985. Weapons of the Weak: Everyday Forms of Peasant Resistance. New Haven: Yale Univ. Press.

Sharp, Lauriston, and Lucien Hanks. 1978. Bang Chan: Social History of a Rural Community in Thailand. Ithaca: Cornell Univ. Press.

Smith, Bardwell, ed. 1966. Religion and Legitimation of Power in Thailand, Laos, and Burma. Chambersburg, Penn.: Anima Books.

Spiro, M. 1966. Buddhism and Economic Action in Burma. American Anthropologist 68:1163–73.

———. 1967. Burmese Supernaturalism. Englewood Cliffs: Prentice-Hall.

———. 1982. Buddhism and Society. Revised second edition. Berkeley: Univ. of California Press.

Steinberg, David Joel, et al. 1971. In Search of Southeast Asia. New York: Praeger Publishers.

Suksamran, Somboon. 1982. Buddhism and Politics in Thailand. Singapore: Institute of Southeast Asian Studies.

Swearer, Donald K. 1976. Wat Haripunjaya: The Royal Temple
    of the Buddha's Relic, Lamphun, Thailand. AAR
    Studies in Religion, no.10. Missoula: Scholars Press.

Tambiah, S. J. 1970. Buddhism and Spirit Cults in Northeast
    Thailand. London: Cambridge Univ. Press.

————. 1976. World Conqueror and World Renouncer.
    London: Cambridge Univ. Press.

————. 1977. The Cosmological and Performative
    Significance of a Thai Cult of Healing through
    Meditation. Culture, Medicine and Psychiatry 1:97–
    132.

————. 1984. The Buddhist Saints of the Forest and the Cult of
    Amulets. Cambridge: Cambridge Univ. Press.

Tannenbaum, Nicola. 1982. Agricultural Decision Making
    Among the Shan of Maehongson Province,
    Northwestern Thailand. Ph.D. diss., Univ. of Iowa.

————. 1984a. The Misuse of Chayanov: "Chayanov's Rule"
    and Empiricist Bias in Anthropology. American
    Anthropologist 86:927–42.

————. 1984b. Shan Calendrics and the Nature of Shan
    Religion. Anthropos 79:505–15.

————. 1987. Tattoos: Invulnerability and Power in Shan
    Cosmology. American Ethnologist 14:693–711.

————. 1989. Power and Its Shan Transformation. IN Ritual,
    Power, and Economy: Upland-Lowland Contrasts in
    Mainland Southeast Asia, S. Russell, ed. 67–88. Center
    for Southeast Asian Studies Occasional Papers Series,
    no. 14. DeKalb: Northern Illinois Univ.

————. 1990. The Heart of the Village: Constituent Structures
    of Shan Communities. Crossroads 5(1):23–41.

————. 1991. *Haeng* and *Takho*: Power in Shan Cosmology.
    Ethnos 56:67–81.

————. 1993. Witches, Fortune, and Misfortune among the
    Shan of Northwestern Thailand. IN Understanding
    Witchcraft and Sorcery in Southeast Asia, C. W.
    Watson and R. Ellen, eds. 67–80. Honolulu: University
    of Hawaii Press.

————. n.d. Assessment of Decision Models. Unpublished ms.

Tannenbaum, Nicola, and E. Paul Durrenberger. 1988. Control, Change, and Suffering: The Messages of Shan Buddhist Sermons. Mankind (Australia) 18:121–32.

Terwiel, B. J. 1978. The Origin and Meaning of the Thai "City Pillar." Journal of the Siam Society. vol. 66, pt. 2:159–71.

————. 1979. Monks and Magic. second edition. Scandinavian Institute of Asian Studies, Monograph Series, no. 24. Copenhagen: Curzon Press.

Textor, R. B. 1960. An Inventory of Non-Buddhist Supernatural Objects in a Central Thai Village. Ph.D. diss., Cornell Univ.

Trocki, David J. 1987. Big Men, Nakleng and Power: The Politics of Violence in the Rural South of Thailand, ed. Carl Trocki. Paper presented at the SEASSI Conference, DeKalb, Ill., July 1987.

Turner, V. 1960. Muchona the Hornet, Interpreter of Religion (Northern Rhodesia). IN In the Company of Man, Joseph Casagrande, ed. 333–56. New York: Harper.

Turton, Andrew. 1978. Architectural and Political Space in Thailand. IN Natural Symbols in Southeast Asia, G. B. Milner, ed. 112–32. Collected papers in Oriental and African Studies, Univ. of London.

————. 1987. "Invulnerability," Local Knowledge, and Popular Resistance: A Thai Theme in South East Asian Perspective. IN Proceedings of the International Conference on Thai Studies, compiled by Ann Buller. The Australian National University, Canberra.

Van Esterik, P. 1982a. Laywomen in Theravada Buddhism. IN Women in Southeast Asia, P. Van Esterik, ed. 55–78. Center for Southeast Asian Studies, Occasional Papers, no. 9. DeKalb: Northern Illinois Univ.

————. 1982b. Interpreting a Cosmology: Guardian Spirits in Thai Buddhism. Anthropos 77:1–15.

Wallace, Anthony F. C. 1961. Culture and Personality. New York: Random House.

Weiner, Annette B. 1988. The Tobrianders of Papua New Guinea. Orlando, Fla.: Holt, Rhinehart, and Winston.

Wilson, Constance. 1985. The Burma-Thailand Frontier over Sixteen Decades: Three Descriptive Documents. Ohio University, Monographs in International Studies, Southeast Asia Series, no. 70. Athens, Ohio.

Wolters, O. W. 1982. History, Culture, and Region in Southeast Asian Perspectives. Singapore: Institute of Southeast Asian Studies.

INDEX

MONOGRAPHS OF THE ASSOCIATION
FOR ASIAN STUDIES

1. *Money Economy of Medieval Japan: A Study in the Use of Coins*, by Delmer M. Brown. 1951
2. *China's Management of the American Barbarians: A Study of Sino-American Relations, 1841–1861, with Documents*, by Earl Swisher. 1951.
3. *Leadership and Power in the Chinese Community of Thailand*, by G. William Skinner. 1958.
4. *Siam Under Rama III, 1824–1851*, by Walter F. Vella. 1957.
5. *The Rise of the Merchant Class in Tokugawa Japan: 1600–1868*, by Charles David Sheldon. 1958.
6. *Chinese Secret Societies in Malaya*, by L. F. Comber. 1959.
7. *The Traditional Chinese Clan Rules*, by Hui-Chen Wang Liu. 1959.
8. *A Comparative Analysis of the Jajmani System*, by Thomas O. Beidelman. 1959.
9. *Colonial Labour Policy and Administration 1910–1941*, by J. Norman Parmer. 1959.
10. *Bankguad—A Community Study in Thailand*, by Howard Keva Kaufman. 1959.
11. *Agricultural Involution: The Processes of Ecological Change in Indonesia*, by Clifford Geertz. 1963.
12. *Maharashta Purana*, By Edward C. Dimock, Jr. and Pratul Chandra Gupta. 1964.
13. *Conciliation in Japanese Legal Practice*, by Dan Fenno Henderson. 1964.
14. *The Malayan Tin Industry to 1914*, by Wong Lin Ken. 1965.
* 15. *Reform, Rebellion, and the Heavenly Way*, by Benjamin F. Weems. 1964.
16. *Korean Literature: Topics and Themes*, by Peter H. Lee. 1965.
17. *Ch'oe Pu's Diary: A Record of Drifting Across the Sea*, by John Meskill. 1965.
18. *The British in Malaya: The First Forty Years*, by K. G. Tregonning. 1965.
19. *Chiaraijima Village: Land Tenure, Taxation, and Local Trade*, by William Chambliss. 1965.
* 20. *Shinran's Gospel of Pure Grace*, by Alfred Bloom. 1965.
21. *Before Aggression: Europeans Prepare the Japanese Army*, by Ernst L. Presseisen. 1965.
* 22. *A Documentary Chronicle of Sino-Western Relations: 1644–1820*, by Lo-shu Fu. 1966.
23. *K'ang Yu-wei: A Biography and a Symposium*, trans. and ed. by Jung-pang Lo. 1967
24. *The Restoration of Thailand Under Rama I: 1782–1809*, by Klaus Wenk. 1968.
* 25. *Political Centers and Cultural Regions in Early Bengal*, by Barrie M. Morrison. 1969.
* 26. *The Peasant Rebellions of the Late Ming Dynasty*, by James Bunyan Parsons. 1969.
27. *Politics and Nationalist Awakening in South India: 1852–1891*, by R. Suntharalingam. 1974.

28. *Masks of Fiction in Dream of the Red Chamber: Myth, Mimesis, and Persona*, by Lucien Miller. 1975.

29. *Dogen Kigen—Mystical Realist*, by Hee-Jin Kim. 1975.

* 30. *The New Jerusalem: Aspects of Utopianism in the Thought of Kagawa Toyohiko*, by George B. Bikle, Jr. 1976.

* 31. *Big City Government in India: Councilor, Administrator, and Citizen in Delhi*, by Philip Oldenburg. 1976.

* 32. *Political Behavior of Adolescents in China: The Cultural Revolution in Kwangchow*, by David M. Raddock. 1977.

* 33. *Philippine Policy Toward Sabah: A Claim to Independence*, by Lela Gamer Noble. 1977.

34. *Code and Custom in a Thai Provincial Court,* by David M. Engel. 1978.

* 35. *Robe and Plough: Monasticism and Economic Interest in Early Medieval Sri Lanka*, by R. A. L. H. Gunawardana. 1979.

* 36. *Burmese Sit-tans, 1764–1826: Records of Rural Life and Administration*, by Frank N. Trager and William J. Koenig. 1979.

* 37. *An Introduction to Javanese Law: A Translation of and Commentary on the Agama*, by M. C. Hoadley and M. B. Hooker. 1980.

* 38. *An Anthology of Modern Writing from Sri Lanka*, by Ranjini Obeyesekere and Chitra Fernando, eds. 1981.

* 39. *Academies in Ming China: An Historical Essay*, by John Meskill. 1982.

* 40. *Kerajaan: Malay Political Culture on the Eve of Colonial Rule*, by A. C. Milner. 1982.

* 41. *Chinese Religion in Western Languages: A Comprehensive and Classified Bibliography of Publications in English, French and German Through 1980*, by Laurence G. Thompson. 1984.

* 42. *Crime and Criminality in British India*, by Anand A. Yang. 1985.

* 43. *Social Protest and Popular Culture in Eighteenth-Century Japan*, by Anne Walthall. 1986.

* 44. *Shaohsing: Competition and Cooperation in Nineteenth-Century China*, by James H. Cole. 1986.

* 45. *Islam in Java: Normative Piety and Mysticism in the Sultanate of Yogyakarta*, by Mark R. Woodward. 1989.

* 46. *The Textual History of the Huai-nan Tzu*, by Harold D. Roth. 1992.

* 47. *Chinese Religion: Publications in Western Languages, 1981–1990*, by Thompson and Seaman. 1993

* 48. *Indigenous Peoples of Asia*, by R. H. Barnes, Andrew Gray, and Benedict Kingsbury, eds. 1995.

* 49. *Gentlemanly Interests and Wealth on the Yangtze Delta*, by John Meskill. 1995.

* 50. *Health and National Reconstruction in Nationalist China: The Development of Modern Health Services, 1928–1937*, by Ka-che Yip. 1995.

* 51. *Who Can Compete Against the World? Power-Protection and Buddhism in Shan Worldview*, by Nicola Tannenbaum. 1995.

* Indicates publication is available from the Association for Asian Studies, 1 Lane Hall, University of Michigan, Ann Arbor, MI 48109.